HOW THEY ACHIEVED

Stories of Personal Achievement and Business Success

Lucinda Watson

edited by Joanne Parrent

John Wiley & Sons, Inc.

New York · Chichester · Weinheim · Brisbane · Singapore · Toronto

Published by John Wiley & Sons, Inc.
Published simultaneously in Canada.

This publication is designed to provide accurate and authoritative information in regard to the subject matter covered. It is sold with the understanding that the publisher is not engaged in rendering professional services. If professional advice or other expert assistance is required, the services of a competent professional person should be sought.

Library of Congress Cataloging-in-Publication Data:
Watson, Lucinda, 1949–
   How they achieved : stories of personal achievement and business success / by Lucinda Watson ; edited by Joanne Parrent.
      p. cm.
   Includes bibliographical references and index.
   ISBN 0-471-38820-3 (alk. paper)
   1. Chief executive officers—United States—Biography.   2. Businesspeople—United States—Biography.   3. Civic Leaders—United States—Biography.
   4. Success in business.   5. Industrial management—United States.   I. Parrent, Joanne. II. Title.

HC102.5A2 W37 2001
658.4'0092'273—dc21
[B]   00-068489

Printed in the United States of America.

10 9 8 7 6 5 4 3 2 1

For my three muses,
Christina, Annabel, and Alexander
and for my best mentor, Felipe Korzenny

CONTENTS

VISIONARIES

EPILOGUE

INTRODUCTION

For the past 10 years I have been teaching people how to sell themselves. What I've learned over these years is that you cannot sell yourself unless you believe in yourself. My philosophy and approach initially grew out of my graduate work in communications. My thesis involved interviewing CEOs about their communication habits within the corporate structure. I now teach at the University of California at Berkeley's Haas School of Business, where I developed a program in business communications and job interviewing techniques.

I often speak with my students about their plans for the future. I hear their dreams and wonder who among them will achieve their goals—maybe even surpass them—and who will not. I encourage my students to believe in themselves, take risks, and follow their passions. Some do this with ease, while others falter and settle for jobs in which they feel safe but ultimately find unsatisfying. As I watch them, I ask myself, What are the qualities that enable people to transcend self-doubt and stiff competition to become CEOs of major corporations or to create visionary endeavors or small businesses that become household names? The search for the answer to that question led to the interviews contained in this book.

There is no doubt that self-confidence and self-esteem are two ingredients necessary for success. The young people I teach are invariably talented and intelligent, but some have self-confidence while others do not. After many years of working with students, I firmly believe that self-confidence and self-esteem can be learned. It isn't always easy to teach these qualities—or to learn them—but I feel part of my job is to encourage students and show them how to build these qualities on their own. The goal of this book is to provide the same kind of instruction for its readers. Through the voices of the diverse leaders in this book—people who learned to believe in themselves—readers will hear the philosophies and practices that made these subjects so successful.

Success is the goal of most people—in their careers, their relationships, and in their lives overall. My definition of success is achievement in a field, as defined by peers within the field. The success stories included here come from many fields of endeavor, and all the individuals reached the peaks of their careers. In my interviews with them, I asked a variety of questions: How did you discover your passion? Who are your heroes, your mentors? How did you achieve all that you have? What role does fear play in your life? What were your toughest decisions? How are today's ambitious young people different from those of other generations?

I discovered that, for each of them, success seems to stem from a single variable: They trust their passion for something beyond themselves and follow it with a full dedication. Almost everyone I interviewed said that to find their passion, they simply remained vigilant in their search. Nearly all the leaders did find their passion, and then followed it with great intensity throughout their lives. Most suffered difficult times but managed to stay on their paths, demonstrating high levels of self-confidence and resilience. They handled conflict and criticism in a positive manner. They used their struggles as opportunities for creativity and finding new ways to approach their endeavors and themselves. All share an inner knowledge that their passion in something beyond themselves is so strong they can only succeed.

Initially my interviewees consisted of up-and-coming, current, or former CEOs—all from major corporations. I then widened the circle to include leaders in creative and nonprofit fields. I met with people who were great chefs and restaurateurs, leaders of large nonprofit organizations, and small business owners who managed to turn their companies into household names. From conversations with this group, I grew to recognize the subtle differences between

Introduction

a CEO, a nonprofit leader, and an entrepreneur. I found that people involved in running large corporations are different from entrepreneurs insofar as their lives must conform more readily to external standards. The people themselves, however, share similar definitions of achievement and comparable visions of success, though the desires that fuel their work may be somewhat different.

The relationship between passion and success is interesting. I repeatedly asked my subjects how they found their passion. Most had no clear explanation beyond the persistence of their search. Yet all found success by believing in and following their strongest desires. Chef and restaurateur Alice Waters remembers going to Paris as a young girl and being swept away by French culture. She later studied cooking and opened the world-renowned California restaurant, Chez Panisse. Faye Wattleton found her passion after college through her desire to improve the status of women. Eventually, she became head of Planned Parenthood, an organization she ran with great success for 14 years before starting her own nonprofit organization, the Center for Gender Equality. Others, like John Sculley of Apple and Donald Kendall of PepsiCo, ran very large corporations for many years. Don remained at PepsiCo for his entire 40-year career; John left Apple and created a new life as a venture capitalist.

The leaders I spoke with were well aware success cannot be achieved in a vacuum. They needed support along the way—financially, psychologically, or otherwise. They found this support through the intensity of their convictions and their awareness of the impressions they made on others. They became effective leaders because people believed in them, and people believed in them because they believed in themselves.

At the end of my interview with men's retail clothier Wilkes Bashford, he asked me, "How many of the people you interviewed told you whether their work or their personal lives come first?" I hadn't asked this question in my interviews because I assumed being immensely passionate about one's work often precludes a rich family life. Yet many of today's businesspeople are concerned with striking a balance between their work and personal lives. It will be interesting to see how this desire for balance affects business leaders and corporate cultures in the future.

Finally, my interviewees come from a variety of economic backgrounds and childhood experiences. Some, like Robert Mondavi and Alice Waters, started out with few advantages; others had a great deal of support. Some discovered their life's work at an early age; others found it by happenstance. Most participants did not have many self-doubts about the nature of their work, but rather about the business and personal risks they had to take in order to realize their dreams. My subjects described periods of uncertainty about their career choices, but uncertainty merely spurred these high achievers on to take the kinds of risks that lead to great change. Passion was the fuel that rocketed them to the top of their fields. Without passion, few would be where they are today.

Three Types of Leaders:
The CEO, the Entrepreneur, and the Visionary

As I listened to the business leaders I interviewed for this book, I heard in their stories the distinct way in which each one rose to the top of his or her field. The one thing they all shared was a strong, directed drive to achieve. Their goals, however, and the primary internal desires that fueled them seemed to fall into three categories. The first group, the CEOs, embody a strong desire to accomplish, succeed, or win. The entrepreneurs, by contrast, are driven by a need to create or express. And, finally, the visionaries, different from the other two groups, desire to contribute or make a difference in the world.

It often took the leaders I interviewed a while to figure out what their goals were; but once in view, they pursued their goals without hesitation. Most of the CEOs I interviewed just fell into their jobs. Some interviewed for work without a specific direction. Many told me they simply knew someone who hired them to work in a large company, and the rest was history. Though they all had great ambition and strength, their direction was more apt to have been shaped by circumstances beyond their control. The CEOs had little time to waste in the corporate maelstrom. When they entered their fields, they displayed the necessary characteristics to make it to the top. Thoughts about what they would do in life were less prevalent than in the more creative or visionary groups. They set out on a path of achievement rather than spending time asking themselves questions about where their lives might have most meaning. Many of the CEOs began work after the Second World War and had a very different mind-set from the college graduates of today. They had an urgency for getting on with life. The luxury of time off for contemplation was not a consideration. I believe one of the reasons for this group's success as CEOs was their ability to survive within a large corporate culture. As a group, they talked less about their childhood dreams and more about the need for achievement. They were more political—in a business sense—than the other groups and more conservative. Most CEOs learned early in their careers it is better to keep silent until the situation is understood and all ramifications of a decision are clear. To function as a CEO, one needs a certain personality type—one that includes a great deal of patience and diplomacy. I also found most CEOs were more guarded emotionally. They knew how to play by the rules and generally agreed with them. As children they focused on and accomplished tasks presented to them by the world rather than spending time dreaming.

The entrepreneurs I interviewed more likely found their passions through a process of trial and error. This group of independent thinkers often started life with an interest in literature or art and seemed to consider themselves loners in childhood. Their thoughts were their companions and dreams, their inspiration. They were also driven by an inner strength that pushed them into trying out their ideas and experimenting with their passions. Unlike the CEOs, they allowed themselves more time to consider which direction to take. When Howard Lester of Williams Sonoma found himself without a job, he took a year off to decide what he would do next. Then he bought Williams Sonoma for a small sum. Bob Cohn of Octel Technologies also took time to consider the path he would take.

The visionaries were a different breed altogether. They dreamed about how they might change the world around them. Born with an instinctive desire to understand people as well as to discover ways to help them, visionaries generally started out in nonprofit areas. Some landed in socially responsible companies, with goals such as curing cancer or building low-income housing. They might have found themselves running a large nonprofit corporation like Faye Wattleton did with Planned Parenthood. Alan Grossman, who ran Outward

Bound for many years, now teaches management of nonprofits at the Harvard Business School. Though some might view her as an entrepreneur because of the success of Chez Panisse, I consider Alice Waters a visionary. Alice's true dedication to humanity shines through in her Edible Schoolyard project, which is actually more important to her life than the restaurant. It offers her the opportunity to make a difference in the world by teaching children how to grow and prepare their food.

CEOS

FRANK CARY

Former President and Chairman, IBM

When my father, Thomas Watson Jr., retired from IBM, Frank Cary
replaced him as CEO. Frank first joined IBM as a marketing representative in
1948. He became president of the company in 1971, chairman of the board
in 1973, and served as CEO until 1981. He presently serves as a director for
AEA Investors, Inc., Celgene Corporation, Cygnus Therapeutic Systems,
ICOS Corporation, Lexmark International, Inc., Lincare Inc., Seer Technologies, SPS Transaction Services, Inc., and Vion Pharmaceuticals, Inc.

At the time Frank Cary became CEO of IBM, I remember everyone
saying he was a perfect replacement for my father because he was so
diplomatic. I wasn't sure why that made him a great replacement, but as
I later understood more of IBM's history, I clearly saw the value of diplomacy. My father's term at IBM was exciting, dynamic, and filled with rapid
developments and change. As a leader, he was inspiring and charismatic,
but also volatile from time to time. Frank, in contrast, was calm, intelligent, and well liked by everyone who knew him. He was a good leader in
a totally different way from my father, and he really inspired trust and
faith in the company.

I hadn't seen Mr. Cary (as I still call him) in many years, but when I contacted him about this interview, he was happy to grant it. His office is now
in an office park in Fairfield County, Connecticut, where most of the
buildings are fairly similar and impersonal—not unlike an IBM plant. It
was difficult to find his office. I had to navigate my way past many non-
human security barriers such as doors with pass codes and phone boxes

with terse instructions. Finding my father's office at IBM was the same kind of experience.

When I at last found his office, Frank, a very genial man, greeted me with affection and interest. He has one of the nicest smiles I ever saw, and his smile is what I remembered most about him. His office displays many mementos from former IBM days and feels like a CEO's office. As Frank reminisced with candor and humor about his past at IBM, I was particularly touched by how much he had clearly loved my father.

Frank had detailed and rich memories about his career, making him an easy man to interview. His conversation is modest and his references to others are generally complimentary, yet he managed to tell a story that was both interesting and thoughtful. I love the moment in an interview or conversation when someone digresses and gets carried away with their memories and stories. With someone as experienced and worldly as Frank, his digressions were especially fascinating as he recounted many memories of IBM, candidly reflected on the company, and noted how it has changed.

Frank made IBM his life and was a great success in the company. He is extremely proud not only of his achievements, but also of the years of dedication and hard work he gave to the company. Many people in business today are as dedicated, but usually because the business is their own. Frank Cary, however, is really a company man, perhaps a dying breed.

Frank Cary

You can never be successful if you don't somehow drum up enough courage to take a lot of personal risks, whether that includes moving from one part of the country to another or standing up to a superior.

I grew up in a little town called Inglewood, California, which in those days was right on the edge of Los Angeles, very close to the aircraft industry. The neighborhood has completely changed over time. It was kind of a villagey town on the edge of Los Angeles then, an independent community that emphasized things like sports, academics, and debating. I participated in these activities at the local high school. Then I went to UCLA where I did undergraduate work. To pay my way through college, I had a great job as a page for CBS.

When World War II came along, I went into the army. I entered as a recruit and managed to get a commission in the infantry. I was very fortunate—I never saw a shot fired the whole time I was in. I served in Japan for about a year after the war. They didn't need infantry officers so they made me a transportation officer. I started out with a company of amphibian trucks hauling stuff from the ship to the shore. Then, when they cleared the docks, they brought the ships to the docks and gave us regular trucks. Before long my company started to go home. I decommissioned the men and then worked with several black transportation companies—three in succession. It was an interesting and valuable experience. Then I flew home and went to Stanford Business School. These early experiences had some influence on my development and on my career.

I changed my career goals several times along the way. My dad was a doctor. He became ill while I was in college and passed away at the beginning of my sophomore year. Up until his death, I wanted to be a doctor. After he died, however, I decided medical school would take too long, particularly since I had to work my way through school. So, I planned to be a lawyer. I majored in political science, got my B.A., and intended to go to law school. When I got out of the army, however, I realized law school would take three years but business school was only a year and a half. I was married at the time, so I made a very practical decision to go to business school. I got into Stanford and have never regretted the choice. I think there are too many lawyers anyway, although a law degree is a good beginning for a lot of endeavors.

I was always a bit of a student of human nature. I learned very early how to get along with all kinds of people and how important it is to be empathic and address people respectfully. That's one of the most valuable things I learned. If I have any wisdom to pass on, it may be that. My father was not the kind of person who got along with people. He was a doctor, but I thought he was a little too rough on people. I believe that you benefit more by approaching people positively. I didn't like some of the negative approaches he took—the way he disciplined me and other things. So I tried to understand people and get along with them. Fortunately, I had a very large cross section of the community in my high school. My class had about 400 or 500 kids and, in those days, only a small percentage of students went to college. I never had any doubt I was going to college, and most of my friends in high school intended to do the same, but we were really a pretty small group. We weren't cliquish, however. I worked hard in school, participated in sports, and learned a lot about human nature. I picked up things from my teachers, my fellow students, some of the people I worked for, and my parents' friends. Then, when I was in the army, there was a larger variety of people to understand, motivate, and get along with. I don't know particularly who or where it came from, but I am a good listener, and I think that helped.

After business school, I thought I was going to be a great retailer, a great banker, or do something in financial services. I thought very seriously about going to work for the brokerage community. I wanted to work for Merrill Lynch, but they only had an opening in Tennessee. Toward the end of school, one of my friends worked for IBM in their summer program. I heard of IBM, but didn't really know much about it. I became interested in the office equipment industry and interviewed not only at IBM but with other firms as well. I concluded this was a terrific industry with a promising future, and IBM was the best company in it. They didn't offer me the most money, but they did make me an offer. I took it, and I think I made the right decision. I started in Los Angeles, the area I wanted, and things progressed from there.

I started training in sales at IBM. It wasn't easy, but it was a stimulating job. At school, I learned about business organization, business function—theoretical constructs. Now I was applying theories with sales reps who were analyzing accounts with data processing information—sometimes accounts of pretty large companies—and formulating solutions to their problems. I'm sort of a puzzle solver, too. I like crossword puzzles, chess, bridge, and anything like that, so I found it very interesting. The training was excellent. I went to both an application and a sales school. I wasn't anxious to knock down doors and make cold calls, but I was very anxious to learn how to use the IBM equipment in productive ways to solve problems for customers. I saw the company had a great future. As a matter of fact, it had an immediate future. No one thought Los Angeles was very good territory when I started, but it was terrific. I made so much money that I considered staying in Los Angeles for the rest of my life. I kept getting offers for promotions, but accepting them would cost me thousands of dollars a year. At one point I told my wife, "We're going to have to decide if I'm going to do this career thing, or if I'm going to be a marketing representative for the rest of my life." I was handling a number of banks and insurance companies and, after a year or two, had some really substantial accounts. I was making about $10,000 a year more than an assistant branch manager and as much as many branch managers. So, it was a financial sacrifice to accept a managerial position. I had to decide whether I was interested in the long term or the short term. Finally, we decided it was the long term, and I accepted my first promotion. IBM was growing so fast that soon after I became an assistant branch manager in San Francisco I was offered a job as a branch manager in Chicago. A year later, I was back in San Francisco as district manager.

I was very lucky in many ways. I worked for some marvelous people. One was a young fellow in Los Angeles named Bud Kocher who was an assistant branch manager. He later became the branch manager in Oakland and then a regional manager, but he died very young. I worked with Bill McWhirter, a branch manager in San Francisco, who was extremely helpful to my career development. He managed his office by providing a good example of every aspect of a sales representative. He would take the time to explain why he did things and how, and to explain the company as a whole—a substantial thing to understand in those days. These two men I worked for early in my career were very important to my development and success. They helped me get an edge on the business and showed me how to be a good sales manager. And, more than anything, the company was growing like a house on fire. They needed capable people. If you were capable, you were offered opportunities. If you didn't take them right away, you didn't necessarily get blackballed, but it wasn't wise to turn down too many offers or people would pass you up.

When we moved back to San Francisco, I was the district manager of the Central Pacific Coast district, which ran from Colorado and Wyoming out through Hawaii. It was the best piece of geography in the country. In 1958, which was a tough year for IBM, the national division didn't make quota, but my district did. We had some terrific offices and branch managers. By that time, Bud Kocher was there as well as a number of senior managers who were what we called wheel horses—people you could count on. We were the only district on the Pacific Coast that made quota that year, so I received a lot of attention within the company. By that time, my wife was saying, "Wait a minute, every year we're moving." So we took a breather. Bob Hubner, IBM's sales manager and a terrific guy, wanted me to move. I turned him down once or twice, but then he made an offer I couldn't refuse. So we packed up and moved east. I began to circulate the halls of 590 [590 Madison Avenue, IBM's Manhattan headquarters] and Armonk [IBM's International Head-quarters in Armonk, New York]. We lived in New York longer than any place we'd ever been. So it all worked out very well, though it was at times frightening. Things happened so rapidly I started to worry about whether my kids could keep up with the progress. They were young enough then, however, so everything was fine. Though they might have been born elsewhere, they all grew up in New York.

My business school background was definitely important to me in my career at IBM. I learned a lot at Stanford in 18 months, things I applied very early in my career. First of all, it was important for me intellectually—I understood modern concepts of business. A lot of business was running then just on the basis of experience, but my business theory background gave me a very important perspective. My Stanford experience was also important because it singled me out as someone who had a good education, since not as many people went to business school in those days. I therefore got a bit more attention than if I had just a B.S. or B.A.

I left IBM at the end of 1980, before we had the personal com-puter. I started the personal computer project before I left, but it didn't culminate until the following year. I was instrumental in putting John Opel in my place. He was a very capable guy who ran the company very well for several years. Looking back, I don't really have any regrets. My wife will tell you the same thing. I've heard her say, "Frank always had the best job in the company, and he always enjoyed it." And I really did. Throughout my career, I wouldn't change a thing. For 38 years, I was really a happy camper.

Some of what happened to IBM subsequent to my departure has bothered me terribly. In recent years, as the company struggled, we had to look outside to choose someone to run it. I think that was the right strategy—an insider would have had great difficulty doing all the things necessary to right IBM. It needed some severe treatment. It wouldn't have been that bad, but we let problems go too long. I have reflected on some issues and wished that I had exercised more fortitude, more stock, or more clout to have changed things sooner. Fortunately, I think the company has recovered. Perhaps I should have tried harder, but it's all history now.

I would tell people starting in business today that it's hard to be overprepared. I think that a good education, diversified personal development, and character are very important to success. You can never be successful if you don't somehow drum up enough courage to take a lot of personal risks, whether that includes moving from one part of the country to another or standing up to a superior. It's very important to be a risk taker and to be courageous about the kinds of things you must do and the decisions you must make. It's also important to have a vision of your goals and be able to communicate that vision. If you want to be successful as a leader, it's important to understand how to set an example and, hopefully, inspire people. A lot of techniques, like effective speaking, can be learned. If you're not a good speaker today, you can't lead a major corporation. The foundations for diversified personal development and character go back to your childhood, to the way you were brought up, and to the kinds of early experiences you had. Mentors also play a big role. I mentioned the people who were important early in my life. Later, Thomas Watson Jr. and Hal Williams played big roles. They were enormously helpful. I had the opportunity to observe them, to see what they thought was important, and how they functioned. It was very, very instructive.

Conclusion

A common theme of the interviews in this book is the importance of taking risks. Frank Cary acknowledges that the courage to disagree with superiors is key to one's success. Frank doesn't believe one attains success by simply aiming to climb the corporate ladder. Instead, success follows from having good business acumen, a vision of your goals, and good people skills, especially the ability to lead and motivate.

Frank describes himself as a student of human nature, and he recounts how early on he learned to get along with all kinds of people. Are people skills so important for the leading executives of companies today? I believe so, as I heard it stressed over and over again from these successful leaders, and continue to hear it stressed in other business circles. For example, two popular business books readily come to mind that discuss the importance of social skills and caring for staff—*Encouraging the Heart* by Kouzes and Posner and *Emotional Intelligence* by Daniel Goleman. It seems the higher you rise in an organization, the more important people skills are.

In reading Frank's story, I can imagine many readers will resonate with his ultimate decision to not move one more time for his career. Today, many career people put their family's interests ahead of a promotion that includes relocation—even if this decision means finding a new job. Frank's story also illustrates that life demands constant focus on values and the vision you have for your life and your career, making sure you are still on target with your beliefs and where you aim to be. How inspiring to hear that at his retirement from IBM he was able to say, "I wouldn't change a thing."

DAN CASE

CEO, Hambrecht and Quist

I heard a great deal about Dan Case, the CEO of Hambrecht and Quist, before I met him. Bob Cohn had suggested I interview him, and in my research I discovered that his brother is Steve Case, the head of America Online. I was curious to know what type of family produced two such impressive young leaders.

I found Dan's assistant to be friendly and open while helping me set up the interview and providing me with background information. This attitude led me to believe the interview would be easy and clear, and it was. When I arrived at Hambrecht and Quist on the appointed day, I was interested to see that the offices all seemed somewhat the same in size and decoration. My first impression was that this place was an active and young environment, which surprised me. I thought the company would be more formal and shrouded. It was, nevertheless, a controlled environment.

Dan resembles Jim Carey to a certain degree. He is tall, attractive, obviously athletic, and filled with energy. He is clearly very bright and doesn't miss a trick, yet he is constantly on guard about what he says. I observed a politician's ability to carefully phrase answers geared to the audience. I wondered if this was because he is very young (40) to be in his position. Regardless, the interview went smoothly. He was easily reflective about his life, and I admired his ability to control his thoughts and emotions.

Dan is successful because he communicates very well and knows how to achieve his goals. As opposed to the older leaders I interviewed, he felt he didn't have words of wisdom for his readers. I found him to be modest in this regard. He did not pretend to know it all and readily admitted he is young and has much to learn despite his achievements.

When he talked about his family I was happy to recognize the same feeling I see in my students at the Haas School at Berkeley. Although he runs a major company, he spends a lot of time with his family. He knows the names of his kids' friends and participates in their activities. I wonder if perhaps this new generation will be better parents, and balance their success with family activities.

When my time was up with Dan, it was clear to me that this was a tremendously accomplished person as well as a very private person.

Dan Case

I was born and raised in Honolulu, Hawaii, attended Princeton and Oxford, and then came to Hambrecht and Quist. I chose Princeton because I had this bias against very large cities (coming from Hawaii) and was afraid I'd get lost in Boston or somewhere like that. In addition, I went there because my father had gone away to college, and I was competitive to go someplace different from him. I had a couple of good teachers whom I respected there. What turned out to be a very lucky thing was my main activity in college turned out to be interviewing people for a student-run radio program, and I was in New York and Washington all the time.

I got into interviewing because I met a guy in my first weeks of college who had started a radio series at Lawrenceville. Those were the days when you had to have a certain amount of public affairs programs on the air, and we basically exploded the niche. Since the stations had to carry such programs, we thought, "Why not make it cool!" And we did.

We were a student-run, "Meet the Press" program. We ran around and told all the politicians and media people we had a significant audience. Then, we told the radio stations we had all these celebrities. The radio stations were the easy part because their alternative was local talk shows. When we offered them U.S. senators and movie stars, they were definitely going to take that.

This was a very formative experience. The game or skill for me was to integrate across [skill] areas. That was a lot of fun. From this experience I learned early in life about different cultures and functional areas. And I learned that when you grow a business fast, you can go broke when there is a difference between revenue and cash flow! We were basically broke the whole time, yet we built this whole business off corporate advertisements. I also learned how to make a consultative intangible sell to major corporations as a college freshman. I was the business guy. I had the strategy in the organization and the money, and my partner was the product guy. He ran the interviews and the radio business. As I think about it, my strength at the time was that I was a conventional overachiever with a willingness to take risks outside the box.

I always had this sense of adventure. In fact, my brother and I started a mail-order and direct-consumer business when we were 12 and 13. We started all kinds of businesses. I grew up in a family where there was a lot of encouragement for achievement and competition within bounds. My brother Steve was the more creative, entrepreneurial character, and I was always bringing strategy and organization to our ventures. That kind of started the ball rolling. I found a partner in college who had the same skill [as my brother] and eventually that happened at Hambrecht and Quist also. Bill Hambrecht, who was my mentor here, is a tremendous visionary, an out-of-the-box thinker, a reader, and has wonderful character. Yet he never enjoyed the details. Fortunately, I think and live in both worlds [of strategy and organization].

I worked for Hambrecht and Quist the summer of 1979, when I graduated from Princeton. I thought it would be a fun place to work. I had a girlfriend nearby in Stanford, San Francisco was a warm and embracing area in which to work, and I wanted to work for a place where strategy, finance, and entrepreneurs met. Bill Hambrecht called me up and said, "I'm on President Carter's Commission on Capital Formation. I see that you've done some academic work on a related area, and you want to learn about strategy and entrepreneurs. I'll teach you about my business if you'll do staff work for me so I can look smart for this commission." I told him it sounded kind of interesting and asked if we could meet and talk. He said, "Sure we can, but we really don't have to. I'd be happy to offer you a job over the phone." I asked him if I would get paid for the work, and he said, "Sure, whatever you think."

So I moved to learn the investment banking business and to help Bill with the staff work, but primarily because I had this girlfriend at Stanford! The girlfriend dumped me the first day I arrived, and the commission never met. However, I was able to focus on learning the business, and I loved it. So I returned in 1991 and 1992 after my two years at Oxford, and still haven't had a "real" job here!

What Hambrecht and Quist is really about is innovation and entrepreneurs; it's about structural change, primarily in technology healthcare business services. A lot of what our mission embraces gives me access, on a portfolio basis, to all the functional areas in which I am interested. And I juggle a lot of projects, which I like. I have thought about doing different things. Yet rather than changing organizations, I've changed jobs within this company. I really love what I do.

I believe the principal values of graduate school are the contacts you make, the pedigree and the education you receive, and the self-confidence it gives you. There are different ways to acquire these, but the one you can only get in graduate school is the schooling. Lots of successful people get the other three another way. In fact, in this funny world of investment banking, I'm sort of considered a rebel because I didn't go to business school. I almost did several times, but I deferred business school for Oxford, and then deferred again to go back to Hambrecht and Quist.

I used to think Oxford and the Rhodes Scholarship, as opposed to the classic Harvard or Stanford Business School, was a disadvantage in the intermediate term if I wanted to move around. It was unconventional and needed to be explained. However, what I found to be the advantage, in the long run, was a much different perspective. So one of these days I'll declare it an advantage!

I think fear plays a role in success, but there's internal and external fear. I think fear of failure is both a motivator and a constraint. I had a pretty straight and narrow and conventional path in some ways. Compared to a lot of my peers in the Princeton and Oxford world, my willingness to take risks was huge. However, when you compare [my risks] to leaders in business or government, mine are pretty modest. I think fear of failure is critical. One thing the world teaches is that failure is good, character forming. Another thing it teaches is that there are plenty of places in the world where you can take 110 percent of what someone else considers to be acceptable risk, for a potential reward of 150 percent. A lot of people never do that, and the hardest place to do that is personally. Basically, I have never viewed the risk/reward ratio the same way a lot of conventional people do. "What was the worst thing that could happen?" I would ask myself. If it didn't work out, I'd start again.

I also think it is very important to have a lot of faith in yourself, if you are talking about the business dimension. It's important for people to take the long view and figure out what really motivates and excites them. Then try to map that out against your experience base. Most of life's great opportunities, be they personal or professional, require energy, discipline, an inner compass, and a long-term perspective.

I think a lot of people are busy achieving, yet they don't know why they are achieving. Actually, one of the interesting problems our generation will face in this episodic/high-adrenaline world is knowing what to do when they get addicted to deals, or energy, or success. When you're 50-something and ready to leave, what happens?

Certainly in this business, one of the things I tell people is that because it's a professional services business, you're at somebody else's beck and call. It's just like consulting, or law, or many other service businesses. Another of my favorite expressions is that working with entrepreneurs in a professional service environment is like wind sprints in a marathon. You often have to speed up, but you can never stop. I think a lot of times people forget the next milestone isn't a place where they can stop. It's just the next milestone. People can have a mistaken, short-term view of what success is.

For me, success is having a great family. It's enjoying whatever game you're playing, and playing it well. Feeling the adrenaline of the victories of your environment, however you define it for yourself. It's coming away with some perspective. Having fun while working hard. It's pretty simple, and it's pretty old-fashioned.

Conclusion

Dan Case is an example of a young CEO with a true entrepreneurial spirit, which he has expressed throughout his life, beginning in childhood. He combines strategic skills with excellence in organization and taking care of details—a rare combination. At 40 he has a perspective about success and his life that is quite self-effacing. What seem to ground him are traditional values and a sense of humor and adventure. Dan definitely seized opportunities when he encountered them, such as the radio station experience in college, and his first full-time position at Hambrecht and Quist. Yet he describes his choices and risks as modest in comparison to government and other business leaders.

What I like about this interview is that it gives the reader a real sense of the world of investment banking and the professional services world. You never stop running and reaching milestones, to follow his analogy to marathon racing. Realistically, it is a demanding field. Know what you are taking on when you pursue it.

Regarding fear of failure, Dan sees it as a potential motivator or constraint. He tempers whatever fears he might have with a sense of resiliency and optimism about life. If things don't turn out exactly as you'd like, try something else. Dan also sees the danger of addiction to power and the charged pace of career success. He acknowledges career success in today's episodic, high-adrenaline world is a two-sided sword. Pay attention to what you really value, be ready to give your best to what you pursue, and take the longer view towards yourself, your family, and your career is a message the reader can take away from Dan's perceptive reflections. It's a valuable one.

JOHN CHEN

CEO, Sybase

John Chen is president, chairman, and CEO of Sybase Corporation, one of the largest global, independent software companies. Under his leadership, the company expanded into four divisions, which provide customers with targeted, market-driven business solutions. Prior to joining Sybase, Chen was CEO and president of Siemens Pyramid, the $3 billion open enterprise computing division of Siemens Nixdorf. In 1995, he negotiated the merger between Siemens Nixdorf and Pyramid Technology Corporation, then a $275 million Unix-based systems company where he served as chairman of the board and CEO. Before joining Pyramid Technology, he spent 13 years at Unisys, where he was vice president and general manager. Chen also serves on the boards of Niku Corporation and Wafer Technology. He is a member of several professional organizations including Business Executives for National Security, Chinese Software Professionals' Association, Asian American Manufacturing Association, and Committee of 100, a think tank of Asian-American business leaders.

I first met John Chen during a flight from New York to San Francisco, where he initially occupied a seat behind me. When a stranger asked him rather aggressively to change his seat, I was impressed by the grace John showed when handling the situation. He is a man who responds with grace and composure to the bad behavior of others.

I interviewed John at Sybase headquarters in Emeryville, California. The modern building with its shiny black exterior is stunning and eye-catching. Inside the building, there is a wonderful flow throughout the space and a sense of calmness. I learned that John is very interested in feng shui and hired an expert to rearrange the space. The feng shui master created an environment that is not only a positive use of space but also provides comfort and privacy for employees.

John and I sat in his office, which is filled with personal mementos. There are several pictures of his large family, and it is clear that despite his enormous corporate responsibilities, he is a dedicated family man. He is conscious of raising his children responsibly, as well as of his obligation to give back to the world by helping those less fortunate. When I first met John on the plane, we discussed his outside interests, particularly his desire to help young Asians in this country. I told him about a student of mine who was very talented but who had been unable to find a job. John asked me to e-mail the student's resume, which I did as soon as I got home. Within a short period, John asked my student for an interview and subsequently offered him a position. My student happily accepted and has been working at Sybase ever since.

Our interview went on for quite some time—I actually forgot I was interviewing John because I became so involved in our conversation. John is very open about his ideas and philosophy and can talk to anyone with ease. He openly expresses himself, which is a somewhat unusual trait among corporate leaders. His ability to engage and share ideas certainly contributed to his great leadership and considerable achievements.

John Chen

Pride comes from clear vision and your best effort. You may not always succeed, but you will be proud of trying your best. And if you really, really try and enjoy the process, 9 times out of 10 you will succeed.

I'm chairman, president, and CEO of Sybase. The background of the company is actually very interesting. In fact, if you look at today's Internet craze, I could imagine some of those companies ending up on a track similar to Sybase's. The company was formed

15 years ago by a number of people from Berkeley, California. They were extremely successful. They were riding on a wave when the in thing was to downsize from the IBM mainframe because of costs and efficiency. It was a whole new era of client/server computing. Sun Microsystems was going strong then, growing from a workstation company to a client/server computing company worth a couple hundred million dollars. A number of companies had complementary software—and one of them was Sybase. At the time, we produced databases to run on these machines that replaced functionally, application by application, the IBM complex mainframe. In those days, the rumor was this would be the demise of IBM, but, of course, the company is still very strong—it just created a different space. Sybase grew by leaps and bounds and soon became one of the darlings of the industry. In 1990 and 1991, it was really hitting on all cylinders. It was the right moment for a paradigm shift. All the Wall Street firms and a lot of the telecommunication companies were using our databases. It was the hot thing. New applications were being developed all the time, so you had to keep steamrolling. It was a little bit like the Internet era now.

By the early 1990s, the company was so successful and the founders and key people made so much money they became very arrogant—at least that's my impression. I was then running a hardware company trying to do business with Sybase. But Sybase was extremely difficult to deal with. The management team was so successful they didn't listen to anyone else. If you went to Sybase for a presentation and didn't agree with or understand everything they said, that would be the end of it. There would be no further discussion. One of the companies Sybase was unable to hook up with was a company called SAP, the leader of the next wave—client/server package application space. SAP actually started to create their solution products on a Sybase database first because Sybase was the dominant player at that time. It didn't work very well, however, in terms of code and performance. SAP wanted to work with Sybase to improve this, but Sybase just turned up its nose. SAP needed a certain type of technology that Sybase refused to provide because Sybase thought the old ways were technically superior. That might have been true, but it didn't solve a business problem. So SAP went to Sybase's competition, and that's how Oracle caught up with Sybase.

Unfortunately for Sybase, in the mid-1990s, most corporations started to worry about whether their software was going to work in the year 2000. At the time, most companies only had homegrown solutions. Rewriting everything was neither efficient nor cost-effective, so they bought prepackaged applications. That's when SAP went from nobody to a dominant player. The companies that supported SAP in packaged applications, like PeopleSoft and others, used the same computing models, and Sybase missed out. At the end of 1993, Sybase started hitting the wall, and instead of trying to work harder to gain back the market, Sybase went off in different directions. It made a string of acquisitions to boost its size and expanded into different types of technologies—development, database, deployment, and wireless technologies. The mergers only worked for about six to nine months because the company never had a strategy or the management strength to integrate the acquisitions. This was 1995 and Sybase was a conglomerate earning over $1 billion in revenue. Though the company produced good technologies, the market was not buying them. The market was buying packaged applications because of the need to solve the year 2000 issues. So Sybase fell on hard times and lost money and market share. Its revenue dropped to $800 million for four years in a row.

I was recruited in late 1997 to reengineer the company and bring it back into the market. The board had just ousted the CEO, and the person who stepped in, Mitchell Pressman, was the chairman of Powersoft, a company that Sybase had acquired. He is a great marketing guy, but he's not an operator. The company needed an operations person to re-create a strategy and vision. It also had to really reengage the fundamentals of its business by making tough decisions on such issues as costs of revenue and productivity per person. At the time I started, we had a very high turnover. Key people left and the operating systems were short-circuited, broken, or in a state of confusion. The company had offices in 60 different countries and over 6,000 employees. It was very inefficient and suffered identity and vision problems. I successfully managed a turnaround of a smaller public company called Pyramid Technology, and returned it to profitability and growth. Based on that, the Sybase board decided I was someone who would buckle down and focus on the business fundamentals, work on building the team, clarify the technology and market visions, generate cash, and return the balance sheets to health. They needed a very hands-on operator, and that's why they picked me.

In the early days of my management career, I always thought everyone else was an idiot and I was so smart I just couldn't stand myself. I graduated from Cal tech where we were brainwashed to think of ourselves as the top 1 percent of the world. We were all very smart, but I have learned to be more humble. The more I achieve, the more I know the truth of the old Chinese maxim that says there are always higher mountains. It's absolutely true. There are always better people. There are always better minds. What you think you do best—and I think I do a lot of things well—there are always those who do it better.

Nevertheless, I achieved a lot and am proud of my work for Sybase right now. I have turned the company around as far as its vision is concerned. I think what I do best is to match reality with expectations—match the vision of what a company wants to achieve with its execution ability. It's not hard to have a vision, especially when you're in an industry long enough. You sense where things are going. From talking to people and through experience, you inherently feel the pulse of the industry. That's why you're in the industry. You sense where it's going to be in five years, whether it's going to grow, not grow, change, or deteriorate. The question is, Can you get there from here? There is no need to have a grand vision if you can't execute it. A lot of businesses fail for that reason. It's not because the individual CEO, president, or management team isn't smart enough. It's that they aren't realistic enough. I think my strength comes from being both realistic and very competitive. I want to be a winner, but I'm willing to see slow progress and take a very long-term approach. I am never simply interested in the short term and don't do marketing hypes. I'm also paranoid. Andy Grove's (the chairman of Intel) most famous line was, "I'm always paranoid." That was how he became so successful. Every day he would get up and worry that someone was going to catch up. I think having some paranoia while also being confident are two ingredients you will find in all high achievers.

Nearly all my achievements come from assembling a great team. I mean this sincerely. I'm not trying to be humble. When I was growing up, I always played team sports. I actually do better in individual sports than in team sports, but I just love being around the team. Whether it was during a down time or an up time, in between matches or in a match, practicing or just wearing the same uniforms, it was all a turn-on. I learned the team is really more powerful than the individual. Of course, most teams need leaders, and I have often tried to be the leader.

A lot of people I respect experienced hard times because their team fell apart. In sports, a team can have great talent, but if the morale falls apart and the team's spirit is gone, they will have a hard time winning. I was very impressed with the Milwaukee Bucks basketball team in the eighties. They were big winners. They had six or seven players—none of them famous. They all did their parts and were cohesive. So I think assembling a team with the right spirit and cohesiveness, especially in a difficult situation like a turnaround, is the only way to succeed.

The 50,000 millionaires in Silicon Valley really concern me. There is high turnover in all the companies, and I think we are missing the spirit of belonging and going through hard times and good times together. There is much more individualism now. This is true in Silicon Valley especially, but also in Route 128 and most high-tech areas. I think we are losing something important. In the old days, with IBM and the other early companies, there was a lot of management training and a sense of belonging. People worked until they dropped to achieve the company's mission. There was never this me, me, me mentality. Of course, people wanted to advance their careers, but it was equally important that the company did well. In the United States, whether it's in sports or in classrooms, we are taught to be competitive, to do better than the next person. That is encouraged from the moment we enter grade school. The trouble is we don't build the fabric of good character and teamwork. We encourage individual risk and everyone to try to hit it big. I'm very concerned about that. Young people today—and I've met quite a number of them—don't seem to value the community in the way society needs them to. They only value their own individual success.

I think the pendulum will eventually swing back. This is one of those gold rush times—everybody wants his or her own part of the riverbed. When there is no more gold to mine and people must make money the regular way, the hard way, I think the spirit of togetherness and loyalty will return. I believe it's human nature to want to be part of something over time.

There are many ways to get rich quickly now, but I am not personally motivated by money. When I'm either retired or dying, I want to look back and say I've accomplished something. I have shared some great spirit with a great group of people. That's what I want. That's what motivates me. I don't want to end up with billions of dollars, living in the best environment money can buy, but feeling I really haven't done much, that I just happened to be in the right place at the right time. To me, the process of building something, the hard work, the uncertainty of whether we will make it, are paramount. That's the reason I took this job. Everyone had written this franchise off, but I believe they wrote it off too early. I think we have a tremendous opportunity to overcome the difficulties, and that process is an experience I'm looking forward to. I would love to be 65 years old and look back to say, "God, I've done well."

I grew up in hard times, not ridiculously hard, but hard times. My parents were refugees from China who escaped communism and went to Hong Kong. My father was an accountant by training. It was difficult for the family at first in the British Crown colony, since none of us spoke English and, of course, my father's accounting degree from China was useless. He learned English at night and did odd jobs during the daytime to keep the family together. It was a struggle all the way and we went through some very trying times. Many others also struggled; there were millions of refugees. I learned to see the progress a people and a community can make. Hong Kong in the fifties was just a piece of rock with a fishing village on it. By the eighties or nineties it became a financial powerhouse and the second largest commodities trading center in the world. This transformation is the result of everyone's hard work. This perspective sharpens my view of the long term. If you just focus on your goal and work hard, you will progress and learn to enjoy the process. That's what keeps me going.

As I grew up, we had to work for everything, whether it was food on the table or an education. Looking back, it was probably the best thing that ever happened to me because it instilled certain values. I don't take anything for granted. I know I need to work and nothing is simply there for me to take. I think one of the shortcomings of the high school education system in this country is that it is guaranteed. Students can just bum their way through school. Of course, if you want to get into Cal, or Stanford, or MIT, or Brown, you've got to work hard. But if you want to go to a second- or third-tier college, you can bum your way through that, too. All you have to do is show up. That's very, very bad, I think. From my background, I learned things are earned through hard work and are not guaranteed.

I was fortunate to receive a great education. I went to a boarding school in the United States and learned to appreciate different cultures. My education gave me a respect for diversity—an understanding that many people do so much. I was taught to become competitive and an achiever—to accomplish something. The colleges I attended were great. I loved Brown. Cal tech was tough, but it gave me an unparalleled sense of self-confidence. I thought I could do anything I put my mind to. So the combination of my childhood background, when I learned to achieve because there was no way to get anything if I didn't, and my terrific education in the United States, really increased my self-confidence. Over time I realized it's important to never focus on other people's accomplishments, just on your own. It's important to have a realistic vision of what you can accomplish and work your own path. I see a lot of people work hard to keep up with and be like others. That's not what's important. What's important is to make a difference in whatever you do. If you do the best you can and feel good about the experience, you will cherish the memory and the process.

All my friends who I consider great achievers and successful people are confident. They know what they want and have very clear goals. They follow both their hearts and minds. When I came to Sybase, I said, "We are going to make this a success." About nine months ago, I called a meeting of our top managers from around the world. I told them the most important quality to have is pride. Pride comes from clear vision and your best effort. You may not always succeed, but you will be proud of trying your best. And if you really, really try and enjoy the process, 9 times out of 10 you will succeed. Every success requires hard work and if you really dread hard work, you'll never be successful, in my opinion. Sometimes the work is gut-wrenching. Sometimes I wake up at 3:00 A.M. screaming. Sometimes

I awake at 3:00 A.M. for a conference call. There is a lot of uncertainty about big decisions—will something go our way or not? It's all part of the process. In some very strange way, you have to enjoy the negative outcome. The ball bounces both ways. Sometimes it bounces your way, and sometimes it doesn't. You can only work hard enough to maximize the chance that it results in your favor. If it doesn't, you have to say, "We've been dealt these cards, let's play it out the best we can." I think every high achiever enjoys the process.

Achievers are also intelligent, but I think the difference in intelligence levels between achievers and nonachievers is really very small. I don't think there's a lot of stupid people out there. Many people may not have the experience or exposure that would make them as current or worldly, but they're not stupid. Others have diplomas to show how smart they are, but the reality is people are about the same.

So, there are a lot of commonalities among high achievers—perseverance, hard work, and a couple of traits not too many people talk about, such as enjoying the process, both the failures and the successes. I think 90 percent of high achievers agree it's not just the results that are important. The path is equally, if not more, important to me. It's like playing a game. If you play a game and lose but did the best you could, you don't feel bad. Sometimes, however, you lose a game because you didn't try, and you really feel lousy. So I think the willingness to keep trying is a big part of achievement. It's actually fun to review some of the failures and what you learned from them. It helped me tremendously. On long plane rides, I always think about the failures that hurt and what I learned from them.

I suppose I care a little about whether the outcome is going to be a plus or minus, but, by and large, I don't care. When you don't care, you're not afraid of failing, and you are optimistic. I am confident enough I will make a difference to this company or whatever I am involved in. Whether it will be a tremendous difference or very little, I don't know, but I know I'll make it better. I'll put my signature on it, and that's important. I know it's going to be better because of me. I just don't always know if it will be enough.

The one thing I learned as a foreigner running an American company is the value of the effort to improve my communication skills. To do well in this country, you have to communicate clearly. Reagan was a great communicator, and actually Clinton's a good communicator, too. He's on point all the time. I try to focus on the message and make sure I'm communicating the most important points, not just improving how I look or talk. When I first came to this country in 1973, I was unable to carry on a decent English conversation. I had a very good vocabulary, but I couldn't speak the language. I would formulate what I wanted to say in my mind in Chinese and then translate it. By the time I got the translation in my head, it was too late. People thought I had nothing to say and would move on. I learned to overcome that and the fear of looking foolish and stupid if I said the wrong words. People would say, "Huh?" and then laugh and say, "Oh, you meant . . . whatever." Sometimes it was very funny, especially my pronunciations. Then I worked on the content and structure.

I still have an accent, but I no longer let it bother me. I am actually proud of my accent. I think it shows my broader appreciation for the world. I don't know the Middle East very well, but I don't look at Middle Easterners the same way I think most Americans do. There is so much about them I don't know, and I am fascinated and want to know more. Most educated people in America feel the same way, but the mass media—what is in the (San Francisco) *Chronicle* and on CNN—is very biased. There is this fear and stereotype of Middle Easterners all being terrorists or religious fanatics, and I'm sure that is absolutely not true. I see similarly false portrayals of Asians in this country. I feel one of my strengths is my appreciation for other cultures, knowing appearances do not always represent reality or the complete picture.

Conclusion

When John became head of Sybase in 1997, it was because they needed an operations person to re-create strategy and vision, an unusual combination and one of the keys to John's early rise to leadership in his career. Clearly, knowing your strengths and when and where they are best applied are important traits to many of the CEOs in this book. In addition, pride and confidence are also important. How does one attain these traits? John suggests pride, in particular, comes from knowing your goal and trying your best.

In his interview, John shares his values for clear goals and outcomes, and the enjoyment for the process. He is as comfortable with failure as with success. He likes to win but has a nonattachment to the outcomes of his efforts. Unlike many business leaders today with their investment in short-term profits, it is refreshing to hear John describe his patience for slow progress and the ability to take the long view of things. In addition, his perspective of nonattachment enabled him to take risks and enjoy himself in all his endeavors.

John also discusses the importance of a great team with a positive spirit and cohesion to ensure the success of his efforts. He feels that the desire to belong to something greater than oneself is a part of human nature, and in the long term, loyalty and team spirit will foster success in one's career. He also sadly observes in the recent phenomenon of Silicon Valley millionaires and quick job changes a lack of loyalty or a sense of teamwork.

A subtheme in this book is the impact of early childhood on these leaders' careers. In the last interview, Frank Cary talked about his father's rough way with people and his decision to do the opposite. In John's childhood, he learned hard work and education were keys to success. And he credits both these factors for the development of his confidence and desire to achieve. It is uplifting to hear John talk of how he values his accent. He feels it shows foreigners his appreciation of the larger context in which he does business. In today's multicultural economy, it makes good business sense to embrace diversity. For John, this sensibility seems to stem from his desire to understand others and enhance his communications with all individuals.

Reflecting upon John's interview, I feel he seems to combine the best of Western competitiveness and realism with the Eastern philosophy of nonattachment to outcomes and wisdom that there are always higher mountains to climb. John is an inspiring CEO.

DONALD M. KENDALL

Former CEO, PepsiCo

Don Kendall is the cofounder of PepsiCo, Inc., and served as its chief executive officer for 21 years before his retirement in 1986. He originally joined the Pepsi-Cola Company in 1947 and became its president and CEO in 1963. In 1965, he engineered that company's merger with Frito-Lay to create PepsiCo., Inc. Under his leadership, PepsiCo., Inc. became one of the largest corporations in the United States, operating today in over 200 countries. Don is currently a board member of Orvis, and Resound Corporation, a director of the U.S.–Russia Business Council and of the Institute for East–West Relations.

Don has a round, jovial face and a beard that is white as snow. He might remind one of Santa Claus, except he is in excellent shape. Keenly interested in physical fitness, he exercises regularly and, though in his eighties, has the stamina of a man in his forties. I was also reminded of Santa when meeting him because of his likable expression and welcoming handshake. He is an exuberant man, with superb communication skills. I could see immediately why he succeeded so admirably as a CEO.

I first met his wife some years ago and hadn't seen him for many years prior to our interview. I drove out from Manhattan to Pepsi headquarters in Purchase, New York and was fascinated by the sculpture gardens around the buildings. The grounds of Pepsi headquarters look like a beautiful European park. Every day visitors from all over the world come to see the gardens, which are filled with sculpture by world-renowned artists like Calder, Rodin, and Moore. The gardens are one of the foremost sculpture gardens in the world. Don, widely recognized for his contribution to the arts, created the gardens during his tenure as Pepsi's CEO.

In addition to guiding Pepsi to its top position in the consumer products industry, Don also made great contributions in the world of international relations and human justice. In 1989, he received the prestigious George F. Kennan Award for his outstanding contribution to improving U.S.–Soviet relations.

A man of unique and diverse accomplishments, he was very easy to interview. He was forthcoming with interesting personal stories and the decisions he made in his career. His memory is sharp and filled with detail. From the moment he began the interview, describing how he left college to join the military and never went back, I realized how very little fazed this man. He spoke with a positive, "nothing can stop me" tone. He always believed in his ability to survive and took advantage of the opportunities life offered. He never suffered from self-doubt, or if he did, it never inhibited him from accomplishing a great deal. Despite his tremendous success, he is the antithesis of arrogance. In fact, he attributes much of his success to luck. He feels he simply took advantage of the many opportunities that were luckily presented to him along the way.

Donald Kendall

Luck and mentors are important, but the most important aid for success is to find work that's exciting. Don't stay in a place that is dullsville for you. Move on.

I was in my second year of college when World War II began. I went home at Christmas to Sequim, Washington. They had barbwire fences up everywhere, thinking the Japanese were going to invade the Olympic Peninsula. There was a big rally in Seattle to support the war and recruit young people for the military. Bob Hope and

Bing Crosby were there. I went to the rally with my father and walked up on the platform right then and joined the navy. I applied for flight school as part of the Naval Air Corps and became a navy bomber pilot. I stayed in the navy until 1947.

When the war was finally over, I had to find work. I couldn't afford to finish school. The navy had a program where you could go to college, but you had to agree to three years' employment in the navy after you got your degree. My younger brother, who was also a navy pilot, did that. He went to Northwestern, and before his three years were up, the Korean War started. He became the captain of an F9 squadron and ended up serving in the navy for almost 20 years.

I didn't want to stay in the navy, so I didn't finish college. I originally came east on terminal leave because of the salmon fishing. The Dungeness River ran through the back of our property in Washington state, and we used to catch Pacific salmon there when I was a kid. I always wanted to go fly-fishing for Atlantic salmon, so I arranged for a week in Nova Scotia. When I was there, my then father-in-law, who was an admiral, kept needling me about how anybody could get a job on the West Coast, but you really had to be somebody to land a job in the East. He was just goading me, but I was young enough to take the bait. A friend I knew during the war suggested Pepsi. He couldn't work at Pepsi himself because he was a Lehman, as in the Lehman Brothers. Walter Mack, who was at Pepsi, had married a Lehman, and they got a divorce. After that, the Lehmans and Pepsi people didn't speak to each other. Nevertheless, this friend suggested I talk to Pepsi. I walked in off the street, was interviewed, and got the job. I started in 1947 at $400 a month.

My career at Pepsi began in the bottling plant, then on route trucks, and finally, I got into syrup sales. I liked it. I occasionally give talks to students and always tell them when you get up in the morning and look in the mirror, if you're not excited as hell about what you're going to do that day, you better go find something else. There's no way you're going to be a success if you're not excited about what you're doing. I think that's one of the problems for young people. They need a job, so they stay someplace even though they're not excited. It becomes routine, and, if it's routine, they're not going to make it. In order to be successful, you must put in a lot of hours and do the extra things. You're not going to do that if you're not excited about your job.

I was very excited about what I was doing at Pepsi and, fortunately, I had a lot of opportunities to move up fast. After I was in syrup sales, I moved into national sales. I moved fast enough in the company that it was always exciting. There was always something new to do and learn.

There are a lot of people who are capable and who should get to the top but don't because they're not at the right place at the right time. You have to be lucky. Of course, it's not only luck. Other things have to happen, too. I was in fountain sales in Atlantic City, selling fountain dispensers. There were about eight of us working the area, and most of the people would work 9:00 to 5:00. Well, in Atlantic City, businesses aren't open from 9:00 to 5:00. Atlantic City's a night town. So I'd go to work and stay until 11:00 or 12:00 at night. I made all my sales in the evening. I sold more dispensers in Atlantic City than the entire crew put together. The only reason I outsold them all was because I worked at night when the owners were available. The fellow who was then running Pepsi heard about my performance, and I got promoted into national sales.

You also must have self-confidence, or you're not going to sell anything. You must have confidence in yourself, and that comes from early experiences. I was born on a dairy farm. I started milking cows when I was six years old. We milked them by hand then. I worked through high school, cutting hay and cutting down trees, clearing right-of-ways for power lines. I operated all kinds of equipment. My work gave me confidence because I had skills and knew how to do things. So I never worried about getting a job. To pass on this lesson, I put my boys to work on the ranch in Wyoming. They learned to operate tractors and backhoes and developed skills and self-confidence. When you have skills and self-confidence, you know you have options. A lot of people, if they lose a job, don't know their options, so they agree to work they shouldn't do.

Recently, a lot of people in Silicon Valley and other parts of the West Coast have started up high-tech businesses, but it's really a very small group of people succeeding at that. For most people, it's important to get experience before they start their own business, unless, of course, they have something absolutely unique. If somebody's got a great idea and they start a company, that's fine, but that's not what happens for the majority of young people. Most young people need experience. I think experience is even more important than business school. People are foolish to go to business school if they have a job where they're really learning and are excited about the company. They will learn more by staying with that company than in business school. I don't recommend going to business school unless there's a particular area, like accounting or marketing, you don't understand. Then you better go to business school and learn that.

I learned about our business on the job and learned administrative things in the navy. I was stationed in Coronado Island a month before the war ended and was training a new combat aircrew. This squadron consisted of enlisted people and pilots who were officers during the war. None of them wanted anything to do with paperwork, so the executive officer of the squadron asked me if I would manage the administration while I was still flying. Instead of sitting in a room like the others waiting for my turn to fly, I'd go to the office and work. I told him I had no experience, but I'd love to do it. As a result, I was an administrative officer and learned how to keep records. The financial end was not my strong point, so I took a correspondence course in accounting.

You can also learn a tremendous amount from people you work with if you simply talk with them. I was working in a plant in Pittsburgh, managed by Fred Sabowski. He trained more people who received promotions than any other plant operator. He used to talk with me until 1:00 in the morning. I'd work all day and, at night, sit down with him. I learned a tremendous amount from him about our business because he took the time to talk with me. I also learned about the bottling business from our franchise bottlers who were in the business a long time. Walter Dawson, who had the whole state of Michigan, was terrific. I spent a lot of time with him. He used to welcome me into his office and talk for hours, telling me stories about the business. I was young then, and several older guys were interested in talking to someone my age, so I also had relationships with bottlers in Denver and Chicago. The man who ran the Louisville area was an engineer. When I made a sale to him for equipment, he pulled out his slide rule. I pulled out mine, also; I had learned to use it in the navy. He couldn't believe some young kid knew how to work a slide rule. As a result, we became very good friends. Ed Lofton, a man I worked for in the early part of my career, was also very helpful, as was Al Steel, a great marketing guy.

In the early stage of my life, my fifth grade teacher was probably the person who most influenced me. She believed in me from the time I was very young and followed my career all the way through. She didn't have children so she paid me a lot of attention. It was a unique relationship. I give her more credit for the achievements in the early days of my life than anybody. My parents were separated, so it was particularly fortunate for me to have someone like her in my life.

Luck and mentors are important, but the most important aid for success is to find work that's exciting. Don't stay in a place that is dullsville for you. Move on. Don't take jobs you're not excited about because you're not going to succeed if you do. It's also terribly important to gain experience in various things to broaden your horizons. Unless you want to be an engineer or a doctor or know exactly what you want to do at college, you ought to broaden your horizons as far as you can. Later in life, you must narrow your focus, so if you can broaden it while you're young, you should. And, when you start in business, you ought to learn as many things about that business as you can, every aspect of it. Don't just concentrate on one facet.

Conclusion

I like how Don Kendall defines luck as taking advantage of opportunities, especially since so many of the interviewees talk about the part that luck played in their lives. Luck seems to be an opportunity that shows itself while working on the job at hand, and the courage necessary to take the risk.

Don began his career at PepsiCo in a bottling plant and through accepting opportunities, working hard, and taking risks, he raised his position to CEO. Like Frank Cary and Bruce Atwater, he began in sales and was always excited about his work. He encourages readers to pursue a field they are excited about. He believes self-confidence is important to sell anything, and he believes his confidence came from his childhood. It came from his farm days when he learned to operate machinery at an early age. Perhaps this sheds light on why outdoor experiences such as Outward Bound are popular in leadership development. Once you physically master rope climbing and other challenges, you add more confidence to your abilities, which can then be transferred to your professional life.

Don's final thought about success is very practical. Learn about business from your experience and the people with whom you are working. There is genuine gratitude to those who shared their knowledge and helped him through his career. Don learned so much about the business by just talking with them—and listening.

JANE CAHILL PFEIFFER

Former CEO, NBC
Former Vice President, IBM

Jane Cahill Pfeiffer spent a 21-year career with IBM, leaving in 1976 as vice president of communications and government relations. Subsequent to that, she became the chairman of the board of the National Broadcasting Company. She currently holds directorships in Ashland Oil, International Paper Company, JC Penney, and the Mutual Life Insurance Company of New York. She is also a trustee of the University of Notre Dame, the Overseas Development Council, and is a member of the Council on Foreign Relations, the Conference Board, and the Economic Club.

Jane was the first woman I heard my father talk about in connection with his business. When I heard her name, I was surprised one of my father's close advisers was a woman. Not unlike other men of his generation, he was somewhat chauvinistic, and I believed this naturally carried over into business. Nevertheless, I was to hear Jane's name many times in the following years, as she became one of my father's closest and most respected advisers.

The first time I met her I was a teenager, and she insisted I call her Jane. This was a big step for me. We were strictly raised to address adults formally. Jane was warm, very friendly, and easy to talk to. She was interested in us as individuals, not just as the children of Tom Watson Jr. She always remembered which ones we were, a tough task since there were six kids, five of which were similar appearing girls. She always took the time to ask about our lives.

When I interviewed Jane, I hadn't seen her for many years, and it was a great reunion. She still has a wonderful, informal way of communicating, which draws people to her. When you are with her, you feel she is fascinated by what you are saying, and I believe she genuinely is. She speaks with wisdom, self-assurance, and confidence, qualities that certainly must have helped her achieve success in business.

The house in which I interviewed Jane was large, rambling, and relaxed—just what I imagined for her. She lived there with her husband, Ralph Pfeiffer, who died the year before our interview. Clearly very much in love, their life together was filled with passion and dedication to their kids and grandkids, as well as to their faith. Jane wanted to be a nun as a young woman, and the faith she developed early followed her through her very successful life. I am sure it helped her deal with some very trying moments as a woman advancing to the highest levels of business in the '60s and '70s.

I always encourage my students to be themselves when communicating, yet very few comfortably follow this advice. Most people are acutely aware of what others (particularly their business superiors) want to hear, and this inhibits their communication. Jane, however, was never afraid to express her views, not even to the man at the top. Though she loved and respected my father, she managed to see both the good and bad in his behavior and was willing to share her thoughts honestly. Jane was a tough cookie and one of the first women to challenge the glass ceiling. She chose a difficult path and succeeded against great odds by the force of her will, and I admire her very much for it.

Jane Cahill Pfeiffer

Much is due to timing, but a lot of it is a desire to work hard and contribute, to not be someone sitting on the sidelines and commenting, but to play a part in what's happening. Have the courage to express your ideas even though some will be rejected.

Probably, I've always been an achiever—not overly ambitious or driven—but a very goal-oriented person. Some of that came from my childhood. My dad died when he was 34, and rather than leaving a lot of money, he left a lot of medical bills. My mother then worked for the government as a dietitian. She worked very hard to take care of the bills, as well as my brother and myself. So I grew up with my mother as a role model, having responsibilities, relishing more responsibility, and cultivating great interests in a variety of things.

I'd been in Catholic girls' schools all my life and wanted to attend a college that would offer me a broader view. In my high school years, I decided to become a nun, but felt it was important to test that desire. A way to test it was to study at a non-Catholic school, so I chose the University of Maryland.

The university opened wonderful new subjects and interests to me. They had a fine theater department, great on-campus publications, and a student government that was very exciting. In the theater department, I worked diligently—directing, writing, and even acting. I participated in student government and was president of my sorority. I also had great professors. For example, I was blessed to have been taught history by Gordon Prange, one of the great historians of World War II and Japan. And I was very close to Charles (Curly) Byrd, the president of the university, and several of the deans.

Interestingly enough, I didn't lose the notion of becoming a nun. After graduation from the University of Maryland, I entered a convent in Berkeley, California and spent about a year there, teaching school. Finally, I decided it was not for me and left. I returned to Washington, D.C. where my family lived.

It was 1955, and a young company called IBM hired several of my friends from school and after interviewing, I joined them. Beginning as a programmer, then teaching, I eventually became very experienced on the 650, an early IBM computer. By the way, the 650 is now in the Smithsonian Institution!

Then, wanderlust got me. I left IBM to tour Europe with two friends. Through good fortune, an IBM executive heard a speech I gave just after T. J. Watson Sr.'s death. He called my mother and told her he would rehire me when I returned. Needless to say, my mother was relieved.

In 1957, IBM participated in the International Geophysical Year. This effort was the beginning of the space program. There were a dozen or so of us in Washington working on the programming for an eventual rocket launch—first unmanned, then with animals, then manned. It seemed at first a bit like Buck Rogers time, but then Sputnik launched. The American space program took off, and it was incredible to be there at the start of IBM's programming and analysis efforts. Dr. Jim Turnock, the manager of Project Mercury for IBM, and Bruce Oldfield, the manager of IBM's Space Center, and a host of wonderful scientists, mathematicians, and engineers were engaged in this work that started from scratch. We looked at old books on celestial mechanics in the Library of Congress to study the positions of the stars, and the moon, and sun. Programs were written for retrieving data from radar and telemetry, to follow the capsule in space. We needed both technical and managerial skills as this program grew over the years from hundreds to thousands of employees and participants. We had to solve a myriad of problems. We had to monitor the best practices of other organizations and figure out how to best communicate with Congress and the public. I really grew up while working on the space program.

At one point, I think I was 25, I went to Bermuda to coordinate IBM's site there. Because we had only radio communication between the mainland and Bermuda and it wasn't always dependable, Bermuda became a backup for Cape Canaveral. I lived in Bermuda for several years. It was a marvelous experience and believe it or not very hard work. In the mid-1960s, I had wonderful opportunities and promotions at IBM, but heard about a program called The White House Fellows. It was an effort by the government to find young people who were marked for success in their careers and give them a year working at the highest levels of government. I was selected and spent a very remarkable and intense year assigned to HUD. It gave me a snapshot of the complexity of managing our country—how our government deals with various social, political, international, and economic issues. I gained great respect for the work individuals at the top of our government do. It was a marvelous experience, and I still stay in touch with Secretary John Gardner, Secretary Robert Wood, and my White House Fellow classmates.

When my year as a White House Fellow finished in September 1967, Thomas Watson Jr. called and asked me to dinner with him in Washington. At the dinner, he asked me to join his office as one of his administrative assistants, and I accepted. Tom Watson's assistants were affectionately known around the company as torpedoes. The day I walked into the Armonk office, a fellow saw me coming and said, "I've always wanted to know what a lady torpedo looked like." It was a very exciting time. Many changes were made in the management structure of IBM, and it was a time of unprecedented growth.

Later, I was elected an IBM vice president, responsible for government relations and communications. The most challenging part of that period was dealing with the antitrust litigation. It put extreme demands on the senior executives, was terribly complicated, and lasted for a number of years. Again, one of the fortunate experiences was to associate with some remarkable people—Burke Marshall, Nick Katzenbach, and Frank Carey to name a few. All have this great quality—they take the time to teach others. I have been blessed with great mentors like Bruce Oldfield and Jim Turnock in the NASA years. So much happened because I went to IBM in 1955—almost by accident—as opposed to another company. IBM was exploding, and all the people who wanted to work hard were moved along. It really didn't matter much if you were a man or a woman. It only mattered if you could get the job done. And Thomas Watson Jr. certainly gave me many opportunities.

My life was truly perfect when Ralph and I married in 1975. Ralph was chairman of IBM's Americas/Far East Corp. at the time. We wanted to be together and with his wonderful children, so I left IBM and started consulting for a number of companies I had known over the years. Jimmy Carter asked me to join his cabinet in 1976, but it was right after I had a cancer operation and shortly after Ralph and I married, so it seemed inappropriate to accept.

In September 1977, Fred Silverman, the president of NBC asked me to join him as chairman. It was quite a change from buttoned-down IBM to the lighter and somewhat less organized ways of network television. But despite the complexities, it was a good experience working with Fred. We made strides in our news coverage and quality programming, and in our management systems.

Fred and I grew apart, and I left in 1980 and returned to my consulting work. But I really cut back a lot. I spent a third of my time in the business world, a third in the nonprofit world, and a third doing everything Ralph and I wanted to do. Ralph was chairman of IBM's world trade division when he retired in September 1986. We both remained involved in entrepreneurial opportunities and charitable commitments. We did everything we wanted to do. Now that he is gone, I will still keep very busy. My life has been a very fulfilling and lucky one. When people ask how did it happen . . . well, I have a very simplistic view. Much is due to timing, but a lot is a desire to work hard and contribute, to not be someone sitting on the sidelines and commenting, but to play a part in what's happening. Have the courage to express your ideas even though some will be rejected. Be willing to assume responsibility, that's one of the foundations of success in any endeavor. I see it in my stepchildren. They are young people determined to take responsibility and make things happen and are willing to work while learning, to do some of the drudgery and preparation work so they understand the process. That gives one a determination to do more. When you really understand what you're doing and are able to bring other people into it, it's very exciting.

Fear, to some degree, is always there, too, but that also comes back to preparation. It is very much like the space program. At the time we started, there was no prior knowledge, no roadmap. We had to take chances and create new procedures, but we couldn't just shoot from the hip. We really had to prepare. We had to learn where to find expert advice and be willing to take the time to assemble that expert advice. Then, we made sure results from group efforts were perceived and recognized as group efforts. To be successful in business, tremendous sharing must occur for the good things and responsibility when things go bad. Success has a thousand fathers and failure has none. IBM used a team approach from the start. Coming up through the ranks of programming and systems work and then later in the communications and government relations area, we always worked in teams. Some of the issues were intellectually too complicated for any one person to have all the best insights and ideas. If we did not operate as a team, there would have been little success. We had people with great intellectual ability and energy, and we enabled them to move forward with new ideas. Sometimes it felt like stepping off a mountainside, but it was fun. Business, like anything else, would be very boring if you did the same thing all the time.

Business is different now than when I started. It's changing. People don't work for the same company all their lives. And, technology, as fast as it's changing today, will seem slow 10 years from now. All young people today must realize that they're in a lifetime learning situation. They will need to continually update themselves. Young people need to develop a conscience and a sense of self. They have to decide how they want to play their lives out. Do they want to contribute and be helpful or are they going to believe it's the game that counts, the win that counts, the money that counts? You have to develop an ethical approach within your own life to enable you to make the right decisions about what's good and what's bad. If you don't develop ethical criteria to balance your actions against, you're going to have a hard time knowing what's right and what's wrong. It is very important to have an early job with a very good company, a company that is managed well, that conducts itself in an ethical manner, and employs quality people. The best thing you can do in your first years of work is to be trained by people who are doing it right. Then you can move on if you wish. Also, it's very important—and it's almost a cliché now—to have fun. Your life has to have a light side to it. It has to have meaning. There must be things you do to give you great joy, so you can take that joy into your relationship with the people you work with, your family, and your friends.

On a broader level, many young people need to realize there is a great distance between them and so many others in our country and our world—a distance in the quality of life beyond measurement. If you look at what's happened to our economy the last 10 years, there is much money at one end of the scale and not very much at the other end. And, there will always be a cadre of people—some old, some middle-aged, some young, some children—who fall out of the safety net. Young people need to find ways to participate and improve the lives of those in need. Many in all our cities, whether it's a day, a week, a month, or four days a year, volunteer for a soup kitchen, a Covenant house, a homeless shelter, an elderly center, or a rehab program. They do something that gets them outside of themselves. They help someone else and learn from it. If your life is spent buying and acquiring things and not helping, I think you'll wake up at some age and say, "What was it really all about?" We don't stay here forever. When I think of my husband Ralph's life and his death at age 69, I realize he was a person who really used all his talent in the best way possible. He was able to face his death at that early age with so much peace. I remember him saying, "There isn't anything I want to do that I haven't done. I'd like to do it a lot longer, and I'd like to do more of it, but it's okay." That was a wonderful example to the children and myself.

My advice to my stepchildren has always been for them to analyze what they're facing, do simple things like writing down their choices, the pros and cons, and then making a decision, knowing it can be changed. Don't get caught up analyzing everything to the point of inaction. Make a decision. You have to force yourself to be decisive. It is a harder thing today than when I was growing up because there weren't as many choices then. You had to work because there wasn't somebody to bail you out if you didn't. People who do the best have a point of view, are willing to set goals, and want to work hard. You cannot procrastinate before final exams. You've got to study and work hard. And that never changes as life goes on.

Conclusion

Jane Cahill Pfeiffer spent an exciting career in IBM, NBC, and consulting. She says she owes it to timing, working hard, and having the courage to be an active player in her organizations. To Jane, it is important to speak your mind in business, although she readily admits that although this philosophy helped her move up the ladder at IBM, it got her fired at NBC!

Jane learned core values and a sense of responsibility, a driving curiosity, and clear goals while growing up with a single mother. Like other leaders in the book, Jane admits to being afraid. During her years in the space program, she learned that the best antidote to fear was preparation, and she carried this lesson with her through the rest of her career.

Jane advanced to a chairmanship at a time when women struggled to advance in corporations. Her advice to individuals today, when the business world is very different, is clear. First, recognize you'll always be learning because technology is driving so much change. Second, develop a strong sense of who you are, and use your ethical standards as a rudder to steer your career course. Third, stay true to yourself even if it has negative consequences, like being fired. Broaden your sense of success to include not only being a recognized leader in one's field, but to living true to a personal belief system—a definition we will also find in our visionaries' interviews.

Finally, Jane reflects how fortunate she was to begin her career in an excellent company, and she advises young people to be selective about the initial company in which they work. This ensures that they learn from the right people in the right environment how to enjoy what they do.

ENTREPRENEURS

WILKES BASHFORD

Owner, Wilkes Bashford Retail Clothier

I've known Wilkes Bashford ever since I arrived in San Francisco 23 years ago. Wilkes has a Peter Pan–like appearance. He looks younger than his years, with a boyish smile and hair without a touch of gray. A mutual friend first introduced us at a large dinner party in Pacific Heights. Wilkes stuck out his hand to say hello, winked his trademark, adorable wink, and said brightly, "Your hair's too long!" I laughed because he was right. People always told me that, but I liked my long hair that provided me a layer of protection against the world and gave me something to play with in meetings. Every time I see Wilkes after our first meeting, he always mentions my hair. It became a running joke between us, and I always laugh and assure him I won't cut it.

Wilkes has the best store in San Francisco. It is the most exciting, cutting edge, fashionable place in town, and he has made it that way. Several branches of his store are in other areas of California, but I always think of the Sutter Street store when I think of Wilkes Bashford. The store is filled with interesting and eye-catching fashion and items for the home. He carries both men's and women's clothes, and the designers are always the newest and the most au courant. You enter the store on the ground floor where the men's department is located and travel upwards through several floors for women's, shoes, and finally, household items. You feel a sense of glamour rising up those stairs like Venus rising from the half shell dressed in Armani. The salespeople in the store are not too aggressive, but always look out for the comfort of the shopper. Wilkes understands fashion and service. He's made his business a great success by overseeing the operation carefully and sticking to his principles. Perhaps his greatest asset is himself because everyone adores him.

I interviewed Wilkes in his office. We were joined by his ever-present small dog, whom he loves. His great concern for animals motivated him to start an organization in Mendocino for homeless animals. Every year he hosts a parade of animals and their owners in Mendocino to raise money for the cause.

Wilkes is a funny man, which made the interview easy. He has a self-deprecating sense of humor and made me laugh constantly. He described his life with a great eye for detail. Like many of the interviewees in this book, he had a belief he could succeed in anything he tried. He has fun with his work. I definitely sensed if he weren't having fun anymore, he would stop. Wilkes never says a bad word about anyone, and unlike others who become successful in a very competitive business, he is nice to everyone. He has excellent manners, remembers past conversations and personal details, asks about your children, all in a very genuine way. These are great personal qualities, which certainly contributed to his success.

Wilkes Bashford

. . . it's difficult for young people today who are bright and intelligent to decide what it is they aspire to. Is it just to become one of these very wealthy people? Or is it to do something of more value in life?

I was born in New York City. My family moved to Hillsdale, in upstate New York, when I was six, and I lived there until I went to college. My father was a teacher originally, but he moved to Hillsdale to help his father with his business, an International Harvester dealership. My grandfather lived in Hillsdale all his life. It was the late 1940s and refrigeration was just beginning. Freeze boxes and all those things were being invented. Farm equipment dealers like my grandfather moved into refrigeration, and it soon became a very big business.

My brother Bruce is a professor at Stony Brook College on Long Island. He's a brilliant kid. He's 11 years younger than I and has spent the last 10 years writing a book on Oscar Wilde, which is being published by a university press. He researched the book intensely. He and his wife spent six months in London going through archives of Oscar Wilde's correspondence and papers, some of which are sealed until 2000, the centennial of Wilde's death. Bruce has been working and working on this book. I told him, "You should have gotten this book out a year ago." But that's the difference between us—he's an academic, and I'm in marketing.

When I was growing up, I caddied and then worked at a golf course clubhouse in a country club not far from Hillsdale. I loved it. Then I went to college at the University of Cincinnati where I was a very good student, graduating first in my college class. I participated in the school's co-op program, which is where you go to school a certain amount of time and work on a job the rest of the time. It's a great system. I'd recommend it to anybody. I started school in 1951, and at that time Federated Department Stores, headquartered in Cincinnati, was by far the most important company in the department store field. Department stores were much more important then than they are now. Since I was in a program where I studied a certain amount of time and then worked a job, I fell right into working for the Federated stores. I worked at what was then Chilatos, and is now Lazarus, in Cincinnati. The co-op program required an extra year to get a bachelor's degree—five years instead of four—and students studied year round. There were no summer vacations. I graduated in 1956 and stayed in Cincinnati at Chilatos three more years, until 1959.

Initially, I really wanted to work in the hotel business. When I first went to college, I thought after I graduated I would go to Cornell's hotel school, the best school in the country for that field. I fell into retailing, however, because of my experience at Federated. I was always attracted to retailing, but my first choice initially was hotel work. I've spent my career since 1956 (so it's 44 years now) in retailing, and I love it. I'm delighted I chose this field and feel it's where my talents lie. As life moves forward, I realize how quickly it goes by, and I would probably recommend for people to do more than one thing in their lives—more than one career. Most people, however, who stay in a field and become successful are too afraid to change. We all have a fear of change. And, if you're really dedicated to your work and do it with intense energy, it's difficult to pull yourself away from it for any reason.

After working in Cincinnati for three years, I decided to move to San Francisco. I got a job with the White House department store in its administration office. Shortly after I started, the men's buyer left. I had experience as an assistant buyer at Chilatos, so the White House people took a chance and offered me the job. I was 26 years old. I did well and stayed with them until they closed in January 1965. There really didn't seem to be the right job for me in another store in San Francisco then, particularly in the men's area. Every position was occupied. I returned to New York for a year and worked with Federated again in their New York headquarters as their men's fashion director.

However, I really missed San Francisco and being in a store. I decided to move back to San Francisco and open my own store, which I did in 1966. I was young, 33 years old, but opening a business in those days was so much easier than it is today. I think I had approximately $30,000. You could do things then that you can't do now because the risk was so much less. The amount of money it took to start a venture then was much smaller. It's a whole different scene.

My strength in this business is that I'm a good communicator. Retail is a people business, and you must communicate well. When I interview people, they always say, "I like people." I don't say that, because I'm not always sure I do. I love animals, and I like a lot of people, but I can't say that I'm in love with the human race. You can be a good communicator and still harbor doubts about people in general. Also, to succeed in retailing, you must be pretty driven. It's a relentless business. There are so many aspects of it. It's not like some fields in which you work to a project's conclusion and then you're finished until your next case or your next whatever. Retailing just rolls on. There's never a time when your job is finished. Retailing is just one seamless project.

Although I studied various basics of retailing at the University of Cincinnati, I think the best way to start in this field is to work as I did. With the co-op program, I went to school for six weeks, and then worked a job seven weeks. From 1952 on, every seven weeks I was working in the store. I was selling. I learned by doing almost everything you can do in a store. By the time I graduated I had some experience, and then I added another 10 years of experience before I opened my own store.

Even today, I am totally involved in all the details and oversee everything in my store. I have people who accompany me to the different markets, but, particularly in the men's area, I oversee everything. It's important to keep a continuity and a look, to give things the same sensibility. We opened a women's department in 1978 and for the first 10 or 12 years, I went on all the buying trips with the women's buyers. I haven't in the last eight or 10 years because my associate, Nina, has been doing it since 1978. I still confer with Nina, but I don't go on very many of the buying trips.

I'd say the most challenging thing about this work is staying ahead of the customers' moods, knowing what their thoughts are going to be. In every market, people change, but particularly at our end of the market, the high end. In the 32 years we've been in business, our customers have gone through lots of phases—people with lots of money wanting to look like they don't have it, people with lots of money wanting to show it off. They go through phases, and we must project what the overriding mood of our customers is going to be. We don't chase trends or worry about what is in this season or going to be out next season, but we do need to know the psychological makeup of the majority of our customers for any span of time. If they're going to change their outlook on life—and people change more than you realize—we've got to be a little ahead of that. We have to anticipate change, not only for what we buy but for how we service a customer and what services we offer, for the mood we give the store, and what our windows look like. That's a challenge. The people who shop here are the top percent of the market, and our biggest challenge is making sure we're in the right ballpark for our customers.

The key thing for us is to focus on our customer: who are the customers and what turns them on. And, at the same time, bringing in new customers. A lot of our salespeople have been here 20 years now, so they're growing older. The ones who started in their twenties are in their forties now. I was 33 when we started, and I'm 65 now.

So one of the challenges is to keep our store young enough in out-look to bring in new customers. Obviously, the great majority of our customers are people who grew up with us. They're aging with us, and fortunately, we've kept a lot of them. We want to keep them happy and, at the same time, bring in new customers.

One of the most difficult challenges I faced was over a rent dis-pute with the city of San Francisco, which owned the building my store is housed in. The dispute concerned what percent of our income we owed the city. Beginning in 1984, we were on the front pages of the newspapers for almost two years. The publicity of the dispute was a challenge to deal with as we tried to minimize its effect on the business. It was the most difficult period of my life, and the most difficult period for the business. We got through it, however, and are in a stronger position today than ever as far as the amount of business we do, the profitability of the business, and our recognition. It's not something I would have chosen, but going through that period, regrouping and recouping, gave us the opportunity to learn a lot. We sharpened our focus and skills and strengthened our resolve to reach our goals. At some point during it all, Willie Brown gave me a T-shirt that said, "Don't worry, Wilkes, this is a onetime only story. Willie L. Brown." Somebody saw me sitting in Le Central the other day. He came over and opened his jacket to show he had on that T-shirt from 1984. I couldn't believe it.

Probably the most disturbing thing to me today—not the only disturbing thing, but one of the disturbing things—is how success is so often measured in terms of dollars. So many conversations among people who should know better are totally about money—how much money somebody paid for their house, how much money somebody is making, how much this IPO contributed to the well. Conversa-tions in earlier decades would have been about literature, or art, or music, or history but are totally dominated by money today. If you go out with a group of people, after 15 minutes everybody starts telling stories about how much money some person made. I sit at Le Cen-tral at lunch (sometimes I like to eat by myself) and, if there are peo-ple next to me, I'll listen to their conversations. It's always about money. I think this is really a dangerous thing for young people. By focusing on acquiring money or being envious of people who have acquired wealth, people miss so much, and it's warping people's values. Maybe it's not as bad as it was in the '80s, but in some ways it's worse. People today have enormous amounts of money. They center their lives around how much money they've got and use their money to show other people who they are. So it's difficult for young people today who are bright and intelligent to decide what it is they aspire to. Is it just to become one of these very wealthy people? Or is it to do something of more value in life?

I feel success happens when you are able to create a life that works for you—a life in which you feel a sense of achievement and a certain inner peace. As you age, your span of knowledge and experience broadens. I don't think anybody knows who they are in their early years, and they'd be lying if they told you differently. I don't even think life begins at 40. It begins later than that. If you've been able to keep things in perspective, listen to other people, and appreciate their points of view, then life begins later than 40. So real success comes with being comfortable with yourself and what you're doing. If you achieve this level of comfort, you will be happy, and people will appreciate you. To me, that's what success is.

I had a number of mentors in my life—and heroes. Willie Brown (currently the mayor of San Francisco) is one of my heroes. I admire and respect him because I appreciate and understand his philosophy of life, what he feels is important and what isn't. I agree with him 99 percent of the time. I like the fact that he in a sense, *created* Willie Brown and yet did not betray himself or anybody else in the process. He's never forgotten his roots. I went back to Texas with him and saw how he treated the people he's known all his life. I think he's done a brilliant job of creating Willie Brown without betraying the essence of who he really is.

Willie Brown and I are alike in another way. Neither of us are very driven by money. People laugh when I say that, but it's true. Achievement is more important to me than money. I just am not driven to be a very wealthy person. I'm not saying that because I'm 65 and not a wealthy person. If I had been driven by money, I probably would have opened a Gap, or something like that. At an early age, I knew that more money is made by appealing to the mass market. You don't aspire to please a small percentage of the market and think you're going to get rich. I think people who made a lot of money have different priorities and outlooks from mine.

In addition to having mentors and heroes of my own, I also find it's important to mentor young people. I enjoy working with FIDM (The Fashion Institute of Design & Merchandising) and spend as much time with them as I can. I was commencement speaker this year for the graduating class. We had an intern here this summer from an eastern school. I like being around young people. They're very receptive. To a lot of young people, our industry isn't as appealing as it really is. The starting salaries are lower than in electronics or the computer industry. The hours are long, and you have to work on Saturdays. I feel I always have to tell people about the virtues of the fashion industry and subtly try to sell them on it. The industry needs talent, and nobody is better able to convey the positive aspects of the business than somebody who has been in it a long time. Although it receives a lot of press, there are some negatives for young people when it comes down to deciding to go into it, compared to their alternatives.

I don't know whether the drive to succeed is something you're born with or if it's acquired along the way. Among people who work at the store, there are some who have a certain type of drive, and right away I know they are going to become more and more valuable to the store. And there are others who come in, who are very happy, and I know they'll be happy for 20 or 30 years, doing well enough so they're valuable to the company, but not aspiring to anything else. Another thing I've noticed as I've had a chance to talk to people who are successful in their fields is that curiosity is a really important trait. I can't read a book without having a dictionary next to me, because if I come across a word I don't know, I have to look it up to satisfy my curiosity. Curiosity leads you to acquire knowledge about a lot of things you wouldn't know about if you didn't have it. People who lack curiosity miss too much to ever really reach their highest potential. To me, curiosity and a sense of humor are two key things in life. Without these, you limit yourself.

With all these challenges, I don't have too much time to be social. I'm here six days a week and am really dedicated to making the store better and better. Doing that takes up a good part of my energy and time. A successful person makes the business or profession a priority, but I think you can do that without giving up a lot of the important things in life. When I have to make a decision, for example, about whether I will go to Mendocino for the weekend where I have a house that I love, or whether I am going to stay here, it's always based on the answer to, "Do I need to be here?" Even at this late date, I still look at things that way. I think that's also the case for other successful people. If you measure success by achievement in your profession, you must make some deliberate choices through the course of your life to put a high priority on your business. If you don't put top priority on your profession, you won't achieve as much.

Conclusion

Values influenced much of Wilkes Bashford's life. He has never been driven by money and sadly thinks it might be a major motivator for many new workers. As John Chen reflected earlier in the book, Wilkes observes the new economy's surge of millionaires, and believes young people today are seduced into choosing a field of work based on material goals and not on their talents and values.

Wilkes has been in retail throughout his career, beginning in a college co-op program and continuing with his ownership of a beautiful retail store in downtown San Francisco. Love for his work came shining through the interview; though at one point, he wistfully mentioned his first career intention of going into the hotel business. Perhaps that is why he recommends trying more than one career in your life. To Wilkes, personal success is being comfortable with who you are. He adds that professional success (at least in his field) means you always make business your priority. Before he can decide whether to enjoy his home in Mendocino, he asks himself, "Do I need to be at the store?"

The drive to succeed is essential to anyone's success, and Wilkes is unsure whether that is something ingrained or learned. He only knows when someone has it or doesn't. It is also important to stay close to the customer (the one who is in your store today and the one who will be there tomorrow). He recommends anticipating the customer's needs.

Learn how to talk to people. In the world of e-commerce and high technology, isn't it interesting so many leaders say that practicing basic communication skills is the way to torpedo yourself to career success?

Wilkes had mentors in his life, and one such hero modeled a philosophy of living and an achievement orientation similar to his own. That is mayor Willie Brown of San Francisco, a very unique individual, indeed. "Be the best that you can be" is what their mottoes could be. Strive to give your all . . . and enjoy the ride!

TED BELL

Former Vice Chairman and Worldwide Creative Director, Young & Rubicam

Ted Bell started his career in banking, and served as the vice chairman and worldwide creative director of Young & Rubicam. His company's clients include Ford Motor Company, CitiBank, and Sears.

I have known Ted since I was 20 years old. I first met him on a lush green mountainside in Virginia close to Randolph Macon College. It was a warm spring day and I had traveled to Virginia to visit Alan Kew, who would later become my husband. I was nervous and ill at ease in this southern college environment. I had really never been on a college weekend before. After nine years of a strict eastern day school and four years of Episcopal high school with communion every day, I was surprised I didn't have to get my mother's permission to be there in the first place.

The first night we went to a large dinner at the college and everyone drank a lot of bourbon except me. I was fairly shocked at Southern life and what seemed like wildness to this eastern girl. The next day, gratefully, the group was much quieter. Perhaps too much. The picnic that had been planned turned into a group nap. Ted was the organizer of the picnic activities and was clearly as disturbed by the napping as I was. I wasn't the slightest bit tired and was delighted at his arrival. I'll never forget my first sight of him. He was dressed in blue jeans and a rumpled shirt and wore an old brown hat cocked to one side.

Ted decided we should make a movie and in about five minutes had written, cast, and begun the film. I don't remember the plot, but I remember how much energy he was able to inspire in this previously napping group. He was, of course, the director. He instructed us to roll down the hill. We did so without hesitation and with great merriment at least 10 times. I never stopped laughing.

We met for our interview around the cocktail hour in Ted's new townhouse on the upper east side of Manhattan. The townhouse is next door to some kind of consulate. One almost feels as if something slightly criminal is going on there which, for Ted, adds to his idea of excitement and is one of the reasons he likes it. Ted met me at the door with a martini in his hand, dressed in blue jeans and a beautiful, probably Italian, cotton shirt. Most of his front hall is taken up by a large grand piano that plays constantly, which gives an eerie feeling to the room, as if a lovely 1930s movie star is about to appear to take over the already moving keys. The front room is sparsely furnished but interestingly so. Each piece has a story that Ted tells with humor and interest. He walks around—or rather lopes around, as he is a tall man with a boyish manner. He is very charismatic and quite handsome in a different way from when he was 22, but he still acts and talks like a kid. Before the interview, he insisted we view on the large television set one of his newest ads for Sony. It was completely magical. All the ads Ted has done have a storytelling quality, enticing the viewer to dream. Ted is the best dreamer I know. He is constantly enthusiastic about his dreams and, even though they are created for his clients, they capture audiences completely. While we watched the video, Ted constantly commented on what was happening as if he had never seen it before. He wanted me to love it, and I did.

Ted's an easy talker and remembers each life event in great detail so the listener really feels a part of what happened. His life has been an adventure for him. He never doubted where he was going or that he would be a success. He never worried about making money, only that he would be interested in the venture. He remains unfailingly excited about his ability to create and continues to inspire those around him. He has written screenplays, novels, children's books, and countless advertisements. And he has more fun doing it all than anyone I know.

Ted Bell

*Be the most passionate person in the room. Not the smart-
est, not the cleverest, but the most passionate. Care more
than anybody and you'll be the one that wins.*

My grandmother gave me the courage to get up every day and believe
in myself. She came to my college graduation and asked me, "So now
what are you going to do?" I said, "That's a pretty good question. I
have no idea." I really didn't. I had no idea. I never had a job in college. Not one. I just had fun. I was probably having too much fun. I
wasn't motivated to work. I had a little sports car, and it was great.

I was an English major, so I told my grandmother, "I think I want
to go to grad school at Princeton, study English, get a Ph.D., and
then teach. But I'm really not sure." She said, "Who's paying for this
graduate school?" I said, "Well, you are!" And she replied, "I want
you to come work in the bank." Our family was in the banking business, and I was the last male heir, so it was assumed I would eventually take over the bank. My great-grandfather started the bank, and
my grandfather was chairman. By the time I graduated from college
in the late 1960s, my uncle was the chairman.

Well, my grandma said, "I want you to try the bank. I know you
think you won't like it, but at least try. If you'll give me one year in
the bank, I will then give you a year to do whatever you want to do.
I'll pay for it." My grandmother was really cool. I started a novel in
my senior year and sent it to a major publisher. I got a letter back
saying, "We are not going to publish this, but we really like it and
would be interested in seeing the completed manuscript." So I
thought that was encouraging. I told my grandmother about it, and
said, "I'll work in the bank for one year, and if it doesn't work out,
then I want to live in Europe and be a writer." She agreed.

So, I moved to Florida, worked in the bank, and hated it. I started
as a check-signature person. This was in the precomputer era. I had
to check the signature cards against the checks for every check in the
bank. It was horrible. I worked in a tiny little room with five women.
They'd look at me, a college graduate with long hair, and say, "Why is

he back here with us in this bank?" I wasn't working in the big main bank, but was in a little tiny bank out in the boondocks. Only one person knew of my family connection to the bank. One woman used to dump trash on the floor for me to pick up.

I did this work for a few months and then got promoted to posting the general ledger. There was this machine with three separate typewriters, like a huge adding machine, and it posted everything that came in and everything that went out. It was very complicated. The guy who was working it was not getting it to the president's desk until 11:00 A.M. I was told to get it done a little earlier. Of course, I didn't know anything, and I was horrible in math, but I went in early and figured the machine out. When the president came in at 9:00 A.M., it was on his desk. That success got me out of the horrible back room and onto the floor, which they call the platform in the banking business.

The only person at the bank who knew of my family connection was the janitor, Jesse. The first day I was there, I walked to the storeroom to get some pencils or something, and he said, "I know who you is. You's Mr. Powell's grandson. I remember you when you was 12 years old. You used to come to the bank on Friday afternoon and pick him up. You Mr. Ted." I said, "Jesse, this is our secret. No one in this bank, other than the president, is allowed to know I have anything to do with the Powell name." And no one else ever found out.

So, there I was on the floor, and Mr. Alvarez, the vice president, would come to Jesse and me every time it rained (and in Florida it rains like every 20 minutes) because it was our job to bring the American flag in and out of the building. It was torture. One day I said to Mr. Alvarez, "Let me ask you a question. I was a Boy Scout; I was a Cub Scout. I never heard this rule that the flag has to come down during the rain." He said, "You know, you're right. But Mr. Powell, the chairman of our company (Mr. Powell was my uncle, but Alvarez didn't know that), was a navy man, and in the navy the flag always goes down in the rain." Years later, I talked to my uncle and told him the story, and he said, "What? That's not true. There's no such regulation in the navy."

By this time, my job was to open checking accounts, which I was good at. The bank was next door to the Wright Brothers Shrimp packing plant, so most of our customers were shrimp packers. They would come in wearing see-through raincoats with shrimp skins all over them. So I would ask, "Would you like the green alligator on your checks, or the red?" In the meantime, when the shrimp packers weren't there, I would read a book at my desk. Mr. Alvarez sat right next to me, and one day he asked, "What are you doing?" I replied, "Reading." He said, "You can't read at work." I said, "Why not? When customers aren't here, there's nothing for me to do." I would bring in whatever I was reading at the time. He said, "Oh, really? I'll find something for you to do. From now on, you're not allowed to have any books on your desk." So then I just started reading the dictionary, because everybody had a dictionary. Every day I would draw a line, and the next day I would read every word for that day. There was nothing he could do about it because everybody had to have a dictionary.

At the bank, we introduced the precursor to VISAs and Master-Cards. It was called BankAmericard because it was created by the Bank of America. My job was to go up and down the trail and sell local merchants on the advantages of a credit card. No one ever had a bank credit card before. It was the very beginning. My only problem was this beautiful Jaguar I received in my senior year at college. I was 21 years old, and I'd pull up, and they'd say, "Whose car is that?" I'd say, "That's my brother's car." Most of my customers were places like ballet schools and repair shops, and here was this kid in a Jaguar. They didn't get it. I was very good at selling those BankAmericards, though. It was my first experience ever trying to sell somebody on something. I would walk in, sit down with a total stranger, and convince him why he should give me 17 percent of everything he made. None of them could understand. So I said, "There are a lot of Yankees coming down here. Their cars break down, and they don't have the cash to pay for it. But if you've got a sign out front saying BankAmericard, they're going to come to you instead of the guy across the street because you'll take their card." I liked selling, but I also liked to write.

I finished my year at the bank, so I decided to go to Europe and start writing my book. The only hard part was when I went to my uncle and told him I was leaving the bank. He said, "You can't leave. Mr. Etto says if you keep going the way you're going, you'll be president of this bank before you're 30." I didn't want it. He said, "Do you realize what it means to be president before you're 30? You're great at this." I said, "I don't want to be great at this. I don't like banking. It's boring, and I don't want to do it, so I'm going to be a writer."

I lived in Switzerland and worked on my book for a year. Every weekend I went to Milan because I had a friend, Birdie, who was a Vogue model and was living in Milan with Tony, a very famous photographer at that time. Tony was always leaving for Africa to do a Vogue shoot. He had this incredible studio in the center of Milan, and I thought, "This is great. I like this." And so I started asking Tony, "What is this whole thing?" All these advertising people would come to his parties. He introduced me to a guy named Luigi Montegheni, who I still know to this day. I said, "I don't know anything about this, but I really want to talk to you about advertising." So Luigi offered me a job. But then his boss said, "You can't hire this kid. He doesn't speak Italian. If he doesn't speak Italian, I'm not hiring him." So I was fired before I was even hired.

Then I went to London and lived in a shitty little room. I took Birdie one morning to show here where I lived, and she couldn't believe it. I started writing letters to ad agencies, telling them what happened in Italy, and how I really thought I would be good at this. I didn't have a portfolio. I didn't know what a portfolio was. Some of them were really nice and talked to me. There was a guy, Malcolm Gluck, at Doyle Dayne Birnbach in London and he supported me. He helped me create a full portfolio—and that's how I got into advertising.

In that portfolio, which I still have, I wrote an ad for Nikon. It was a picture of a sunset, and the copy was, "If there was only one sunset every 25 years, I'd get my dog and I'd go to the beach with my Nikon." The idea was that if the sunset was such a beautiful thing and it only happened every 25 years and you wanted to take a picture of it, you'd better have a Nikon. That was the concept.

I knew then I wanted to do great ads. I didn't want to move up the ladder. I didn't want to be chairman. I didn't want to tell people what to do. I didn't want to be a boss or anything. I just wanted to do great ads. As I started to get further along in my career, then I wanted to get young people to also want to do great ads. The trouble a lot of people have is their ego gets in the way of their success. They don't get joy or pleasure seeing others succeed, and as a result, nobody wants to work for them. But if you are truly generous with your time and energy and help young people succeed, then everybody wants to work for you.

I never worried about whether I was going to be a success. I always thought I would be. I had total confidence. I always knew I had taken the right turn. And I've been really lucky. Things have never gone badly for me in my career. (I'm looking for some wood to knock on.) I've never felt insecure about my talent or my ultimate success. I've never worried about that. I just had this feeling I could do ads and I was really good. My first job was at a little agency in Hartford, Connecticut. My salary was $7,000 a year. I remember the creative director coming up to me after hours when they were closed and asking, "Do you like this idea?" I thought, "Wait a minute. I'm this kid making $7,000 a year, and the big guy is coming to ask my opinion about whether something is good."

There actually was one time when I felt I should consider something else. A friend of mine in the movie business asked me to write a screenplay with her. I wrote this screenplay in a very short time and loved it. I also had the good fortune to sell it. Everybody in advertising wants to sell a movie. Everybody writes screenplays, and I sold my first screenplay just like that. I said, "Wow, if I can write it that quickly and sell it, maybe I should have been in the film business. I should have been in Hollywood." This was around the time I got married. I really seriously thought about moving to L.A. and working in the movie business. It might be really good there. I could write and then ultimately direct feature films. And then I thought, "I'm doing great in advertising. Do I really want to live in some crummy little apartment in West L.A. and spend all my time pitching ideas to seedy agents?" (I know some people in the business are really nice.) Anyway, that was the only time I really contemplated leaving advertising to do something else.

I think creativity is a critical component in success, no matter what field you are in. I think Bill Gates is amazing. I think [Sumner] Redstone is a very creative guy. John Reed is probably a really creative guy. Although you have to be creative, you can't be successful in the upper end of advertising unless you can sit down with the CEO of a major corporation and talk intelligently about their business. Really good creative people in advertising are people who understand business in an almost instinctual way. They just get it. I can sit down with Jack Nassa or Alex Trottman, CEOs of the largest companies around, and talk to them about business. I know what Alex is doing right and what he's doing wrong. I just have an instinctive understanding.

I am really passionate about what I do, and everybody knows that. People sense it. They feel it. I think it's a key thing to have. You need a strong vision of what's good, bad, and the right thing to do— and a passion for it. It's as though we're all in a boat, with our hands on the oars, waiting for someone to tell us where to row. It doesn't matter if you're right or wrong as long as you say, "Let's row this way." You might be headed for the rocks. If you sense something funny, you say, "I hear waves breaking on the shore. Let's go that way." It doesn't even matter. It really doesn't. As long as somebody is saying, "Just row this way." And if you hit a rock, you say, "Let's turn around and go the other way."

I'd say my leadership style is passion for what I do, which inspires people to follow. I also have very high standards. I learned this from Bill Burns, who was my boss at Doyle Dayne, one of the most legendary guys in my business. He had this capacity to get people to think the way he did. He couldn't see everything in the company, and he couldn't be at every meeting. All he wanted was to have the people in the company, when they made a decision, ask themselves, "Jesus, what would Bill think?" You can't be in every meeting, you can't be at everything. Ads are sold by us right now in India. Do you think I'm looking at them? I'm not. But there are people out there who say, "I don't think Ted would like that."

For me, success is going to work every day and feeling really happy about what I do for a living. First of all, you've got to be lucky enough to pick a career you are good at. Or, like in my case, just drift into it. Most people in advertising drift into it. When you grow up, your parents either want you to be a banker, a lawyer, or a doctor. Nobody says, "Advertising." It's not the kind of business that makes people say, "I want my son to be an ad man." But advertising is fun.

I think young people coming into advertising today are different. There are big schools around the country for advertising now. But what's really happening in advertising is an amalgamation of disciplines. Advertising and the movie and entertainment businesses are all coming together. As the future unfolds, they'll be essentially doing the same thing. When Steven Spielberg puts a Ford Explorer in the heart of Jurassic Park as the vehicle driven through dinosaur country, the movie also becomes an advertisement for Ford Explorer. Everything is sort of coming together. Jeff Berg from ICM met with me a year or two ago, and then a guy with Digital Domain, Jim Cameron's company. They both wanted to talk about how to marry movies and advertising. They were thinking maybe the people who write ads should write movies because ad people know more about what's going on in the culture than 22-year-old screenwriters sitting out by the pool.

When I was a kid, I always felt separate from everybody. Not arrogant, but I always felt I was different. I don't know how to explain it. I wasn't a kid who played softball in the afternoon and ran around riding my bike. I did that stuff, but I also spent long hours in my yard in Fort Lauderdale. In the afternoon, I would climb to the top of this tree. It would sway in the wind, and I would just sit there for a long time. I felt totally removed from everybody. Then, when I was in the sixth grade, I started writing short stories. I didn't have my own room. I had a room with my brother Mike, so there was really no place for me to be alone. I was really into writing, so I would literally sit in the back seat of the car and write while everybody was running around or riding bikes. I'd turn in these short stories to my sixth grade English teacher. She loved me and would put my stories up on the wall. Everybody would read them and say, "Oh, that's great. I can't believe you wrote that." I felt like I was a writer from the time I was 11 or 12 years old.

Advertising was perfect for me because I also had good instincts about the business and confidence that I could sit with the bigwigs. When I was young, a unique thing happened when I was befriended by Mike Laranthal. Mike was a friend of my grandfather's. He was a very powerful man and a very successful lawyer in New York. He was on the boards of a lot of big companies. He was a founder of Eastern Airlines with Lawrence Rockefeller and Eddie Rickenbacker. He would take me with him to New York from when I was nine until about 13 years old, and we would go to Rockefeller Center, where Eastern Airlines was located. I would sit around and read while he'd go to an Eastern board meeting. Then we would have a dinner or cocktail party at the hotel, and then we'd go to "21" with Larry Rock-efeller, Eddie Rickenbacker, and high-powered businessmen. We wouldn't have dinner until 10:00 P.M. They all talked business, and I just sat there listening. I was just a kid, but I was very comfortable. They talked about the airline industry and their plans. So I learned not to be intimidated by powerful men. At 10 years of age I sat and listened to powerful men talk about business. I probably soaked it up and didn't even realize it.

Of all the ads I've done, my favorite so far is one for Memorex of a girl, a waitress, saying good-bye to her boyfriend. The actor was this very cool-looking guy who later became a big TV star. In the ad, he's standing in the desert near this dusty old 1955 Porsche and a sign that says, Diner. He's looking at the girl and says to her, "Look, I'll be see-ing you around, okay?" And he walks over and gets into the Porsche. This beautiful girl is crying because he's blown her off. He gets in the car and tears off, heading down the highway into the sunset. Then the car stops, reverses, backs up. The guy gets out of the car, walks back-wards, and walks back into the camera and says, "Look, I'll be seeing you around, okay?" Then the camera widens to reveal the girl who is crying is watching this scene over and over again on Memorex tape. And a voice comes up and asks, "Is it love, or is it Memorex?" She's torturing herself watching this. That's my favorite.

My advice to young people is to just be passionate about what-ever it is you do. Be the most passionate person in the room. Not the smartest or the cleverest, but the most passionate. Total passion. Say thank you. Say please. Don't take the credit, take the blame. Do all that stuff, that's good. But if you're the most passionate person, you'll probably win. Care more about it than anybody and you'll be the one that wins. People love that. People gravitate toward that.

Conclusion

Ted Bell lives, works, and talks passion. To Ted, passion is having a vision, self-confidence, and most importantly, a love for your work. Success is communicating this passion to everyone and being happy with what you do for a living. It's waking up every morning and saying "Yes!" to the day.

As he grew up, Ted knew he loved to write and gained a belief in himself from his grandmother who always believed in him. He interacted with powerful businesspersons and developed business acumen at an early age. Yet Ted never had a clear career goal in mind. In fact, he drifted into the advertising business where he luckily found a vehicle to express his talents and experiences.

Reflecting on factors to career success, Ted points to creative people with an instinctual understanding of business, a talent he sees in the elite business leaders of today like Bill Gates, Sumner Redstone, and John Reed. He also feels generosity with your time and energy to others in your field contributes to success. When colleagues experience your efforts to help them, they truly want to work with you. This, in turn, helps you develop a winning staff.

Ted's observations about the current changes in the advertising business are quite insightful and useful to individuals considering this field. Today, he observes, advertising is an amalgamation of disciplines—advertising, the movie industry, and the entertainment businesses all coming together. Keeping in touch with the business world and apprised of its many changes obviously contributes to one's success.

SUSIE TOMPKINS BUELL

Founder/Former Owner, Esprit Clothing Company

Susie Tompkins Buell was the cofounder and co-owner of Esprit de Corps, a clothing company located in northern California. Susie started Esprit in 1968 as the Plain Jane Dress Company. Within a year, her then husband, Doug Tompkins, joined in running the company. In 1979, the company name was changed to Esprit de Corps. It grew to become one of the country's leading manufacturers of junior sportswear. The company was not only successful, but under Susie's direction, it also addressed political issues that concerned its customers, such as the AIDS crisis. Susie sold the company and retired from Esprit in 1996. She married Mark Buell, with whom she lives in northern California. She remains very active in politics and social causes, focusing primarily on women's and children's issues.

I interviewed Susie at her remarkable home on the bluffs above the ocean in Marin County, California. Her home, which is filled with mementos from both her friends in politics and her family, reflects Susie's great sense of style. It's a low-key style, but a very interesting one. The house is an inviting and charming ranch house, furnished with California-casual furniture. Every corner of the house reflects a well-thought-out visual plan. The photographs on the walls are all specially arranged. Even the bathroom fixtures are unusual and dramatic.

On the day of our interview with a strong wind blowing, we decided we would still enjoy doing the interview outside. We settled into chairs on the hillside and, while we were talking, threw tennis balls for Gracie, Susie's adorable Jack Russell terrier.

Susie's home is often filled with children, grandchildren, friends of children, friends of Susie's and Mark's, visiting dogs, and whomever or whatever might be in the neighborhood. She attracts people because of her openness and charm. She has the ability to make anyone feel at home with her. She often asks disarming questions that seem to come from out of the blue. I found myself answering her from my heart because that's how she communicates—very intimately. Susie has a fresh stream-of-conscious way of communicating, changing from one subject to another quickly, and yet it's easy to flow with her. She is incredibly astute in her observations and intuition about others, which contributed to her great success in anticipating fashion trends and styles.

Susie Tompkins Buell

. . . people who are lucky enough to be in a position to choose their careers should ask themselves, "What interests me? What makes me really excited?" Then they should get creative and never take no for an answer.

For a while, as a kid, I wanted to be a nun. I think it was when I was most impressionable, when I was going to Catholic schools. Later on, I wanted to be a mother, and then a wife. I never had any big goals, but I was very restless. I had a lot of energy. I always wanted to be somewhere else, somewhere I wasn't.

My first jobs were baby-sitting and wrapping Christmas boxes. During high school, I had my first real job at the Metropolitan Life Insurance Company. I wanted to earn money to buy a car because my parents would either pay for college or a wedding—but those were my only two choices. I never liked school and wasn't a good student. I probably had something that would be described now as attention deficit disorder. I wanted school to end so I could start living and experiencing my life.

So I got married to get away, gain independence, and so on. I met Doug Tompkins and was very interested in him. He was such an adventurer. Like me, he was never satisfied with where he was. We both always wanted to try something else. I thought he would be so great because he would never settle. He would always reach out further. We got married, but Doug was so independent he was gone right away. I wasn't happy with being alone. I thought if I had a baby, I'd be happy—someone would love me and want to be near me. We had Quincy and then Summer and, around the same time, started an outdoor equipment store called The North Face. It was really Doug's enterprise, but I always helped him.

When our kids were little, I was very restless. I knew I was a good mother, but I still felt I was missing something. A friend of mine in Europe was trying to work as a model, and I went to visit her. I was about 26, and it was my first trip to Europe. I was buying for the ski line at The North Face and was very taken by the style and fashion of European women. Their clothes were very simple, but there was a certain femininity and very stylish look about them. I didn't understand why we didn't have clothes like that in America. I came back and another friend, Jane, was looking for a job. I said, "Why don't we start our own company and make clothes like the ones I saw in Europe?" And that was what we did.

We called our line Plain Jane. The dresses were very little, very nipped-in close—not feminine in the way you think of feminine now, but tailored, snug, and great looking. Very modern, kind of mod. That's what had been so fashionable when I was in France. We found a patternmaker and looked for fabric. People laughed at us because we were just two girls trying to start a company, and neither of us had any fashion training. Jane was very ambitious, but I was just curious and helpful. I wanted to do whatever it took to make things happen and trusted whatever we did would be fun. It didn't matter if it made money.

Meanwhile, in 1967, Doug and I became bored with The North Face and sold it to two brothers. We owed money so we didn't make very much in the sale. Doug bought a used Ferrari with the money we did make. So here we were, two kids with a baby, no money, and debt. It was a time, however, when there was a lot of freedom to do what you wanted, to express yourself. It was okay to be an adventurer and explore life to see what it was you wanted. There was no pressure to know your long-term goals, to say, "I'm going to be this or that" or "I'm studying here or there." It was good because I believe we grow from our mistakes more than any other kind of education.

So we decided to sell the Ferrari—it was an old used Ferrari, not some fancy thing—and start a new women's clothing business. Doug put an ad in the paper and in the middle of the night the phone rang and some guy said, "I want to buy your Ferrari. When can I see it?" He came over right then, and he and Doug went out. When Doug came back three hours later, he said the guy wanted to buy the Ferrari for cash. He also wanted to know if he could back us in the business, as Doug told him we needed a financier for Plain Jane.

In the beginning, we found contractors in Chinatown to make our dresses. We didn't know what we were doing, but it didn't matter because nobody else was doing it. As long as we were making something nobody had ever seen before—and people wanted it—we couldn't go wrong. We had a friend who worked in PR or advertising at Joseph Magnin, the department store. She made an appointment for us with the head buyer for the junior department, and he loved our dresses. Magnin bought them and put them in their windows. They were so excited. It totally launched us.

After that, the dress business just kept growing until one day dresses suddenly went out of style, and everybody started wearing jeans. We were in L.A. showing our holiday line and shopping in a store called Judy's. It was a very happening place in those days, and all the salesgirls were wearing jeans. Since the little tiny dresses were still in stores, they were wearing dresses over their jeans. We knew we couldn't make jeans—that's an entirely different business. Also, we didn't have time because we were going into the market the next day. So I called up our pattern maker and said, "From the same fabric of every dress we have, make a pair of pull-on pants that you just slip into. Get them down here by tomorrow. We're going to sell them as pant suits." And we did. We sold zillions of them.

I love solving merchandising problems like that. I love discovering things. I love finding new ways of doing things. When you have a problem it's great because you must figure out a solution. Fashion is evolution. You have to always figure out what's next, and it's fun. You're not always right, but in the fashion business you can always recover. You

71

have next season to try again. I can't stand the problems I faced years and years later in which it's really fighting with all these egos. I just couldn't deal with that and that's what did me in at the end.

So we got away with selling these pants that went underneath the dresses for a season or two. But girls were wearing jeans and smocks then, so we started something called Sweet Baby Jane—cute little smocks that went with jeans. Then we decided to start making T-shirts and thought we should go to Hong Kong or India and make them off-shore. That was absolutely a new thing then. Customers loved them. And we soon found out about other things we could do in India. One thing led to another. So eventually we went to Hong Kong and started making T-shirts and woven shirts. Then we made some of our dresses and, finally, we even made jeans there.

We had some difficulties at each stage, but in those days you couldn't go wrong because the market was so hungry for new products. As long as items didn't have three sleeves or five legs, we could sell them. I always had a good feeling for color. I chose a lot of great colors and had things embroidered. There just wasn't young, fun merchandise like ours. We couldn't make enough.

We needed a corporate name for the business so we chose Esprit de Corps but it wasn't put on our labels for a long time. For about six years, we had all these little catchy name categories for our clothes like Plain Jane, Sweet Baby Jane, Rose Hips, Jasmine Tee. Then I had the idea for incorporating our different labels and coordinating our products so they matched and made sense. Instead of having a shirt line that didn't have any matching bottoms, we packaged things so a store could buy from us in a different way. At the time, clothes were really sold by category. We'd market jeans or shirts. We wouldn't do a collection. We really started the collection idea before anybody else. I got the concept from fashion and wholesale apparel shows in Europe and from how the Europeans marketed. We started marketing items that were coordinated—the pants were made in the same colors as the tops—and now it's just the way it's done. But in those days, it wasn't. Once again, it was all about marketing and planning how to present and package the products.

So instead of having five labels, we had Esprit Sport and the Esprit Collection. Esprit Sport was T-shirts and knits, very sporty. The collection was a casual line of dresses and linen fabrics. That's how we came up with Esprit. We took our corporate name, put it on our labels, and it was very, very successful.

Doug and I learned as the company grew. For a long time, as we were learning ourselves, the market was also developing. We grew up with the industry. By the time our company was 10 years old, we had 10 years' experience. We learned a lot, and the stores learned a lot. We were coming up with good ideas—ideas that were just kind of common sense—like coordinating colors, silhouettes, having conceptual collections, and other things that made shopping easier for the buyers. With its great name and image, Esprit couldn't do anything wrong until about 1986. That marked the the beginning of the fashion industry price wars. The Gap was great at it. They copied everything hot in the world at a great price. So if you were an original, you had to get your prices way down. Even for a successful brand name, people still want value. People always want a bargain. We were known for color; we really brought color into the market. But it wasn't difficult for other companies to come up with interesting color palettes. And by then, many European services guided manufacturers and helped them figure out what to make. The fashion industry became much more professional.

In 1990, with some partners, I bought Esprit from my husband. Five years later, I sold out because the company basically outgrew me. It has a life of its own now. For years and years, I felt so responsible for that company. It was like a baby, like a child we conceived that really needed us. It needed Doug, me, and all the people we had around us who were hand-chosen and good. But now it's on its own. It has its ups and downs, but it will never have that surging time again. I don't think that's possible in the industry now.

When we started out, I never thought about whether we would be successful. Neither did Doug. We just pushed ahead. What drove us, I think, was figuring out as we went along how to make it happen. You have a good idea for a product. You figure out how to make it and how to sell it. Then you figure out how to really produce it.

Now I think being successful is understanding what your purpose is—what you want to accomplish by the end of your life. What will make you comfortable when you know your life is ending? Is it that you accomplished things, that you did good work, that you helped people? I'm concerned now about the world, our community, and the condition of the earth and humanity. That's what I want to engage myself in today. I want to solve some of the problems and make the world a little less painful for people because it's a pretty scary place when you stop to think about it.

I realize, however, one's definition of success depends on where you are. If you're sitting here like me with all this splendor under your belt, you're going to talk about health and peace of mind. If you're in the rat race, you're going to talk about being bigger, getting more power, being there first, having the most of this and that, controlling and conquering everything. That's what happens when you're in business. You must be first and have the most of everything. But I don't think that's interesting anymore. Not at all. When you get off the business treadmill and start looking at the bigger picture, first you look at your life. Then you look at your environment and the world around you. You try to get a grip on that and it's awesome, it's amazing. But I don't think you can see all that when you're on the treadmill. All you can talk about when you're on the treadmill is perhaps spending a little more time with your family. That's about as close as you can get to what's really important. As long as you're in business, you're playing that game.

Having business success, however, gives you tremendous opportunities to meet people and do things. Because I've been successful, I can get almost anybody on the phone. That's a real opportunity I wouldn't have otherwise. I can make connections because I've got credibility from my success. It gives me more ability to do good work, and to me that's what's really important. Today, I enjoy bringing women together and getting them to understand we've got to support each other. That's my favorite thing right now—being there for women and getting them to recognize the power we have when we pool our talents, our interests and our understanding and work together.

I've created a foundation and its focus is women in education. I've been very supportive of the school of journalism and photojournalism at the University of California at Berkeley, for example. I'm committed to educating women so they can take responsibility for the people in their lives. I believe if you educate women, they're going to educate their kids or not have kids they can't afford to educate. They'll also educate the men in their lives. And, hopefully, with more responsible, educated people, we can solve some of the problems we face.

The best advice I have for young people is to get involved with something that really, really fuels their passion, something they get excited about and can throw themselves into deeply. And work hard. We used to work 14 hour days, seven days a week, week after week. But it was fun because we were passionate about it. We were exploring. That's another thing that makes work fun, breaking ground. I know this advice is idealistic. Most people in the world have to work simply to put a little bowl of rice in front of them. But people who are lucky enough to be in a position to choose their careers should ask themselves, "What interests me? What makes me really excited?" Then they should get creative and never take no for an answer. Of course, it's also important to keep things in perspective so you don't end up a lonely, old curmudgeon because all you did was work.

I don't have any regrets today. Sometimes I miss the adrenaline from work, but there are all kinds of wonderful, satisfying things to do when you're not working. A whole kind of soul-searching is opened up. I never would have gotten married again if I were still working, and my second husband, Mark, wouldn't have either. When we stopped working, we had a new perspective. If you're an executive, you're working a minimum of 14 hours a day. Even if you're home, you're on the phone. You can't put quality time into your life because there's simply no time left. So how do you have perspective? You don't.

There really isn't gentlemanly behavior in business anymore. You can't trust anybody, and that's not the way it's always been. When we started out, we didn't have contracts. There was loyalty. People liked us because we were enthusiastic. People bent over backwards to help us. I don't think that exists anymore. I go out of my way now to support small companies, but sooner or later they will get eaten up or bought. It's better now to be bought and then go out and do it again. Since I sold Esprit I've thought of a half-dozen companies I could start. I realize if I did, however, I would have to open concept shops and then sell them as soon as they took off. If I didn't sell, the companies who wanted to buy me would end up copying the concept anyway and wiping out my smaller shop. They could pay more rent and make the product for half the price. I had one great idea but to succeed I knew I would have to give up everything for six or seven years, and I'm not ready to do that. In order to succeed now in a business where you create products or have a concept that could be rolled out, you have to think about packaging it and then selling it as soon as it becomes successful. And that's kind of sad.

Conclusion

Susie Buell was restless as a young mother and had a sense of merchandising and adventure! The germination of the idea for Esprit de Corps started with a trip to Europe and her observation that the United States did not have the same kind of clothes as Europeans. "Let's do it!" seems to be Susie's mantra, and she progressed with simple merchandising ideas that eventually matured into retail concepts and her success. Susie says she was lucky the market was hungry for new products in the 1970s and 1980s and even into the early 1990s. She now sees how retail has changed and how her success story cannot be duplicated in today's marketplace. There are new rules for retail success, just as there are new trends in advertising as described by Ted Bell.

At this time in her life, having sold Esprit de Corps in 1995, Susie defines success as understanding your purpose in life, what you want to say you've accomplished by the end of your life. She is very honest when she further reflects her definition is based on where she is in her life. Susie says she has the luxury of thinking about health and peace and is very grateful for this freedom. She recognizes that others are at different stages in their lives and careers, and may be putting in the 14-hour days she once did to achieve career goals. Their definition of success would probably be very different.

Susie's advice on career success is similar to Ted Bell's. Be passionate and creative, and in addition, be realistic about the time it will take to succeed. Finally, if you are in the merchandising business and are developing a great product, be ready to sell it and move on to other products. Keep the spirit of adventure.

BOB COHN

Former CEO, Octel and Lucent Technologies

Bob Cohn, the founder of Octel Communications, served as its chairman and CEO until Octel's acquisition by Lucent Technologies in 1997. At the time Octel was acquired by Lucent, it was the world leader in voice mail systems, serving over 120 million people in 70 countries. Mr. Cohn, who earned his M.B.A. from Stanford University, worked with McKinsey and Company from 1976 to 1979 and, before founding Octel, was employed by Acurex Corporation. He is currently on the board of Saba Systems and Chapters Online. He also serves on the boards of Business Executives for National Security, the Castilleja School, and the National Conference for Community Justice and is a member of a small advisory panel to the United States Department of Defense. Originally from Canada, Bob now lives with his family in the San Francisco Bay Area.

I first met Bob during a flight from San Francisco to London. I had an aisle seat and was talking with a man across the aisle when Bob decided he wanted to sleep. He asked me to be quiet in a way that made me smile rather than feel irritated. Later, when we were about an hour from London, we talked. We discussed everything from how to enjoy life after achieving success to how to raise children in a household of plenty. Bob, an extremely bright man, listened carefully to what I had to say and then commented thoughtfully, often disagreeing with me. It was a challenging and provocative conversation and thoroughly engaging.

I interviewed Bob at his home in the Bay Area. He lives in a delightful colonial house near a college town. Though he has a fairly simple lifestyle and is very down to earth, he does keep a full time assistant and a cook. His favorite vacation spot is a camp in northern Canada, where he travels to each summer with his children. His house is furnished rather formally, but a large, shaggy dog hovers about, lending a more casual air to the place. As the interview shows, Bob is very deliberate and thoughtful about his life decisions and has a great memory for detail. His path was not as direct as some, but he always sensed he would make the right decisions. And, unlike many people who make a great deal of money in a very short time, Bob is not arrogant about his success.

Last fall, Bob was kind enough to host a lunch for some of my students at his home. He greeted us very genially and made everyone feel welcome. We sat around his long, formal dining room table and enjoyed a delicious lunch while he spoke about his career. One bit of advice he gave the students made sense to me, but I wonder how many people are really able to follow it. His advice is to decide how much money you need for a life that contains everything you desire. When you determine what net worth amount provides this, then promise yourself when you reach that point, you will stop pursuing wealth and start giving back to the world. Bob has really done this, and I admire him for it. Many people make some money and the taste of it makes them want more and more. Bob, however, is both a prudent and philosophical man who lives with forethought and sensitivity.

Bob Cohn

People usually plan their vacations more carefully than they plan their careers. I'm a compulsive planner, but there were times when I had no idea what I was doing.

My grandfather started a business shortly after he came to Canada, and my father also ran his own business. When I was a kid, I really liked going there and seeing our name on the door. I always wanted to run a business myself. I also loved medicine—I actually helped diagnose my mother's brain tumor when I was young. In high school,

I became very interested in entertainment. I managed some bands in high school and kept them booked constantly. I arranged for some big-name performers to play at our school and a nearby college and put my band in with them. I was fascinated with the music business.

So by the time I started college at the University of Florida, I was really interested in three things. I wanted to be a neurosurgeon, run my own business, and make movies or do something in the entertainment business. After a while, I concluded the people in the entertainment business might not be the sort of folks I would enjoy being around for the rest of my life, even though I still found the industry fascinating. That narrowed it down to either medicine or business. I started in pre-med and, unfortunately, had a not-so-inspiring organic chemistry teacher who didn't speak the language very well. I didn't know if I could cut it.

That summer—it was 1967—I worked for my uncle in his fur factory in Canada. I really liked working there. It was the biggest fur processing factory in the world. You don't hear about fur factories, because coat makers buy furs at auctions and send them to the factory for processing. My uncle does all the processing for most of the major coat manufacturers. My grandfather started the company and my father, a chemist, helped develop it.

At the time, no one had heard much about computers. I had a friend, who today is a really neat nuclear physicist, who was then attending a university near the factory. For amusement, he asked me to visit the computer lab while he ran his programs. He was using an IBM 360 model 50, the biggest thing you could find at the time. It replaced an old IBM 1620, which they left in another room. Anybody could play with the old one and my friend encouraged me to try it. I knew nothing, so he taught me how to program it while he waited for his programs to run on the big computer. It was very hands-on. You punched your own cards and fed the cards into it. It would then punch an object deck and run a print deck, which you put through a printer. This was really early stuff, but I understood it. The computer had such a slow cycle speed that I debugged my programs by putting an FM radio on the computer. You could hear where it was in the program on the radio just by the noises it made.

In the meantime, my uncle and grandmother wanted me to work in the office rather than in the factory. I didn't want to work in the office, but they insisted. They had me check their payroll system, which was a very complicated, piecework payroll system with a lot of variables like how long the employee was with the union and what type of fur they processed, and so on. It took a half-dozen people almost two weeks to run one payroll. My uncle asked me to check the payroll for the last five years, I'm sure thinking that would keep me busy all summer, so I programmed the computer to do the job.

It took me about a month to learn how to program it. It wasn't a complicated program—the data was simple—but it was tedious work. When it was finished, I could check an entire payroll in an hour. I checked several years of payroll and found thousands of dollars in mistakes. I was thrilled with myself. When I told my uncle I was finished, he said, "What are you talking about? You've only been doing this for a couple of weeks." I pulled out the printouts and showed him all the mistakes I found. He wanted to know how I did it, and I told him I did it on the computer at the university. He was furious. He had no concept of computers and thought I had taught the computer his business. He thought computers were intelligent beings! So it dawned on me, particularly as I started meeting a lot of his friends, that most people in business at that time knew nothing about computers. That summer I decided not to study pre-med, but to learn all about computers. If I was going to be in business, I couldn't imagine running a business without them.

The problem was that you couldn't really study computers in those days. The closest I could find was University of Florida's industrial engineering program. As a part-time job, I started working in the University of Florida's computer lab. It turned out that I almost had more knowledge of programming computers than most people on earth at that point. I asked the professor who started the computer lab how I could learn more about computers. He suggested classes in industrial and systems engineering, his department, to get a good overview. He soon asked me to work with him, teaching FORTRAN to his college seniors. Then he developed the first computer science curriculum at the university. I graduated with a degree in computer science because I had either taken or taught all the courses in that new curriculum.

I didn't study computers only because I was fascinated with them. I studied them because I really wanted to either start or run a business and wanted to learn what computers did and what you could do with them. I didn't want to be in my uncle's situation—he thought these machines were brains that were going to take over the world.

I finished school in '72 and wanted to enroll in business school. I applied to two schools but didn't get into either one. So I thought, if I want to start a business, I better learn how to get money. There wasn't really much venture capital in those days, so I decided to work in commercial banking. If I learned how to lend money, I would know how to borrow it. I wanted to work in a bank that had central-ized commercial lending so I would be able to get involved with larger deals, not just loans to the local dry cleaner. Unless you went to Stanford or Harvard or had a great M.B.A., Chase Manhattan or CitiBank wouldn't hire you, and in the early '70s, branch banking wasn't allowed in most states. California and Maryland were two states that did have centralized commercial lending, so I got a job with the Maryland National Bank in Baltimore. I paid my own recruiting expenses and only earned a salary of $7,800 a year, but it was fabulous. I really learned a lot. They gave me the books of vari-ous companies, and like the stereotypical guy with a little green eye shade, I would spread out the books and make spreadsheets with old-fashioned calculators.

After I was there for about a year, I also started to make sales calls to companies. When I would try to get a new customer, they would always ask what Maryland National had that another bank didn't. Would we lend them money when another bank wouldn't? Would we lend money more cheaply than other banks? I had to say no to both. I told them we would provide great service, but really didn't have anything specific to offer. I tried to get the bank to do all kinds of things in order to create corporate customer loyalty. I pro-posed a frequent flyer–type program—each time a company used the bank, they would earn credits for things like personal loans for the executives or discounts on other loans. We couldn't pay them interest on certain accounts, but I thought we should give them bonus points they could cash in for something else. They never did any of those things. I think they thought I was a very strange duck.

One day a man entered the bank with a really interesting com-pany that made frit, a powder that when put on metal and heated, coats the metal like porcelain. Frit is used on things like washing machines and dryers. At the time, there weren't many people producing it, and this man made a killing. He was getting old, however, and wanted to sell his business. A buyer made him an offer for the business, and he wanted someone in the bank to see if it was enough. I don't remember the numbers, but if the business had for example $10 million in revenues, he was making $5 million in profit and had been offered about $5 million for the company. I learned how to do discounted cash flow analysis with a slide rule in my industrial engineering courses. There were no calculators then that performed operations like that. I used all the formulas to analyze his company and told him, "You've got a profit stream of $5 million a year. Do you know what that's really worth?" He didn't. I told him if he bought a bond that paid $5 million a year in interest at 5 percent, he would have to buy a $100 million bond. By the same token, his business was worth $100 million. He was stunned. He had been offered $5 million. The potential buyer saw a money machine and an owner with no financial knowledge. I wondered how many more people were out there like this man.

My job also included making decisions on loans. A customer would come in and say, for example, he wanted to open another branch of his department store and needed a $1 million loan. I'd ask how he knew the amount he needed. He'd answer $1 million was about how much it costs to run a branch. My job was to decide if he could pay back the loan. I would ask a lot of questions, and every time he'd answer a question, I'd spend five hours doing a spreadsheet. Then he'd answer it differently, and I'd have to do it over and over again, constantly changing the numbers. I noticed the bank had a time sharing computer they rarely used. I wanted to write a program to do the spreadsheets and was able to get some time on the computer and a terminal on my desk. I wrote a FORTRAN program that did spreadsheets. It was similar to what Excel does now, not quite as fancy as Excel, but very effective. Then, people would come in and say they needed a $1 million loan, and I could do an analysis fairly quickly, including spreadsheets of their income statements and all the variables. I could project the x number of years it would take them to pay off their loan and figure out how much they really needed. We could run another quick analysis to see what would happen if one of the projections didn't pan out so well.

People suddenly received a real service at our bank that they couldn't get elsewhere. When I made sales calls, I could say, "Here's how I can help. Let's go over your books and I'll tell you how you're doing." This was really thrilling to people. You couldn't do that kind of thing then.

After a couple of years, I applied to business schools again. I applied to 10 schools, got into nine and chose Stanford. I left the computer program I wrote with the bank, and I'm told they used it for years. So by the time I went to business school, I already saw the value of computers to business, and I always did from that point on. They could really be put to use as a tool.

Throughout those years, I tried to make sure I had my dance card punched in all the right places to start or run a business one day. I wanted experience in international business, so I took a year between undergraduate school and working at the bank to live in France. I wanted fluency in a second language and familiarity with the humanities and other things I hadn't learned in school. I traveled throughout Europe, but was based in France. I learned French so I could eventually work somewhere abroad and learn international business. Between my first and second year at Stanford, I tried to get a job in an international business in Europe. European companies didn't usually hire American business students for the summer. I wrote about 30 letters and only about five of the companies even responded to my letter. One letter, however, hit a desk at exactly the right time. The man who received my letter at the Rothschild Bank in France ran the Division of Financial Affairs and Relations. He employed four French people who had been to American business schools, and he had gone to Harvard himself. He was irritated that the people at the bank couldn't quite think like Americans and wanted to hire an American, and about that moment my letter landed on his desk. His main concern about me was whether I could speak French. Of course, by then I spoke French fluently. This man attended school with a fellow who was then the dean of admissions at Stanford. He called the dean and asked if I could really speak French. The dean checked me out and assured him I could. I was hired for the summer, and it was a great job. I acquired a better understanding of international business and received exposure to things I never saw before. The man who hired me became a very close friend and eventually the godfather to my oldest child.

When I graduated Stanford, I considered working for an international company. My resume read international banker because I'd been in banking and I'd worked abroad in a bank, so I thought I better not because I would get pegged as a banker. Instead, I needed some line management experience, but I didn't know from where. I was offered a summer job for a consulting company that I turned down, but now I thought consulting might be good. I would learn to solve management problems from people who knew how to put out fires. Some consulting firms were solving problems most businesspeople didn't get to attack until they made it to the top of a very big company. So I worked for McKinsey and Company for a couple of years, and it turned out to be a good choice. I learned how to write, organize, design, and make articulate presentations that can hold and engage an audience and how to be very analytical and focused. McKinsey is very good at teaching easy-to-understand, journalist-style writing so you get the point across without superfluous garbage. They teach you all these skills for two years, and after that you learn how to become a partner. I stayed two years, was certified as a consultant, and ready to be trained a partner. I used computers to do certain evaluations, did a lot of strategic planning, and fixed a lot of problems. I enjoyed it. I was very good at marketing, strategic planning, and organizational structuring. I woke up one day and wondered if it should be my career. I wasn't certain I still wanted to start my own business. My wife reminded me I traveled nine months out of the year with McKinsey and asked if that was really a lifestyle I wanted.

So, I was still undecided, we were living in Canada at the time, and I became fascinated with McDonald's franchises. They were money machines, and I thought it would be cool to own one. I did some studies of these fast-food stores for McKinsey and knew there were not many in Canada. Although my wife never told me what career to pursue, when I became interested in owning a McDonald's franchise, she said, "With all due respect, I don't want a husband who flips hamburgers for a living." I explained these stores made millions, but she was still skeptical. I actually applied but wasn't accepted as a franchisee. You had to put up a fair amount of money—I think it was $250,000—and you could not have inherited or borrowed it. You had to have earned it. I hadn't earned that much money at that point. Burger King had the same requirements.

Right about then, an electronics company from California contacted me about a marketing position. They wanted someone who was out of business school for a few years and found me by looking at old resumes of Stanford graduates. This was 1979, and there wasn't much going on in Silicon Valley then. Several years earlier, I had a job offer from a Silicon Valley company called Rolm. I didn't take the job, but I became friends with the founder of the company. We kept in touch and ended up vacationing together after my wife and I moved back to Canada. About the time that I received the letter from the electronics company in California, we traveled to California for a vacation and the Rolm founder was there, too. We left the frozen tundra and arrived in nice, warm California. My wife, by the way, is always cold. She wears a sweater in the summer. So we were in sunny California and my friend from Rolm asked me about my plans. I told him about all the travel at McKinsey. He thought it sounded like a perfectly horrible job and suggested I come to California and work for him. I explained what I really needed was line management experience. I had all the education I needed, all the staff, banking, and consulting experience, but I was either going to manage something or not. I was at the point in my career when I had to get that experience. If I didn't, I might as well stay in consulting. I told him about the company from Silicon Valley that contacted me. He said to check it out, and he would set me up with some other companies at the same time. He introduced me to a venture capitalist who introduced me to a couple of start-ups in the area. The two possibilities I considered most seriously were with Intel, which was only a couple hundred million in size then, and another little $50 million company. They told me I would have been the first M.B.A. ever hired at Intel. The position was for a production control manager for their factory that made the 80xx series of chips. They really wanted me, but I hesitated because the people who would work for me were convinced you didn't need an M.B.A. to succeed. I was going to be the proof. I didn't need 40 factory workers trying to prove a person with an M.B.A. was useless. The other company was run by a man with an M.B.A., so I knew that wouldn't be a problem there, but they had other problems. I worked for that company, and the experience was phenomenal. They were doing everything wrong, and I had to turn things around.

My strength is really in marketing and strategy. This company had a neat market niche, making specialized measurement and control instruments. They were using computers and making machines for use in very rugged locations. I became the marketing manager for this group, and it was like a McKinsey study. In two months, I figured out where their strengths and weaknesses were and located their market holes. I talked to customers who told me what we needed to do. I studied their competitors, who were ignoring us, and devised the product that ended up being the most successful product they ever had in that division. It weighed products while in motion at high speeds as they came off production lines. If a product is underweight, companies can't ship it because if a weights and measures inspector finds an underweight package in a store, the company is fined and must recall all their packages. So it was a real critical machine. If it wasn't working at all, the production line would shut down. If it was making errors, the company risked losing a lot of business. This product sold more units in a shorter time period than any other product the company had. The only problem was the engineers hadn't built it right. We shipped 500 of these worldwide in a month, and they were breaking down everywhere.

The company had a serious engineering problem. The service people were servicing the machine incorrectly, the manufacturing was laid out wrong, and the design was bad. I knew we had to standardize the design first. We couldn't fix the other areas until the design was right. We went through several engineering managers and a general manager because we couldn't fix this design. They finally brought in a guy who used to run FMC central engineering labs. He didn't have a clue how to solve the problem, but he knew a guy who could, Peter Olson. Peter Olson weighed 350 pounds, smoked four packs of cigarettes a day, and charged a lot of money as a consultant. He came in, asked a lot of questions, looked at the design, and said, "For $100,000, I'll solve your problem in two weeks. For every day I'm late, I'll take $10,000 off the bill and for every day I'm early, pay me a $10,000 premium." My bosses were upset he was so expensive, but I told them the company would fail if they didn't fix the problem.

Our engineers didn't know how to fix it. I was assured by them several times that the product was ready to ship, and then I tested it and made it fail every time. Besides, if Peter Olson didn't fix the problem or was 10 days late, his fee would be zero—what did we have to lose? Earlier, I stopped production and had a massive argument with the general manager about this product. He said his Cadillac failed several times and when it didn't work, he'd take it in for warranty repairs. I argued we couldn't consciously ship a product that was defective. I even quit over it, but agreed to stay on for six months because I didn't think it was appropriate to leave in the middle of this mess. They ended up firing the general manager, so I decided to stay.

Peter Olson solved the problem in a week. He didn't show up for work for about four days. I thought perhaps he was drawing a complete blank, or maybe we'd been had. But he eventually showed up, worked all day and night for several days, and solved the problem. The machine was just designed really badly. He not only made it work, but tripled its performance and made it the most reliable product of its kind in the world. After that, I wanted to know Peter. That machine was one of the company's lower-end products. I wanted to design the high-end product with the same parts, using the same boards and the same soft display. I wanted to make the machine simple enough for a guy with a third grade education who couldn't speak English to use. Also, we sold this machine all over the world and never put the displays in other languages. I suggested that we have content-sensitive soft displays that could be in any language and would only display what the operator needed to decide at each moment. I even got a patent for that concept.

While we designed the second product, I got to know Peter Olson. I knew if I were going to start a company, I would need a great technical person. And Peter, as it turned out, was looking for a president. So we played this little mating dance for a while until we broached the subject. Then we started to discuss the industries that interested us. The industries included measurement and control instruments, process control computers, medical instrumentation, aircraft avionics for nonairliners, telecommunications, and microcomputers. This was 1981, and the Justice Department was all over both AT&T and IBM. I followed the cases and thought AT&T was going to lose and IBM would win. I thought everybody would get involved in transmission or PBXs when the phone company split up, not white-collar productivity. So we wanted to do business in white-collar productivity. A friend of Peter's had been involved in something called voice mail. We had no idea what it was so we went to an office automation trade show in Las Vegas. Everything there was designed by techies who seemed convinced everyone else in the world was also a techie. It took half an hour to learn how to even touch at least half the products. I knew the average executive, who couldn't operate a computer, would never come close to this stuff. I wanted to produce something a 50-year-old noncomputer person would want to use because it actually solved business problems.

The technology that enabled voice messaging had just come on the market a couple of years earlier. I thought voice mail was interesting and could solve real problems. If we could make the right product with this technology, we'd have something big. I used to think I was born too late and all the great ideas had been taken—there was nothing left. Now, I could hardly believe there really was this big gap in the market. I started researching the field and learned there were quite a few companies trying to fill this gap. I called all these companies—Wang, IBM, Voice & Data Systems, and a company called VMX, in Texas—and asked for material on their voice messaging systems. They didn't ask me why I wanted it, but just sent me all their sales literature. Wang was so busy they sent me the sales manual for their product. They were all so proud of their work they made their technical papers available, and I got copies of them all.

When I looked at what these companies were doing, I thought they all missed the mark. The products they designed were too big, too complicated, and didn't solve the real problem, which was how to answer somebody's call. I roughed out a product spec and asked Peter to design a product that could do voice mail for larger corporations, which could sell for a low enough price. I figured we had to sell the product for $50,000 retail through distributors, and we could finance our own growth if we made a large enough profit margin. Peter thought about it and said he could do it. He couldn't really explain clearly why he could do it and others couldn't, or what the approach would be. He just said other companies were thinking about it all wrong. I won't relay the details, but history shows he was correct. I wrote the business plan, and we tried to raise money to start the company, but it was very hard. Peter had been with a company before this one, and he had a reputation as a really eccentric person. People were reluctant to invest money in a company he was involved in. I wrote the plan for Octel between November 1981 and March 1982, and we eventually found money in July 1982. As it turned out, the company's growth worked out exactly the way the plan said it would. We were only off about a year.

I retired in 1990, after we crossed the $100 million mark in the company. We were always very profitable and grew at such an incredible rate we beat out all our competitors. Wang and IBM left the voice messaging business. We completely eclipsed everybody. A lot of it was luck. They didn't focus much on our business, and that's all we did. Early on, I put in a management team that could grow the company. I wanted people who had experience in a $100 million company, people at a much higher level than our company in its early stage. I didn't think the management we had could grow at the accelerated rate the company needed. When we crossed the $100 million point, I figured we now needed someone who had been in a billion dollar company to get ours to grow to his level. He would know how to reconstitute the management team and structure the company. I just didn't feel comfortable taking it further myself. Plus, I had two kids, with a third on the way. My kids didn't know who I was, and I wanted them to know. So I retired.

Looking back, I realize I had a talent I didn't know I had, a talent I thought everybody had—vision. Vision is the ability to identify an opportunity no one else can see, visualizing how to get there and knowing when you're not on track. I also have natural merchandising skills. When you've lived in a house for a while and all the lights are off at night, you can walk through the house without tripping over anything because you can visualize where everything is. That's how blind people get along. They have vision. They get to their destination because they've scoped everything out. In the same way, some people have marketing and strategic vision and can identify where to go and what they need to get there. Other people can't do that. I never understood why they can't, but they can't. We hired a man who had been executive vice president of Hewlett-Packard. He ran a multibillion dollar division of that company, had a Princeton engineering degree and a Stanford M.B.A. But he fell flat with us because he didn't have the vision or the merchandising skill.

The ability to motivate people is also critical. For a long time, I didn't realize I had the ability to inspire people. I thought everybody was like me, but they weren't. I knew how to explain where we were headed in a way that made people want to get there with me. I think that's a talent good CEOs have. It's a natural talent. Inspirational presidents can get people to identify the hill and then convince them to go take it. But someone who explains a million details in a very dull monotone bores people, and they don't want to go anywhere with him. I don't know why some people have these qualities and others don't. It's probably genes to some extent, but not entirely. Even though I always had an ability to explain things, my training, in particular the McKinsey work, helped me learn to synthesize complicated things and explain them simply.

People usually plan their vacations more carefully than they plan their careers. I'm a compulsive planner, but there were times when I had no idea what I was doing. A good first step to decide on a career is an intellectually honest inventory of yourself. I did this in the '60s. I listed the things I really wanted and the things I didn't. What I found was some things I wanted opposed each other. For example, it was not a value to want money in the '60s, but I decided I would like a lot of money. If I wanted to be socially or politically correct but still wanted money, I would have had a contradiction inside myself. Or, if you really enjoy teaching young children and that's your career choice, but you'd also like to own a $20 million home in Beverly Hills, it probably won't work unless you marry someone with a lot of money or inherit it. So you have to reconcile your conflicting priorities. You must get your eye off the $20 million home or change your career choice to something that will earn money for the house. After you reconcile those opposites, you should take your inventory again, focusing on not rationalizing your current behavior. Most people rationalize whatever they're doing at the moment is the right thing for them. To be really honest in this inventory, however, you can't rationalize this way. You must accept the possibility that what you're doing is absolutely wrong for you. After you've done these inventories, it's easier to make a career choice. It's still hard, of course, when you're only 17 or 25. I had some idea at 17 or 18 about what I wanted to do in life, but if you think about it, we are adolescents then. We're not asking an 18 year old to do career planning for a lifetime. We don't have a clue about life but are supposed to plan a career. We take advice from people and get degrees. We take an interesting job because it pays a lot of money or it's some classy thing we feel good telling our friends about. If we start getting good at it, even though it is not what we really want as our life's work, we end up making it our career. If we're really lucky, we like it, but if we're not lucky, we wake up six years later in a place we absolutely hate.

Another way to plan a career when you're young is to imagine what you might feel proud of having accomplished at 50. You can also imagine what a 50-year-old employer is looking for in the person they're hiring for the job you really want. What education, what track record and reputation would that employer look for? That's the stuff you've got to do. If you get a job offer from George Lucas at the Skywalker Ranch postproduction studio, and it is not your real career goal, then either quickly redo an inventory to see if your career goal is wrong or thank George a lot for the offer, but don't do this. Or if somebody offers you a great job for a lot of money selling pianos, but it doesn't have anything to do with your career goal, don't accept it. Be less concerned about money, the name of the company, or the position you take and much more concerned with how this job builds your reputation and experience toward what you really want to do in life.

It's also important to work for people who are good teachers. Even though you might be offered a good position, if it's for a bunch of loose cannons who don't know what they're doing, you will make a lot of mistakes and won't learn much from them. If you work for the right people, however, they will teach you well, and you'll be able to visualize how these people solve problems. You'll then have the right values and skill sets. You'll be able to predict what that person would do in a similar situation. You pick the right mentors by picking the right job. Someone may have no intention of mentoring you, but if he or she does the job well, you can learn from watching him or her.

If you take a cushy job, you'll never really succeed. It's like buying bonds—if you buy a 1 percent bond, chances are you will earn 1 percent. If you take a little more risk, you'll get a better return. So push yourself harder. Take a job that's on the right track, but you're not sure you can do. Just keep pushing yourself to grow.

Conclusion

Unlike several of our entrepreneurs, Bob Cohn had a clear vision of his goals. Bob knew early on that his strengths were marketing and strategy development, and he wanted to start or run his own business. Bob made decisions based on his goals and talents, adding more skills in each position he took. It is interesting, though, that despite such clarity and careful planning, Bob mentions times when he had no idea what he was doing. He even feels his path to Octel was not a straight one at all!

Bob began his career in his father's fur factory where he had his first experience with computers. He then took a job in a bank in order to learn about venture capital, followed by a position with McKinsey. Next he thought about buying a McDonald's franchise, thinking it could be cool to own one. Instead, he accepted employment in the Silicon Valley where he brought all his computer, financing, and consulting skills together— first working for someone else, and eventually creating his own company, Octel. Then Bob retired 10 years later!

Bob's career advice is to be strategic about your choices and to not just follow the money, which our former CEOs and entrepreneurs likewise emphasize. Instead, know yourself, sort out your priorities, and develop a plan. Along the way, learn skills that will help reach your ultimate goal. And even with such a carefully planned approach, remember a spirit of experimentation will be helpful, like the time he went to a lab to fool around with computers. (This advice reminds me of Thomas Jefferson's remark, "I'm a great believer of luck, and I find the harder I work the more I have of it.") Finally, Bob notes the real success differentiators are the talent for having a vision and the ability to inspire others. And like Ted Bell's comments on passion and business sense, Bob sees these talents as instinctive.

RAY KASSAR

Former CEO, Atari

Ray Kassar hasn't slowed down since he started Brown University at 16 and finished at 19. After graduating from Brown, he worked in Burlington Industries' training program for two years. Ray then went to Harvard Business School, received his M.B.A., and returned to Burlington, where Spencer Love, the founder and CEO, groomed him for a top management spot in the company.

When Love died at an early age, Ray remained at Burlington for several years. He left to start his own company, which he ran very successfully for several years, until selling it to take a position at Atari as president and CEO. When Ray took over the company, Atari was losing money. Under his leadership, the company was doing $1.5 billion in sales within three years. After four years, revenues increased to $2.5 billion, with earnings of $4.5 million.

I first met Ray because he knew my mother on Long Island when they both were young. When he moved to San Francisco, he invited me to dinner. I found him entertaining and charming. An entire upstairs room in his house was filled with Atari games, and we had enormous fun playing with all the new games. It was the late '70s, and video games were still uncommon. We all became like kids around them. I had Ray over to dinner on another night, and after dinner I decided we should play some games. Ray was the perfect guest. He willingly danced and played, even allowing two of us to roll him up in a rug. To this day I can't remember why we did that, but I do remember what a good sport he was.

Ray knows everyone. He has friends all over the world and in every field of business. Pictures of movie stars, royalty, and of course, family, along with other objects that reflect a sophisticated life of travel and entertainment fill his home. His house, which sits on a hill in San Francisco and has the most spectacular view of the city I have ever seen, is both glamorous and comfortable. Those two qualities also suit Ray perfectly—he is both impressive and friendly, simultaneously. He is easy to talk with, open, and yet very aware and sensitive to others.

Ray's success is in part certainly due to his wonderful charm and ability to make everyone feel at ease. He has an expectation that everything in life will go well, and this optimism encourages those around him to believe the same. And he inspires trust. People meet Ray, like him, and want to do business with him. He's the kind of guy people love. You know he will always be genuinely friendly when you meet him.

Ray Kassar

Ask questions, and don't take anything for granted.

I was born in Brooklyn, New York and went to school there. I graduated from Boys High School, which was a very good school, and won a scholarship to Brown University. My English teacher at Boys High School was an alumnus of Brown, and he suggested I apply. I think it was a combination of his recommendation and my grades that got me in. I started Brown when I was 16, and graduated at 19. I was very excited about the whole idea of going to this great school. It was during World War II, so they had accelerated semesters, which is why I finished at 19.

I didn't know what I wanted to do, but I was very ambitious and a very hard worker. I just knew I was going to do something. Interestingly enough, my father was a laid-back guy, happy with whatever he had. He had no ambition at all and didn't care about money. My mother wanted the best for us but didn't push us, so there was never any pressure to be successful. I don't know where I got my drive to succeed, but my brother had it, too. It's curious because we had no pressure environmentally or parentally. In fact, my father discouraged college. He thought it was a waste of time. My mother was very proud of my grades and my scholarship. I'm sure that, in his way, my father was too, but he acted neutral about it all. If I wanted to go to college, it was fine, but he thought it was a waste of time. My father's family immigrated from Syria in 1911 and were in the silk business. They had silk mills in Patterson, New Jersey, but lost everything during the depression. So my father worked sundry jobs like handyman and cabdriver. We didn't have much, but I never felt deprived. There was a lot of love. I had a very happy childhood.

My father wouldn't let us take summer jobs. He thought it was a terrible thing for a young person to work. At college, however, I needed to support myself because I had no money from home. So I worked two jobs. I was a steward in the fraternity house, and I had the best job—running the switchboard from 12:00 to 8:00 in the morning. I never slept. I made $25 a week on the switchboard, which was a lot of money then for a kid. It's equivalent to maybe $300 or $400 a week now.

After college, I had a set of fortuitous circumstances. My roommate at Brown was Bob Love, whose father was founder and chairman of Burlington Industries. We had been living together for two years, and I never knew Bob's family was wealthy. He always borrowed money from me, never had any money with him, and his clothes were very tattered. Then one Christmas, he said he was going to see his father in Florida and asked me if I would like to come. I told him I couldn't afford it. He was very vague and said he thought we could work it out. It turned out we went down to Florida in the company plane. His family owned a huge villa in Palm Beach. Don David, the dean of Harvard Business School, was also a houseguest that weekend. While I was there, Bob's father offered me a job and the dean of Harvard Business School offered me a scholarship. I don't know what I did to impress these two guys, but that's a true story. So when I finished Brown, I started work at Burlington as a trainee in North Carolina. I went from mill to mill to learn the business for nine months. Harvard was to come later. The dean wanted me to gain two years of work experience. So I worked at Burlington for two years, and they gave me an official leave of absence to attend Harvard Business School.

When I returned to Burlington, I became a sales trainee in New York. I loved it. It was exciting. It was fashion. It was New York. I met interesting people. I soon became Burlington's youngest vice president. Then, Spencer Love suddenly died on a tennis court in Palm Beach, and the treasurer of Burlington became the new president. At that time, I was group vice president of the home furnishing division and made more money than the new president, so he immediately demoted me. The general impression at the company, except for the people who worked with me and knew my work, was that I got where I was because of Spencer Love. I was furious because I really worked very hard. I wanted to quit, but thought if I did, they would say, "That's right, that's why he left." So for three years, I had to prove myself all over again to Charlie Myers. After that, I was promoted and everything was fine. I was vindicated. It was rough because I couldn't see the point—no one respected the new CEO—but I felt I owed it to Spencer Love. It would be a terrible thing to quit and let people think I got where I was because of Spencer Love. That's why I did it. I had to prove my worth.

As a manager, I was willing to be innovative and had good people skills. Those were my strengths. Of course, I was also lucky to be at the right place at the right time. Spencer Love was truly my mentor. I worked very hard because with Spencer Love that's what you did. I worked from 7 A.M. until 7 P.M. I worked nights and weekends, willingly. He liked that I was a kid who came from nothing. I worked my way up, did well in business, and people liked me. I was never intimidated by him and told him whatever I thought. People were typically very afraid of him. Like all great titans of industry, he was a legend. People were very intimidated by him, but I was very comfortable with him. In fact, that first weekend in Palm Beach I remember Bob, my roommate, said I acted like I'd been living this life all my life. The first dinner was extraordinary, and Bob waited for me to go crazy, but I just took it in stride. He couldn't get over it. I think Don David and Spencer Love were also surprised that a 19-year-old kid was so comfortable with them. When I think about it, it was amazing—I was just myself. It must be something in my genes. I think I would have succeeded even if there hadn't been a Spencer Love. All Spencer did was give me the opportunity. I was very interested in textiles because my father's family had been in the textile business, so there was a link.

I just felt comfortable. It seemed like Burlington was my home, and I had a very happy, exciting career there.

After three years, it was time to choose a new chairman. There were three contenders. One was Bill Klopman, who ran the apparel division. Then me, who ran the home furnishings division, and one other fellow. I was the youngest by maybe 12 years, so they picked Klopman, even though I made more money for the company. My area accounted for one-third of the sales and two-thirds of the profit. Apparel was two-thirds of the volume but only one-third of the profit. I gave the company 28 years, and I thought there was a message in their decision. I decided to strike out on my own, and I left. It was a gutsy move. I started a company that was the first to import men's and women's apparel from Egypt. I called it RA Kassar Corp., and it did very well.

One day, prior to leaving Burlington, I had lunch with Bill Sarnoff, a classmate at Harvard and good friend. He told me that Warner Communications had just bought a company called Atari, and they were looking for someone to run it. He asked if I was interested. I was actually insulted. It was a $27 million company—why would I leave Burlington for that? After I left Burlington and started the Egyptian company, he called me again. He asked me to do him a favor and meet with Manny Gerard in the office of the president at Warner's. I told Bill I didn't want to waste their time, but finally agreed to go. Manny is one of those nonstop talkers, and he convinced me to travel to California for the weekend, take a look at the company, and give them a report. I went to Sunnyvale, met Atari's founder, Nolan Bushnell, and looked around. I was really fascinated. It was a whole new world for me, totally engineering and technology based. I came back and told Manny it was kind of interesting, but I didn't think I was the right guy. I wasn't a high-tech person or an engineer. He said they needed a business person like me. He asked me to make a proposal. They would consider anything. I told them I wouldn't give up my company but would be willing to go to Atari one or two days a month. I made them a crazy proposal, asking for things like a driver so I didn't have to drive from San Francisco. They agreed to everything.

After the first month, I realized it wouldn't work. It wasn't fair to Warner's. I couldn't really give them a full evaluation of Atari in one or two days a month. Because I had a good person running my company, I decided to stay for six months at Atari, as long as I could come back as needed. They appreciated my honesty and agreed. At the end of the six months, they thought I would recommend the liquidation of the company, but I told them they had a great opportunity. I gave them a report and encouraged them to invest in the company. They asked me to stay on, but I really wanted to return to my company. Finally, I agreed to finish out the year. When it was over, they wanted me to become president, working for Nolan Bushnell. I said I would only consider staying if I ran the show and Nolan left. He was the old regime and a problem for me. So, they got rid of the old regime, and I became chairman and CEO of Atari. In retrospect, they were right. I was the perfect choice because I was a nonengineer. I was a business guy and wasn't embarrassed to ask dumb questions. I had to sell my own company because I was so involved in Atari. It was fun having my own enterprise, but it wasn't meant to be.

When I arrived at Atari, the company was doing $75 million in sales and losing $15 million. There wasn't a chief financial officer. There was no production manager. There was nothing. I had to build an infrastructure. Also, the products they made were very defective. When I arrived, they had just shipped about 100,000 video games, and 80,000 came back. So I worked on quality control also. Within three years, we were doing $1.5 billion, within four years we were doing $2.5 billion and earning $4.5 million net, after reserving another $.5 billion. We made so much money.

I guess I was effective because I'm tough in business. I appear easygoing and laid-back, but I'm tough. Also, I'm both a hands-on person and a strategist, which I think is a little unusual. Usually it's one or the other. I'm just there constantly. I love business. I'm good at delegating also, but if I'm not getting results I move quickly and cut my losses. If a guy isn't doing a job, I have no compunction about firing him, as long as the facts are there and it isn't an emotional action.

In the case of Atari, I think I was successful because I knew nothing about the business. I didn't have any preconceptions. The last thing they needed was another engineer. That was their problem. Everybody was an engineer and nobody was focused on the bottom line. Nobody asked, How do you make a profit in this business? Or, where do we go from here?

I was with Atari from February 1978 until June 1983. I had a noncompete clause for five years after I left, so I couldn't really do anything. They were afraid I would work for a competitor, so they paid me handsomely. I invested and became a consultant.

It was a difficult transition. Steve Ross, the chairman of Warner's, never interfered with anything I did initially. We were a fully owned subsidiary of Warner's, and Steve was my boss's boss. He never came out to see Atari and never wrote me a memo or anything. In the five years I ran Atari, I had two phone calls with him. The first phone call was the beginning of the end. He called me and said he was trying to get Spielberg to make movies for Warner and had just made a deal with him to make a video game out of the movie *E.T.* He guaranteed Spielberg $20 million—not against royalties—just a flat-out guarantee. He asked for my opinion. I told him it was the craziest thing I ever heard of. We never guaranteed anybody a flat fee—even for Pac Man. On top of it all, he wanted us to produce the video game for Christmas, and it was July 1982. I told him our lead time was six months. He said, "Well, you've got six weeks." I told him it was impossible, but he said he already made the deal. It was done. I called my guys, and they thought I was crazy. Spielberg came up three or four times to help, and we produced a game. It was a turkey. Steve insisted we ship five million of them. So we shipped five million and five million came back. That was the beginning of the end.

There were a series of things like that. We got so much publicity I think Steve was resentful. He came out for the first time and started to take over. We never spent any time alone together, so I asked him to my office for five minutes. He came in very reluctantly. He doesn't like to be alone with anybody. I told him I sensed he was unhappy with my performance. If that was true, I wanted him to just tell me, and I would leave. He said I was doing a brilliant job. So I asked him to stop the interference. Well, it got worse, and I was fired in June 1983. I think they started to be dissatisfied with me because Steve didn't like my objection to the Spielberg deal and told him what I thought honestly. No one speaks to Steve like that. I also think it is a cyclical business. Kids were getting a little tired of the games. It was a combination of those two factors. They called me to New York on a Thursday. I saw Manny Gerard, and he couldn't really come out and say I was fired. Finally, he said, "Well, maybe it's better if you resign." I told him if he was trying to fire me, he should just tell me. He said Steve wanted him to fire me. I said fine. I was pretty upset—not for being fired, but for the unprofessional way in which it was handled. The next day, Manny called me at the Mayfair Regent where I was staying. He said he spoke to Steve, and Steve wondered if I would stay for another three months since they didn't have anyone to replace me. I said, "Manny, you've got to be out of your fucking mind! You just fired me and now you want me back." Can you believe that! I said no, and went to Europe for 10 days. They hired someone and, of course, it went downhill.

Steve Ross is a very complicated guy. He is charming and very low-key. I think he was nervous because at one point Atari represented 60 percent of Warner's profits and 40 percent of their sales volume. Suddenly, this little thing called Atari was the whole news about Warner Communications. I received a lot of press. I didn't want it, but couldn't help it. We were the Nintendo of that time, and everybody was writing about us. Steve didn't like that. He had a huge ego, and I think that was part of the problem. I have absolutely no regrets, however. The experience was terrific. It was the beginning of a new industry that took the country by storm. It prepared kids for the computer generation.

As for the future, there's one more business I want to do. David Ferguson and I are working on an Internet concept called Shoppers IQ. He's doing the technology, and I'm running the marketing. If it's successful, I think it will be quite exciting. There's nothing like it on the Internet. I still have a lot of energy and am ready to run another big company, but I'm afraid someone will say I'm too old. I don't think about my age, however, I just think about building things. I'm pretty much involved in this project with David, but if some large company with a lot of problems approached me, I would seriously consider a position.

Things have changed a lot in business today. In my day, there was corporate loyalty and loyalty to your employees. I would get a lot of calls from headhunters when I was at Burlington, but I was indignant anyone should think I would leave the company. I've had two jobs in my life. If you tell that to someone today, they think you're crazy. People bounce around two or three times a year. I've seen people who have had 10 jobs in three years. It's desirable, apparently. In my day it wasn't, and that's a big change. There's no loyalty anymore. I don't think we will swing back to that, either. There is too little to be gained by staying in a job today. The environment and circumstances have changed. Today most employers, and certainly those in high-tech, almost feel the more companies you work for, the better prepared you are. I don't necessarily agree with that, but I think that's the mind-set now. The rest of the world is becoming like us. Europe is now beginning to restructure—they're lagging behind us, but they're getting there—and Asia will at some point.

I still strongly recommend the business school experience to young people today. One thing I learned in business school is how to ask a very good business question, to hone my communication skills. Also, I never had any intimidation, but if I did, I lost it at Harvard. I would ask anything of anybody, in a nice way, of course. It's also important to be curious about your work. Ask questions, and don't take anything for granted.

When I was growing up, my heroes were historical figures. I loved reading history books. I was interested in people who ran countries—prime ministers, presidents, people like Napoleon. I admired success and was fascinated by how people achieved different objectives. In the business world today, I admire people like Jack Welch of General Electric, Roberto Goizueta of Coke, people who have really achieved a lot and built empires. There are many, but the one person I admired the most, of course, was Spencer Love. He was born in Cambridge, Massachusetts, where his father was a math professor at Harvard. He borrowed $3,000, went to North Carolina, and founded Burlington, which he built into the largest textile company in the world.

Conclusion

Although he wasn't clear about his career direction, like other entrepreneurs, Ray Kassar just knew he would achieve something with his life. There was no pressure to succeed from his family, but he had an inner drive. So when opportunity presented itself to him at Burlington, he embraced it. As he said, "I was lucky to be at the right place at the right time."

Ray brought a talent for innovation and excellent people skills to Burlington. He also brought an ability to make tough business decisions and a gutsy nature. After 28 years with the company, he called it quits and started his own import business. From there, he took the top position at the engineering and technology-based company, Atari.

Ray bases his success at Atari on his fresh perspective about the business. That is, he had no preconceived notions how to make the company successful. Instead of providing answers, Ray asked questions, and he turned the company around. After Ray left Atari, he tousled some with Steven Spielberg and a new business venture with Time Warner. When he saw it wouldn't work, Bob left and started his own consulting business. And now he's looking at one more business to pursue, an Internet start-up.

What an adventuresome career! Ray's career advice is to discover and know your talents. Ray, for example, was good at building things, which one can see is a recurrent theme in his career. Learn to ask good questions and become an excellent listener. Be curious, don't take anything for granted, and ask for what you need.

The world of work is changing, Ray reflects in the interview. Loyalty left the business community. This is a thought shared by other CEOs and entrepreneurs. However, Ray's life and success encourages one to find career success, which might just mean honoring the old work value of loyalty.

HOWARD LESTER

CEO, Williams Sonoma

Howard Lester was born in 1935. He received his B.A. from Oklahoma University and then worked for IBM in Oklahoma City. He started his own computer programming company a few years later, which he soon moved to Dallas. At the age of 32, he sold a second computer software company to a Los Angeles firm, CSC, and worked with them for five years. He then purchased another software company, Centurex, built its business, and sold it to a publicly traded company in 1975. After taking some time off, he decided to buy a small, floundering San Francisco–based company called Williams Sonoma, which he built into a $2 billion enterprise. Lester is also a director and founder of Il Fornaio USA, a contemporary Italian restaurant chain, and serves as director for the electronics retailer, The Good Guys, CKE Restaurants, and Harold Stores Inc. He is a trustee of the San Francisco Museum of Modern Art and is on the advisory board at Berkeley's Haas School of Business, where he endowed the Lester Center for Entrepreneurship and Innovation.

I first met Howard about 15 years ago at a dinner party at the San Francisco home of Lita Vietor. Lita was an extraordinary woman—beautiful, elegant, charming, and a very talented hostess. She collected the most interesting people around her, and I always had a great time at her stimulating and fun dinner parties. The night I met Howard was no exception. When I first noticed him, he was standing by himself at the side of the room, watching people. I found him appealing because he seemed perfectly comfortable with himself and very independent. Tall and attractive, he looked as if he couldn't care less about anyone around him. He gave the impression of a Wyoming cowboy, who'd rather be roaming his ranch astride a big horse than at an elegant dinner party.

I still remember his greeting—not the exact words, but how he cut right to the heart of who I was. He said something about my family history, commenting it must have been interesting. Many people comment about my family background (often offensive), but Howard was simply genuine. I was intrigued rather than insulted, and interested in talking to him. We developed a friendship that night and stayed friends over the years. His conversation is always direct, honest, and intelligent. There's little frivolity or small talk. No matter how much time passes between our meetings, he always gets right to the heart of things by asking something like, "How's your love life?"

I interviewed Howard in his office at Williams Sonoma, an unpretentious building in San Francisco. The space is surprisingly modest and informal. It is uncluttered, with simple furnishings, and an open, relaxed atmosphere. Howard was easy to interview. He has a great memory for detail, interesting reflections on people, and a very open attitude about his life. He calls a spade a spade and tells his story with a frankness that is arresting and engaging. Although his life is a classic American success story, he is a modest man. He reminds me of my father, who never really saw and believed in his own success. The qualities that made Howard a successful entrepreneur are the very ones that make him a likable man— his independence, self-confidence, sense of humor, and a never-ending drive to achieve.

Howard Lester

Failure is just not an option. You don't consider it. You visualize success and do what is necessary to achieve that vision.

My first job was a paper route, which I started when I was about 9 years old, during the Second World War. I remember delivering papers the day Roosevelt died, in 1945. I had a paper route until I was about 15, and even at 9 or 10 years old, also worked summer jobs. I mowed yards, worked in a drugstore, on a highway crew patching roads, and for a homebuilder as a bricklayer's helper. My best summer job was working on an air force base taking compaction tests on runways. I made the most money there, and it wasn't hard. I don't remember a single summer during high school when I didn't have a summer job. We didn't have much money so I always needed to work. I didn't have the luxury of going to camp or anything like that. My father was gone, and my mother worked. I liked some of the jobs more than others. I probably would have preferred doing nothing—to have gone swimming or off to camp—but I didn't resent having to work. All the kids I knew worked just like I did.

I continued to work in college, at the University of Oklahoma, in Norman, Oklahoma. I worked for a wonderful fellow who owned a hamburger place on campus. It was a little horseshoe counter, where we sold hamburgers for $.15 each or seven for $1.00. At night, we'd sell them in the dorms. I was a cook, a waiter, and everything. I earned $.75 an hour, which was quite a bit of money in 1954, and all I could eat. Needless to say, I ate a lot of hamburgers. Unfortunately, we were known for the fried onions we put on top of the hamburgers, so I smelled like onions for four years. No one ever told me lemon juice eliminates the onion smell. When I dated my first wife, she could smell me coming for blocks!

I had no idea what I was going to do after college. I was just kind of getting through and didn't have much ambition for anything in particular. I didn't even finish school right away, but dropped out, and after about three years, was drafted and sent to Europe for a couple of years. Then I returned to finish my degree at the University of Oklahoma. I started going out again with a girl I dated before I left school. She was a terrific girl. One night, we sat and talked at a drive-in, not a movie drive-in but a food drive-in, and I'll never forget her saying, "Lester, I don't think this is going to work out. I want to marry a man with a purpose, and you don't have one." That was the end of that romance, but it made me think. I realized I probably didn't have a purpose, and I had better get one! So I started thinking seriously about things to do. For a while I thought about being an attorney, but was never really serious about that. Even though I didn't know what I was going to do, I always had a lot of self-confidence. I wasn't worried about failing or being able to take care of myself. I never really had those doubts. I felt I would ultimately be successful at something.

After I finished school, I worked for IBM in Oklahoma City for about a year and a half. I thought IBM was a terrific company, but I was always thinking of new business ideas. While at IBM, I had an account at a bank in Oklahoma City, which had purchased a 1400-series IBM computer that was only utilized about half the time. I had the idea to use the computer during its downtime to perform services for the bank's customers. It was the first time you could actually write programs for computers. They now had operating systems, so one program could serve 100 different users. Prior to that, they were basically unit record equipment. I talked the bank into developing a program to run all the billing and office work for doctors and made an arrangement with them that I would sell the automated service and the bank would pay for the programming and everything on the side. This soon became a popular application for banks and other people to do later on. And it led to a bigger idea. Two of my friends and I formed a company in Oklahoma City. We raised $100,000 and entered into a joint venture with Republic Bank in Dallas, which at that time was the biggest bank in Texas. We developed applications to serve their customers, such as doctor's billing or payroll, and became their automated customer service department. They paid us so much money per month or a percentage of the gross sales, whichever was greater. In 1962, I left my job at IBM, became the president of this little company, and moved to Dallas. I was 27. I never really had a complex about starting this business, I was just excited. I thought it would really work and was in line with what I wanted to do.

We got some other banks involved, including one in Memphis, Tennessee. We did a lot of work with Marine Midland Bank in New York State and with a bank in Jackson, Mississippi. We had offices in each of these banks. After a while, I moved from Dallas to Memphis, where we moved our headquarters. We had mixed success. We were way ahead of our time conceptually, but ultimately the banks wanted to run the business themselves rather than an outside company. We finally sold the company back to the banks. Also, the way the business was structured, we were never going to get rich. We made a moderate profit, but worked awfully hard for it. There was just no leverage for us, so we sold our little company and each took our respective shares, which weren't worth much.

So there I was in Memphis, looking for something else to do. I went to the First National Bank of Memphis and asked for a license from them to sell to other banks the software we had developed. They agreed, and I made an arrangement with them. I formed another company, wrote a brochure, mailed it to banks, and waited for the phone to ring. Sure enough, it did ring, and I started selling this software. That was really the first time software was sold as a package. We initially developed it for General Electric equipment because most of the banks had GE equipment at the time. Then, in 1965 or 1966, IBM announced a computer line called the 360. I wanted to convert all our systems to that because I felt it would be the next generation of equipment and we'd have the bulk of the market. I made a deal with the bank in Jackson, Mississippi for me to design the software and them to furnish the people. In return, I would give them a royalty—something you do when you don't have any money. I started selling this software in advance, collecting a little money down, and using that to finance the development. When we finished, I was ready to deliver, but IBM was not. The language our program was written in was COBOL, and IBM couldn't make their COBOL compiler work. My system wouldn't work until they could do that, so I couldn't deliver. Since I had sold about 20 copies of this package at $35,000 each and had already spent the deposits, I was very worried. It wasn't good.

Around that time, I received a call from a fellow in Los Angeles who was with a company called Computer Sciences Corporation (CSC). At the time, CSC was a fairly small ($20 or $30 million in sales) very elegant systems house that specialized in writing compilers and operating systems for IBM, GE, Sperry Rand, and companies like that. CSC wanted to reach into the applications software business. They sent a man to do market research, and everywhere he went people would say, "You ought to get in touch with this guy Lester. He's been doing this for several years." So they called me, and I met with them. They agreed to finish all the software and deliver it if I would sell them my company. I sold them the company and signed a five-year employment contract with them to run a department called Applications Systems, which was to do all the same things I had been doing. This was 1967, so I was 32. I moved to Los Angeles and had a great career at CSC. I did a lot of enjoyable and challenging things for a young guy and kind of grew up there. CSC became the second or third largest systems house in the world. They now do $3 or $4 billion a year.

In January 1972, after I'd been at CSC for five years, I left. There was a little company I wanted to buy when I was at CSC, but Bill Hoover, who ran the company, didn't want it. I was kind of hard-headed about it so I left, moved to New York, raised a little money, and bought the company myself. It was a company that produced software for banks, so it was familiar. They had outstanding software and some really good people, but didn't know how to sell their product. I thought it was a good opportunity. I moved the company, which was located in Reading, Pennsylvania, to Southern California and landed a big contract with Bank of America and BankAmericard. The company became the largest supplier of applications software to banks in the country. We changed the company's name to Centurex, one of those good high-tech sounding names. Again, we were ahead of our time. It was before software became what it is today. It was still hard to sell. The MIS departments of most banks preferred to develop software themselves rather than buy software packages. We wanted them to buy packages because we knew first-hand just how hard developing software is, but they didn't. It was an uphill battle. We did a good job, however, and if we had stuck around we probably would have been a fairly significant company today. We received several offers to sell, however, and did in 1975 to a publicly traded New York company, Bradford National Corporation. Bradford was closely tied with the banking industry and, at the time, was doing some very clever things. We got a good price for the company, and for the first time in my life, I made some real money. They weren't such a big company, only $150 million in sales, which seemed big to me at the time, but they really had a great, great strategy. If they had executed what they had planned, they would be a major player in the consolidation of the financial services industry today. Their management was flawed, however, and they didn't follow through. Initially, I wanted to be part of what Bradford was doing and worked for them as an executive vice president for a year and a half. I ran the marketing and pulled together all the products.

I commuted to New York, which was miserable. My marriage was going to hell, so in the summer of 1976, I quit and moved back to Los Angeles, where I had really never left. I didn't do anything for a year or a year and a half, except play golf.

I'd been around computer stuff my whole career (I was 41 or so then) and I didn't want to go back into it. The other territory I knew was the banking industry, but I didn't want to go back and say, "Well, I've got another hat on." I never thought of myself as a salesman, I thought of as myself as a businessman, but I felt like I was turning into one. Though I was a good salesman, my strong point was creating vision. I was creative and good at getting new things off the ground. I was weakest in all the little details it takes to get something executed. I could get it done, but I didn't like it, which is not too different from most entrepreneurial sorts, I imagine.

For about six months I loved not working. I'd get up every day and I'd say, "Boy, I can do anything I want today! I'm not answering phone calls, or worrying about something not happening." In the computer business you always have big customers with a lot of leverage over you. They pound on you if things don't work right. You constantly try to satisfy them because you can't afford to lose them. If my little company lost BankAmericard, for example, it would have been disastrous. So for six months I felt pretty good, but after that I started waking up and thinking, "I don't have anything to do today, and all my friends are working." I'd spend time at the Los Angeles Country Club, and the worst day was Monday because I could never get a golf date. So I started to feel the urge to do something. I really didn't know what, I just knew I didn't want what I had done before. I'd been there and didn't want to do it again. It wasn't consistent with my self-image, and intuitively, I knew I needed to grow and do something different. I thought about what was really important in life and realized money was not that important. Of course, money is important when you don't have any, but once you have a nice house and certain fundamental things, it's not important to make a billion dollars, at least it wasn't for me. What was more important to me was being excited about getting out of bed in the morning, loving what I do every day, looking forward to it, and enjoying it. For the first time in my life, I really contemplated a different set of values. Up until then, I tried to make a living, be successful, and take care of my kids, all of those things. Suddenly, I wasn't worried about that any more. I had enough money. I didn't need to worry. I thought more about what makes me happy. I had a whole different set of priorities. So I started a search and looked at all kinds of things. I knew the banks and the bankers, so I told them what I was looking for, what kinds of resources I had, and asked if they knew of anything—companies that had loans, or were in trouble, or other opportunities such as someone wanting to retire. For about a year, I talked to people and looked at different companies. I briefly got involved in a few ventures. One was a machine that used sulfuric acid to regenerate dry gas and oil wells. It was fascinating. It was the first time I had the luxury of spending time doing stuff like that.

Through one of my bank contacts, I found a little company for sale called Williams Sonoma. I flew to San Francisco and met with the lawyer who was handling the deal. It was a small company, which was only doing about $4 million a year in sales and was probably on its way to bankruptcy. The Marcus family from Neiman-Marcus owned half. Mr. Marcus died and his wife, Betty, wanted to sell it. I thought it was a neat business! I talked to a couple of women who ran the store in Beverly Hills, and they were very encouraging. One of the software applications we did back in the beginning was for retailers to do their open-to-buys and billing for their charge customers, so I knew a little about the financial side of the retail business. I spent two weeks in Emeryville, California at the Williams Sonoma offices, trying to understand the business and devise a plan if I were to buy it. I got this vision—to me the company looked like it could be a little earner. Instead of losing $200,000 to $300,000 a year, I felt with some basic improvements, the business could make $200,000 or $300,000 a year and would be a lot of fun to boot. The idea of a retail business was really appealing to me. It was the frustrated consumer in me coming out. I knew the stores could be displayed better. They also didn't have any systems, and I could install systems and plan inventories.

With a friend of mine, Jay McMahau, I bought Williams Sonoma. Jay was the only guy I knew in the retail business in Los Angeles. I played golf with him, and one day I asked if he would look at my business plan and tell me if it made sense. After he looked at it, he said he wanted to buy the company with me. At first I said no. I wasn't putting that much money in and didn't need him. But he said, "Come on, it'll be fun. Let me do it. You may need some deep pockets." So I agreed. I didn't care about the money. He put in $50,000, and today his stock is worth $250 million. We bought it in June 1978 for $100,000, and the market value today is about $2 billion. It's been a good run, and it's been fun. I moved up to the San Francisco Bay Area, and I've loved every minute of it. It's given me exactly what I hoped for. There have been very few days that I am not excited about my work. I love the customers, and I truly enjoy the quality. There are many retail businesses that may make more money, but I don't think any company is as proud of what they do as we are. We run a business in which we treat our customers the way we like to be treated. We don't sell things we don't think are good. I learned about an entire new industry, but it's a pretty simple business, really, not like the systems business. You need good instincts about it and about the people you hire, but it's not a hard business. You basically buy low, sell high, and make your customer smile by treating them the way you'd like to be treated.

Why did success happen to me and not the next guy? I've thought a lot about that. Mentors didn't really play a role in my life, as they have for others. The only fellow I ever worked with for an extended period of time was Bill Hoover, the chairman of CSC. I have deep respect for him and learned a lot just by watching him run a business, but I'm not sure I would call him a mentor. He was just a guy I worked with for five years. Some of our ventures were only moderately successful. In fact, they were probably closer to failures, but I think you probably learn more from doing something wrong than from doing it right. For me, however, failure was really never an option, and I would guess this is a pretty constant thread among high achievers. Failure is just not an option. You don't consider it. You visualize success and do what is necessary to achieve that vision. If you worry a lot about failure, it's hard to visualize success. It's kind of like playing golf. You visualize the shot and you take it, but if you visualize hitting the ball out of bounds it's real hard to visualize that perfect shot. People who visualize probably also spend a lot of time fantasizing. I've never had a great experience in my life I didn't previously fantasize about. It's amazing, really, but I think that's what creative people do. I fantasize about next year and the year after that, about where we are and how much money we're making and how many stores we have. If you do that, you're always in an inquisitive frame of mind. If you're planting seeds, some corn will grow. If you're willing to talk to people and ask questions, when an opportunity comes along, you react to it. You've probably already fantasized about it. It's not like having an engineer's mind that goes from A to B to C to D. Those types of people are so narrowly focused they miss out on the good stuff. Opportunities hit them in the face and they do not see them because they're so focused on the one little thing they're trying to do.

Some of this creative thinking can be taught. You can teach the process of what you do and teach people to be inquisitive and see more than the norm. I'm sure we're all different and have different kinds of minds, which is why psychological tests work. If someone is smart, however, they have the ability to imagine. I tend to talk about people who are the way I am, who have an ability to imagine, but there are different kinds of entrepreneurs. I know very successful entrepreneurs who are not imaginative in the way I am, who are more like plotters. They just keep plotting. The one thing I know exists in those people, however, is they don't even think about failure. I can, I can, I can—they think that way. Dick Riordan (the mayor of Los Angeles) is like that. Whether you can teach people to have the confidence so they don't consider failing, so they're not needy—I don't know. I often wondered this as I raised my children. I don't know the answer. But you can teach some of it, and Haas (the business school at Berkeley) is doing a good job. More and more great kids are coming out of the program. As they get more knowledge about how to find the steps up the ladder, it increases their confidence. I saw two young women yesterday who have an Internet start-up, and it's just terrific to hear their pitch. They've raised money and everything. I think we're going to have more successful entrepreneurs in the next century than in the last century.

I like working with students. It is fun, and I wish I had more time to do it. But how much you're born with and how much you learn, who knows? I think mental confidence is such a big part of it. If you're afraid of failing, you end up staring failure in the face all the time. You do stupid things all the time. For the first 90 days after I left my job at CSC, I said this was the dumbest thing I ever did. I just built a big new house in Rolling Hills and had new cars and all that stuff. I left a great job making a lot of money for this stupid thing that could go under. Sixty days later, I could barely make payroll. But you can't think twice.

There was this fellow who worked for me at CSC. He was probably more capable than I am, but I happened to be the person who recruited him from IBM to CSC. Soon he wanted a bigger job and CSC wouldn't give it to him. So he got a huge job at Xerox. We remained good friends, and I kept talking to him about joining me in my little company. He had this big job, was married with two kids, and had a little ulcer problem. I finally talked him into coming West and was going to give him part of the company. He had to return to Xerox headquarters in Greenwich, Connecticut, for his final debriefing. Xerox tried to keep him, but he still left. I picked him up for a little meeting. We went to a place in Vermont my investor owned. We didn't have any preparations. We just sat at a table and talked. When we went back on the airplane, he didn't talk the whole time. Over that weekend, he called me and said, "I can't do this. I just can't do it. All I can think of is how stupid I am for leaving Xerox. I need the support system." So he didn't join me. He went back to Xerox and eventually became the chairman of a very successful computer manufacturer in northern California. I still see him occasionally. He couldn't do it. He had all the confidence in the world to do what we needed him to do. He would have been wonderful and made a difference for us, but emotionally he couldn't deal with an entrepreneurial environment. I think that's true of a lot of people. They're not cut out for it emotionally, whereas I thrive on it. It didn't bother me that I didn't have a big office. I was never scared. So, that's my story and I'm sticking to it.

Conclusion

Howard Lester's career vitae makes it difficult to believe he did not have a goal in college. Howard said he always knew he would be successful, but he just didn't know in what! Fortunately, he joined a great company after college, and he began to use his real talent, namely thinking of new ideas. This was the beginning of his career, and he soon formed joint ventures in software applications, and bought and sold new companies.

The first part of his career was in the computer world, and he could have stayed there. Instead, at 41, Howard quit work, took time off, and did some soul-searching. He realized through self-reflection he was messing up his marriage and was veering away from his career passion—creating visions. Since he had enough money to take care of his family, Howard decided to explore other career options with no preconceived notion of the outcome. Eventually he found a little company he could turn around and have some fun with. With a friend, he bought Williams Sonoma, and it has been everything he hoped for—the products have quality, he loves his customers, and most importantly, he loves getting up every morning!

Howard's advice about success is to keep an inquisitive frame of mind, talk to people, and ask a lot of questions. Put yourself in the path of opportunity and focus on being successful and not a failure. Mental confidence is what he calls it, and it comes from experience and practice. Howard says being successful as an entrepreneur also takes the emotional capability to work in that environment, and he realizes not everyone is cut out for it. Likewise, Howard recognizes two types of successful entrepreneurs—the visionary, like himself, and the plotter. Know which method suits your style and talents seems to be the message here.

In summary, Howard's career illustrates how essential it is to occasionally reflect on your values and priorities. Make sure your career is in line with them, and if not, make the appropriate adjustments. Know your strengths and use them in your work. Don't be seduced by other job or company offers; stay the course of your own talents. And most important, visualize success for yourself and use that positive energy to realize your dreams.

NICK NICKOLAS

Venture Capitalist

Today Nick Nickolas describes himself as a private investor, but he spent a stellar career in business as a CEO and president of several companies. He joined Time Inc. in 1964 and was elected treasurer in 1971 with responsibility for the company's financial affairs in cable and pay television. He served as president and chief executive officer of Manhattan Cable Television in 1974. In 1976, Nickolas was appointed president of Home Box Office Inc. (HBO), Time Inc.'s pay television subsidiary. In 1981, Nickolas was assigned responsibility for strategy development of Time Inc. He was elected to the Time Inc. board of directors in 1983 and served as chief financial officer. Named executive vice president in 1984, Nickolas ran the company's video operations, including American Television and Communications Corporation and HBO until becoming president of Time Inc. in 1986. In January 1990, Time Inc. and Warner Communications Inc. merged to form the world's leading media and entertainment company, with major lines of business in magazine and book publishing, cable television, film and home video, television, and recorded music. Nickolas then served as co–chief executive officer of Time Warner Inc. from May 1990 until February 1992.

Nick is currently a director of the Xerox Corporation, the Boston Scientific Corporation, DB Capitol Partners, and Priceline.com. He also serves on the boards of several privately owned media companies. He served as a member of the board of Turner Broadcasting and of the President's Advisory Commission on Environmental Quality. Nick is also chairman of the board of the Columbia University Graduate School of Journalism, a Trustee of Environmental Defense, and a member of the Council on Foreign Relations. He graduated from Princeton University and received an M.B.A. from Harvard Business School.

I served on the board of directors of Sarah Lawrence College with Nick. He is an attractive, well-dressed (snappy as my mom would say) man with dark hair and interesting and very dark eyes. Thin and fit, with quick movements, he also seems athletic. He initially sparked my interest because he spoke out in board meetings with a distinctive, independent voice. I was also struck by his high energy level, both physical and mental, and the sparkle in his eyes. He has high expectations and focuses on the job at hand rather than socializing with other board members, as some people on nonprofit boards do. When you talk with him, he is very intense and curious and remembers all details of the conversation, but he's not interested in small talk nor is he one to linger over a stalled deal or a problem. My first impressions of him were interesting, dynamic, curious, and alive, and that was borne out as I learned more about him in this interview.

Nick is a man who tried many things in his life, and is never afraid to move from one project to another. Like other entrepreneurial types, he seems to constantly be out in the world searching for his next project. Earlier in his career, before the current popularity of video cassettes and cable television, he worked in fields not many people were yet involved in and helped shape them. He is very curious about life and his varied activities reflect this.

Nick and his family have a really sleek-looking house in Colorado I have always admired. It seems ahead of its time in terms of modern architecture. He is very involved with his kids—he knows their friends, their likes and dislikes—and is passionate about his wife.

My interview with Nick was the only interview for this book conducted over the telephone. Nick was very cautious in his responses initially. It is difficult for people to freely express themselves over the phone, knowing their words are being recorded. It is a tribute to his verbal ability and his organized thinking that the interview turned out so interesting despite that limitation.

Nick Nickolas

Making hard choices, saying no to certain things and yes to others is what differentiates great people from mediocre ones. It's true leadership.

What I do now is assist bright, entrepreneurial, younger people to launch their dreams. What that requires is both capital and what I call hands-off advice and a willingness to let them take control. I'm involved mostly in media and technology-related businesses. Where, in my earlier life at Time Inc., we helped start ventures like a new magazine, today I am more likely to help start a new Internet service. I function in a much more nurturing way now than I did in the past. What I do today is the opposite of the command-and-control structure I knew for so long in the corporate world. After 30 years, I decided I wouldn't do that anymore. Now, I have a very free-floating kind of existence. I'm connected by phone, fax, and e-mail to a growing network of incredibly interesting younger people who know a lot more than I do about what they are doing.

As a little kid, I was always working. I didn't have time to think. I was the first-born child of immigrant parents, and even though my parents were young when they came here, the work ethic was still everything. My dad went to Annapolis and became a career naval officer, so we were basically poor, given the military pay. He was stationed all over the world and was away at sea a lot when I was a kid. My mother, however, was an extremely strong-willed lady. We were just workers, but it's really intriguing what happened to us. My younger brother is listed in the Forbes 400 wealthiest people in America this year. He built his company from nothing 10 years ago and has made a billion dollars in high technology medical equipment. It must have been in the water or the air. Nobody ever told us we had to do all of this. I didn't spend much time screwing around, though I wish I had now. I had no idea what I was going to do when I grew up. There was no plan.

When I was a kid, I used to clean glasses in the bars of the officers' clubs. I couldn't serve drinks, but they let me wash glasses and bring the empty beer kegs in and out. I was good at getting things done. At Annapolis, my father was a noted pen and ink artist, and the Naval Academy yearbooks were full of his drawings. In our family, working with one's hands and manual work were highly valued. I could repair simple things. If the refrigerator broke, I would fix it instead of calling somebody. I still value those types of things. Another thing that was valued in my family was being a self-starter, being self-initiating rather than sitting around and waiting to be told what to do.

My hero as a kid was Ted Williams. I was born in New England, and anybody who lived a while in New England loves the Red Sox. Williams was the left fielder for the Boston Red Sox, and probably one of the greatest hitters that ever lived. He was a phenomenally great athlete, but was also the opposite of a hot dog. If you watch a football or baseball game today, when somebody makes a good play or a home run, they do high fives and all that. They hugely overdo it. It's nice to have the public celebrate you, but I think it's more important that you simply do a job well, not celebrate it. I have tremendous admiration for people who quietly do their business. I've been drawn to the kind of people, like Ted Williams, who don't need everyone's attention. They just go out and do it! My brother's that way. I am extremely turned on by people like that.

I don't really know what my parents expected of me as a child. I probably have some kind of a block about it. In the early 1950s, we lived in Europe, in Copenhagen, for about four years. I went to school in the Danish school system and learned the language. There were very few Americans around and no embassy schools in those days. When we moved back to the States, I was about 15 and enrolled in an American high school as a sophomore. I felt completely like a fish out of water, having lived in Europe during the last four years. I remember my dad saying, "You're going to go to Andover next year, if you can get in." I didn't know what Andover was and was very unhappy about the idea of being locked up somewhere. Nonetheless, when I look back on it, I realize it was a turning point in my life. Andover opened my eyes to a much larger world than I had known—a much more interesting and varied world. My brother went to St. Paul a year later. They wanted us in different schools. That's the only reason I think my parents had aspirations for me. They never said, "Here are our aspirations for you." They didn't even talk about things indirectly. What they did was give me a great education, and then let that take me wherever the hell it did. I had to get all my education through loans, by the way, which I didn't pay off until 10 years after I went to work for Time in 1964.

Nobody could have been more surprised than me as to my success. I always knew at some level I would go into the world of commerce as opposed to education or law. I also always knew I was a capitalist. I guess it started in the New England winters shoveling people's driveways for a quarter. Even though my father was a civil servant and didn't exactly provide a role model for a capitalist, I just knew I was one. When I graduated from Princeton, I decided to attend business school. IBM offered me this monstrous fellowship with full pay for Wharton. I turned that down for Harvard and borrowed my way through, because in those days I thought Harvard was the best. Whether it was, who the hell knows?

When I finished Harvard, I decided the kind of place I really wanted to work for was one that I could have tremendous respect and admiration for what they did and for their products. So, I took the lowest paying offer and worked for a journalistic enterprise, publishers of magazines. I was not particularly driven by money in those days, even though I didn't have any. All I had was debts. The advice I give young people today is to pick a company whose products they can absolutely fall in love with rather than be lured by some promise of short-term advancement, or money, or the best vacation policy or health plan. They can get that anywhere. If they go to a place where they feel compassion and excitement, they'll probably end up with the right company. They can worry later about what real job they will end up in. I know it sounds trite, but if you go to work every morning, or most mornings, really excited about the place (after all, you spend more than half your life there) it's got to be a place that turns you on. And if you're really excited, your performance will be better than it would otherwise. It's absolutely human nature. It isn't rocket science.

I don't think I really had a mentor as a young person. I would like to think my parents were my mentors, but they were my parents. A mentor, I think, is a different animal. The first person who really took an extraordinary interest in me was a guy named Jim Shepley. He was hired by George Marshall to be a chief aide at the end of

World War II when the Marshall Plan was put together. He was a journalist with a college education, who crossed over to the business side of publishing. He was the UPI bureau chief in Washington, worked up through the ranks at Time, and eventually became president of Time, Inc. Still basically a journalist, his nickname was brass knuckles. He was one rough, tough guy.

The only insecurity or fear I can recall in my career was having so many school loans to pay off. I have really never been afraid. I know that sounds macho, but it's true. I started like everyone else, at the bottom, yet I always had the gumption to put my ideas out, no matter how outrageous they seemed at the time. When I look back at my early career, I think that characteristic defined me and distinguished me from everyone else. There were plenty of others with good ideas, but they didn't always surface. I was unafraid of being ridiculed. If I had a good idea (or what I thought was a good idea), I made sure it got on the table. It is a little surprising in retrospect. My brother is the same way, so it must be a family characteristic.

Things are tougher today than ever for a lot of reasons, whether it's in politics, business, education, or whatever. We all struggle with inadequate resources to do what is necessary. And in that situation, the best leaders find ways to focus their institutions so they can concentrate the resources they do have on what is needed or what is good or terrific about the institution. That requires making choices, which is a hard thing. You have to say, we can't do everything. We can only do so much, so let's focus our best people and our financial resources, however limited they may be, on these few targets. We'll let our competitors do the other stuff. Making hard choices, saying no to certain things and yes to others is what differentiates great people from mediocre ones. It's true leadership. Look at Clinton, for example. I voted for the guy, but he tried to do everything. His agenda was far too ambitious, and in my view, that is the principal reason it failed. I'm a political independent. I don't register with either party. I'm attracted to anybody with the focus and drive to accomplish something. There are very few politicians today who I admire or are my heroes. I actually can't think of one because they are usually all over the place. I don't have a lot of heroes in other fields either. My brother is probably one of my heroes because he's really directed and focused. He is in a huge industry, healthcare, and for 10 years he has believed this country is involved in the escalating costs of healthcare. He designed his company around the slogan, "Better Outcomes for Less Money"—better patient outcomes—and he's deadly serious about it. Every bit of energy in his company is focused on that principle. If it doesn't fit the principle, they don't do it, no matter what it is. He doesn't get distracted. He doesn't get seduced by the siren of more money or more this and more that. It's got to fit what he wants his company to excel at. The more power people get, the more apt they are to be seduced by the trappings of success, the press, or whatever. There aren't a lot of people who can resist that and keep their values intact.

If I could have done anything differently myself, I think I would be an entrepreneur at a much earlier stage of my life. I would become a risk taker, on my own, at a much younger age. When you work for a corporation, how much of a risk are you taking? If you want to just get along, you can get along and survive, but if you want to do something dramatically different, you must take risks. If I could go back and relive my life, I might do things differently, but I probably would still end up in the same place. Instead of working all the time, I would goof off and do more nonbusiness things in the earlier stage of my life. I would have been a ski bum—but I don't mean just screwing around. I mean travel, reading, exploring Indian pueblos, fishing, and things I like to do. I'm doing a lot of that now.

My advice to people in business school or those now going into business would be to first really think about the kinds of products you want to be identified with. For example, the last product in the world I would want to be identified with is tobacco. I smoked for years so I don't mean to make a moral judgment on other people, but it's not for me. I don't want to sell Dr. Pepper, which to me is water with crap in it. Who wants to spend their life doing that? You must have a value system that says, "I would like to be identified with this. I am comfortable and passionate about spending the next 20 years being identified and part of the effort to do XYZ." I think that's how people ought to think about their futures—not about the starting position, the salary, the vacations, or the boss. My advice to young people in these situations has always been to knock on the door, get in, take any job they offer you—any job! Sweep the floor. Do anything to get into that place, because once you are in that company or institution, if you strongly identify with what they do, you won't have to worry. You'll get the right position once you know more about how the place works. Who do you want to be with, what kind of people do you want to be identified and associated with? What kinds of things are going to turn you on, excite you, make you feel good about yourself and the contributions your company makes to the quality of all kinds of things? These choices are really the most important.

Conclusion

Nick Nickolas began his career in a company he respected and admired. Nick advises this is the smartest business decision a young person can make today. Choose a company whose products you love. Join a place where you feel compassion and excitement, and you have the optimum career start.

Like Frank Cary, he also advises people to have the courage to express ideas, and pay no attention to the potential consequences of remaining true to one's convictions. He cites his brother's business strategy of staying focused on his product to illustrate the importance of not getting distracted from business vision and goals. Nick acknowledges in today's world the many more distractions than in his career days, yet he believes success is dependent upon not trying to be all things to all customers.

Nick reflected in his interview the influence of his childhood experiences when he learned the values of initiative and the competency to fix things. His heroes are unassuming yet competent people, like Ted Williams the baseball legend. I must admit I had to ask one of my sports friends what not being a hot dog meant, and learned it was a compliment to Ted.

At this stage in his career, Nick helps young businesspersons realize their entrepreneurial goals, and he truly seems in his element. His only career regret is he didn't become an entrepreneur himself earlier. Perhaps helping others to realize their dreams is one way Nick can recapture some of those years.

BRADLEY OGDEN

Restaurateur

My favorite restaurant in the Bay Area is Lark Creek Inn, Bradley Ogden's main restaurant, in Larkspur, California. Located in an old Victorian house under several tall redwood trees, with a lovely garden open in the warmer months, Lark Creek Inn has undoubtedly the best atmosphere and some of the best food in the Bay Area. People come from all over to dine there because Bradley Ogden made it so charming. The food served at the restaurant is American cooking at its best, using the freshest ingredients and the simplest flavors.

Lark Creek Inn, Ogden's first restaurant, opened in 1989. Prior to that, he was the executive chef at Campton Place in San Francisco. Campton Place is considered one of the best restaurants in the city and still maintains the distinctive style Ogden created. There are now four restaurants in the Lark Creek Restaurant Group, which are co-owned by Bradley and Michael Dellar. One of the restaurants, One Market Plaza, was named Best New Restaurant of 1993 by *San Francisco Magazine* readers. Bradley is recognized as a pioneer in the culinary field for his work in transforming traditional American food into sophisticated, updated fare. He is a spokesman for various companies and organizations including the Dairy Board, the Raisin Board, and Quaker Oatmeal. He also serves as a consultant to American Airline's Chef Conclave and has participated in numerous discussion panels on the culinary arts. He and his wife, Jody, wrote a book entitled, *Bradley Ogden's Breakfast, Lunch, and Dinner.*

Bradley is a slight man with brown hair, crinkly eyes, and a devilish grin. He radiates energy and looks 16 instead of the 40-something he is. It's hard not to be charmed by his boyish modesty and shy smile. He greets people in his restaurant in a gentle and authentic way, quietly approaching to say hello and suggest a certain dish or wine. There's no one I know who doesn't like him. His personality has certainly contributed to his success. I am sure there are times when he is exhausted and really not in the mood to chat with his patrons, but he is still always warm and friendly with his guests.

Wherever Bradley is, so is the most delicious food imaginable. He was prepared to serve me an amazing meal during our interview, but I insisted we sit at a quiet table without any food. Had I allowed him to serve me a meal, I knew he would concentrate more on whether I was enjoying the food than on what he had to say. One of the reasons he is so successful is because he focuses on pleasing people. Bradley gets enormous pleasure from seeing others enjoy their food. Every time I dine at Lark Creek Inn, something new is on the menu, and Bradley always comes over to say hello and offer my friends and me a free appetizer or a glass of wine. He is truly generous to everyone. Last fall, I took a group of M.B.A. students there for lunch. He created a special meal for us with a printed menu card and three elegant courses. The students will never forget the meal or his generosity of both his time and the superb food and wine. As we ate, he regaled us with descriptions of his life in the restaurant business and the joys of an entrepreneur.

During our interview, Bradley kept getting up to check things in the restaurant or talk with his assistant. I think he did this in part because he was somewhat uncomfortable being interviewed. He is a very modest man who rarely talks about his own success and always gives credit to those who help him. Once he relaxed, however, he told his story with enthusiasm, conveying the same confidence and willingness to take risks displayed by other entrepreneurs I have met. I loved his stories about his past successes, as well as some of the disasters he faced in the kitchen. It is clear he is the father of invention when need be. When I asked him about starting Lark Creek Inn, he described it simply as something he just did and didn't really worry about. Bradley grew up in a family where hard work was expected of everyone, and he hasn't stopped.

Bradley Ogden

Too many people want success too fast, and they want it for the wrong reasons. I've found that the most successful people are also the most humble. Their passion for life and the reasons why they do things are different from just wanting money. Their goals are different. And those are the people who are really the most successful.

My first restaurant, the Lark Creek Inn, in Larkspur, California, opened in 1989. We have five restaurants today. Almost four years after we opened Lark Creek Inn, we opened One Market in San Francisco. Then we opened Lark Creek in Walnut Creek, followed by Lark Creek, San Mateo. Our newest restaurant is opening in downtown Santa Barbara. The Pacific Hotel Group of Los Angeles is building a 100-room, upscale hotel, and they asked if I wanted to do all the food and beverage in it, and I accepted. It's going to be like a Lark Creek Inn, and we're involved with every aspect of it. It's our fifth one, and we're looking to open some others down the road.

It's a little easier to supervise our staff when the restaurants are local. There's a tighter control on things. It becomes a little more complicated when you have to take an airplane to check your restaurant. We have some very talented people, however. We like to hire and train professionals and promote from within. I'm in touch with all our restaurants at least biweekly. It's challenging. Sometimes members of my staff come here and spend a few days with me, or I visit them. I was on the road a lot more in the beginning when we only had three restaurants, and I wasn't accomplishing anything. I was in the car more than I was in the restaurants, so I decided it would be more beneficial for me to just stay put. My partner is in the city, and my main office is here in Marin. For the last two years, I've really been focusing on the Lark Creek Inn.

Employee growth is very important, and education, training, development, and creativity are all a big part of our business. Our training formats are really huge. Each month we meet in the restaurants. We review the P&Ls with all our management staff. Our key managers have percentages of the business. That is unusual in this industry, but the only way to keep talented people is to make them responsible owners of the business. Otherwise, it's just a job, and they'll go someplace else.

If I were hiring a chef I didn't know, I would invite him or her to spend a few days in the kitchen working with us, and prepare a meal for us. We would then get to know the person. Most of the time, however, before that even happens, you know them. It's pretty much word-of-mouth in this business. The good ones are usually working, so it's not hard to check them out. It's pretty easy to entice employees to the Bay Area, Marin, or in the city. Everybody wants to work in San Francisco or Marin. However, it is a little more challenging in the suburbs.

Our head chefs have a lot of creativity in terms of planning the menus. They have a structure to work within, obviously. Our menu has certain influences—it's American, it's farm fresh, and there are particular ingredients we use. I don't want a chef to add something to a menu that doesn't make sense for our restaurants, or to which our customers can't relate. It needs to be functional, understandable food, but within those limits, we encourage creativity. Of course, we don't just throw something on the menu and make that the test point. Usually, we communicate new ideas, try them out, and talk about them. Sometimes, though, when we go to the market and find some wonderful ingredients like beautiful Black Mission figs or Turkish figs, and even though we may have duck that day, we decide to do a duck dish with pearl pasta and grilled fresh figs, or make a little fig jam or a little fresh fig tart. We do that a lot. We take advantage of the local market on Thursdays and Sundays in Marin, and what we get from the market goes on the menu that night. We also have farmers who drop things off at the back door. Every week, we have what we call creative meetings to discuss the menus.

This management structure allowed a big part of our business growth. We want our ideas to continue to grow and expand so we take each step very carefully and make sure we have the right people in place to grow. We don't want to just build restaurants for the sake of building them and not continue our high standards and quality of our product.

My partner, Michael Dellar, knows business, and I know food. We created the business together and do everything together. For us to still be partners after 10 years is pretty amazing. It's interesting how we started together. We weren't looking for each other. I was at Campton Place at the time, and he was with Spectrum Foods, as the vice president of operations. He left to do consulting, and I was still at Campton. We knew each other because we were both on the board of the American Institute of Wine and Food (AIWF), and he was a frequent customer at Campton Place. One night in 1988, we dined together in Marin with our wives—my wife, Jody, who is very much a part of the business now, and his wife, Leslie. We talked about what each of us was doing. I received a lot of opportunities for different things and was looking at properties at the time. He was also thinking about opening a restaurant. So we just said, "Why don't we pool our talents and go into partnership together?" And that's what we did. We've been partners for over 10 years, and it's like a marriage. There's a lot of give and take. Like anything, if you want to keep it going, it takes a lot of work and effort. Fortunately, we complement each other very well.

I've experienced 17 openings of restaurants and hotels, so I learned in the school of hard knocks. Everybody thinks an owner doesn't have to work as hard, but in reality, you work twice as hard. What I like to do most is the hands-on part of the business—creating and cooking. That's my forte. To be successful, however, you also have to be a good teacher and educator. You need to be there with people, you have to handle a fig and explain to your employees what a fresh fig is. That's why I go to the market every Thursday and Sunday with my staff. I don't ever want to stray from the essence of what we do. Farmers' markets have always been a part of what good food means to me. I've always believed that's the best way to cook. When I was at the American Restaurant in Kansas City, I shopped in farmers' markets when nobody else was. So, it's all about training, developing, educating your staff, and continuing to motivate them. We have a great business structure that includes management meetings every month. We also train our people to deal with computer and accounting issues and to watch every penny. We budget everything, with as tight controls as possible because it's too easy to let the money fly, and suddenly you're in the red and closing your doors.

Our business is more challenging today than ever. There are a lot of great chefs now. More restaurants are opening, and the consumer is more educated about good food, so the demand for excellence is higher than ever before. It's probably the riskiest time for us now. We were in our heyday during the first four years, and it's easier when you are new. Everybody pounds on your door because they want the new thing. To continue that, it's important to establish yourself, but it's even more important to continue your commitment to excellence. You can't take shortcuts. You must make sure you scrub the wall before you put the paint on it. That's how we operate. It's why we spent $25,000 for a little room—we don't want a draft to upset our customers. It's so important to continue improving what you do and never rest on your laurels. That's why today is more challenging than ever.

I worry about the toll our continuing growth takes on me. Sometimes I wish I could sell it all and do a little B & B someplace, or start a cooking school, or take a year off. I can't tell you when I last enjoyed two weeks off in a row. It seems like it's been forever. The most I get is three days here, four days there. We can't take a month or two-month sabbatical because there's always something going on. We do little trips here and there, which we usually coordinate around an event I'm doing someplace. I've only been to Europe a few times and have never been to Italy. I'd love to go there. I've been to Paris a couple of times, and London, and Scotland. My first trip overseas was to Barcelona in 1986. I went with Alice Waters. There were six chefs and three food writers, and we were the guests of the local government. Colman Andrews, the editor of *Saveur Magazine,* Ruth Reichl, the reviewer for the *New York Times,* and Perry Butler, a good friend of Colman Andrews and a food writer in Los Angeles, were there. The chefs were Alice, myself, Larry Forgione, Jonathan Waxman, Lydia Sheae, and Mark Miller. We spent 10 days together and got along perfectly. No one wanted to do a dinner because we were having so much fun, but that's what we were there for. We went to the rombleaus (the market) and prepared a dinner on a Friday night. There was only a little kitchen, about four feet by four feet square, and we had to cook for 50 people. We each did a couple of dishes, and I did a little quail appetizer. I used a couple of wobbly grills, which were outside in a cobblestone alley. While I was grilling the quails, the grill fell and I had to scoop the coals up into a pile. There I was trying to grill 50 quail on these dinky little grills with everything falling over. It was a picture worth a thousand words. Then, in Barcelona, everyone likes their food well-done, and since I normally cook quail to medium-pink, a lot of them came back. We also tried making homemade strawberry ice by hand over a big bowl of rock salt and ice. It was quite an evening.

I grew up in northern Michigan, with six other siblings. We didn't have much growing up. We occasionally ate Sunday dinners all together when we were young and had typical Midwestern food, like pot roast. My mom made the greatest meatloaf and pot roast. Even though we didn't have much, what we did have was always the very best. There was a big emphasis on freshness and quality in my family. We did a lot of fishing and hunting as kids. I also remember how my dad would get us to stand in line, all seven of us, and we'd turn the old hand crank on the ice cream machine. I loved the homemade banana ice cream. My dad was really a gourmet at heart, even though he owned a rock 'n' roll business for 25 years in Traverse City, Michigan, where we lived. He would often pop into the kitchen to make homemade breads, which were really good. I looked forward to anything homemade, and look back fondly on those days.

In 1972 and 1973, I returned to Michigan and cooked for about 40 kids on a farm. It was sort of a cult thing. We had 440 acres of land, organic gardens, fresh trout ponds, and fresh eggs. I cooked all vegetarian food, with some fish, for a summer, and I lived there for a year and a half. During that time, I also worked as a chef for a couple of Holiday Inns and another little resort. Meanwhile, I got married when I was 20, and I've been married for 24 years now. We had one child at the time, and another on the way. I returned to cooking school, graduated with honors, and won the Richard T. Keating Award, which was for the student most likely to succeed.

It was a fluke I got into the food business. When I finished high school, I went to drafting school for about four months. I dropped out, and my brother and I both started flipping eggs at the local Holiday Inn in Traverse City. Traverse City, by the way, is the cherry capital of the world. Alice Waters also has family there and lived there for a while. Anyway, after we started flipping eggs, my dad saw an article in the *Detroit Free Press* on the Culinary Institute of America in Hyde Park, New York. He figured it was a good place for us—if we learned how to cook, he said, we could always get a job. So I spent the summer in the Holiday Inn's kitchen, and it felt like I had been doing it all my life. I had so much fun. Then we went off to chef school. My brother dropped out after about four months and joined the navy. I left for a few years, but returned and graduated in 1977. During my years there, I was always thrown into management positions, even at an early age.

My first job after school was for Gelbert Robinson, in Kansas City. They had Houlihan's and a gourmet restaurant called Plaza Three, where I was supposed to start as a sous-chef. A flood hit the area, however, and wiped out the restaurant. They put me in another one of their restaurants, which was great because I ended up working on the menus and other things for the reopening of Plaza Three. I helped open that restaurant in 1977, and worked there for about a year and a half. The executive chef of the corporation, who hired me, was also an instructor at the Culinary Institute of America, where I had gone to school. I left Gelbert Robinson with him and together we opened three restaurants and a hotel in Springfield, Missouri, during a span of two years. I was offered the chef position at Plaza Three, which I declined because I figured I'd learn more and develop more with the guy who hired me.

Then, in December 1979, I returned to Kansas City to become the chef at the American Restaurant. I worked there for almost five years. Our consultants were Joe Baum, Barbara Kafka, and James Beard. Joe Baum was really my mentor, if I had to pick one. Fortunately, I've had a few over the years. Of course, working with James Beard and Barbara Kafka was also great. We received a lot of accolades at the American, and it was a great learning experience.

I went to New York a few times with Joe Baum. He was really a taskmaster and a fanatic on details. He owned Windows of the World, the Four Seasons in New York, the Rainbow Room, and was president of the Restaurant Associates. He had me in tears a few times. I remember one time, in 1980, when I traveled to New York with Joe to redesign our luncheon buffet. We did this three-day eating stint then—Balducci's, De Luca's, Four Seasons, the Coach House. It's amazing how food brings back the memories. I remember my meal at the Four Seasons. I wrote everything down. One dish we had was a chilled sugar snap pea soup with a basil sorbet in the center. It was like eating right out of the garden. The basil was so fresh, and the sugar snap pea soup had a little bit of mint. It was really delicious. We also had a smoked trout dish with apple fritters and a little applesauce. The night we were supposed to eat at the Coach House, a couple of generators fritzed in Lower Manhattan. It wiped out all the electricity. We were on the doorstep of the Coach House at 7:00 P.M. when the lights went out. I was with James Beard, Barbara Kafka, Joe Baum, Dennis Sweeny, and Michael Whiteman. The owner said, "Come on in, guys. I'll put the candles on and make you dinner." It was pitch black, with candles all around. It was kind of scary. The Coach House was famous for its pepper steak and black bean soup, so that's what we had. For dessert—I'll never forget this as long as I live—we had a huckleberry and blueberry tart. The blueberries and huckleberries were just picked. The chef pureed huckleberries (which are like miniature blueberries, but they're tiny and wild) and blueberries, then added a little honey to bind them. Then he made a layer of the blueberries and huckleberries with just a little honey glaze. He warmed it and served it to us with one scoop of crème fraiche ice cream. It was the most incredible thing.

In 1983, I left the American Restaurant to move to San Francisco and open Campton Place with Bill Wilkinson. Bill, who is owner of Greenleaf Produce now, was general manager at Stanford Court and worked with Jim Nassikas during the heyday of Stanford Court. I had recently been on my first trip to San Francisco for a huge food and wine event at Stanford Court in May 1983. Ten chefs were brought in to represent different regions. It was the first time chefs from all over the country really got together. Alice Waters, Julia Child, and Robert Mondavi were there, along with Paul Prudhomme, Larry Forgione, Jonathan Waxman, and Mark Miller. The American Institute of Wine and Food (AIWF) was involved; it was when they were first getting off the ground. There was a birthday dinner for James Beard, and we all prepared this huge meal. Jimmy Schmidt and I, who represented the Midwest, did the entrée. It was during this event that Bill Wilkinson convinced me to open Campton Place. I didn't really want to move to San Francisco. I figured on earthquakes and San Francisco falling into the water, but I flew out to discuss it on July 4th weekend in 1983. Bill and I saw eye-to-eye.

He offered the right price, and I moved out a month later. We opened the restaurant in October 1983. It still is a great place. I recently took my staff there for breakfast. The same cooks I trained, who didn't know how to flip an egg then, are still there. I worked there for six years before I opened Lark Creek Inn.

About three or four weeks after we opened Campton Place, Patty Unterman reviewed the place. She was with Ruth Reichl and a couple of other people of profound magnitude. It was her first time in the restaurant. I served the Dungeness crab chowder on the menu. It was delicious, tasted great. She loved the chowder, but she called me over, and said, "Brad, I have to let you know that you left part of the sachet bag in the soup." I thought, "Oh, my god!" I tried to save myself and said, "That's part of what they do in Kansas City. You didn't know that?" We all learn from our mistakes, hopefully.

I remember another time when I was at the Plaza Three Restaurant. I had just started and Ken Hill, the president of Gelbert Robinson, was in for dinner. I made Apple Charlotte. To make it, you take a whole loaf of pomalova bread, trim off the crust, hollow out the center, and save the top. The top is a one-half inch rectangle, which you can put back on. Then, you fill the inside with an apple pie mixture, butter the whole thing, and bake it. It comes out golden brown on the outside. We served it with a vanilla rum custard sauce. The sauce came out perfectly, and it was really, really tasty. The Apple Charlotte was a beautiful golden brown, cooked perfectly, and that's what Ken Hill had for dessert. He came in the next morning, and Dan Durrick called me over and said, "Brad, Ken Hill was in for dinner last night and said everything was wonderful. He had the Apple Charlotte for dessert." I thought he would rave how wonderful it was, but he said, "Unfortunately, it tasted like garlic." I had accidentally used some melted butter on the line without tasting it—I had used the garlic butter. I learned very quickly to taste everything after that.

I've been married for 24 years and have three wonderful children. I am very fortunate to have a wife who has been a big part of my success, if not *the* part of my success. That's the truth. She kept me grounded. I often like to jump into things, but she's kept me out of trouble. I have three boys, who also make me very happy. One of them, Chad, is in the business, even though I tried to discourage him. He's at the Culinary Institute of America. That's very rewarding in a lot of ways. For years he said, "I don't want to be in this business." For his first 20 years, I was never around. I was always working. I generally leave home at 7:00 in the morning, and I'm not home until 1:00 A.M. I used to survive on five hours of sleep, but now I need at least six. Luckily, I'm a high-energy person with a lot of drive. I've done it for 18 or 20 years, because I love the business. If I didn't have that passion for the business, I couldn't do what I do. Many people want to be successful and have their name out there, but expect to do it in 40 hours a week. That's not what it's about, however. It's really about taking care of the customers and pleasing them with good food. You are lucky to have people come to you and pay you to be in business. Some people only see the fame and the glory of it all, but the real essence of this business is the passion and the vision. An analogy would be this: You're at the market with two peaches. One is sort of rock hard but will be ripe in four or five days, and the other is perfectly ripe. If you handle the ripe one correctly, get it back to the kitchen, and serve it now, you'll have this wonderful, delicious flavor, like it just came off the tree. If you do that every single day—pick that piece of ripe fruit and serve it every day—you'll be successful. If you take something that's not ripe, you have no idea what it will be like four days from now, even if somebody tells you it will be delicious. There's no way it could be as delicious as something you pick right off the vine.

So simplicity is not necessarily simple. It's a passion and a desire for excellence. Simplicity is easy to talk about, but it's harder to maintain quality at that level. The easier way would be to buy the unripe peach. In four or five days, it would be ripe, but you would probably use it before it's ripe. The challenging part of this business is keeping the expectations up and regular customers coming in the door saying, "Wow, that corn tastes like it was just picked."

Obviously, I am proud of owning my business. But what is really important is the quality of life I have been able to establish—what I stand for and my commitment to excellence. I own four restaurants, but I could own 10 restaurants and it wouldn't mean as much if I couldn't treat my customers and staff at a certain level—rewarding their lives. If something doesn't come from a soul-satisfying experience, then it's not worth it. That's the way I feel. It's not just about making money. That's not it for me. It's a whole lifestyle issue. It's also what we can do to help people's lives in the area. It's simple things like donating time and energy to the school systems, or charity. I do thousands of those things. We work for national charities like Meals On Wheels, March of Dimes, Red Cross, AIDS. I ran a golf tournament for three years for diabetes. We also do a lot of local fund-raisers for community schools, the fire department, and other local organizations.

I think it was grounding for me to grow up in the Midwest. There's a way of life there, and you sort of gain a spiritual grounding. We had open land where we could hunt, and fish, and run. You could do that then, but you can't today. My kids didn't experience the way I grew up. There are too many areas today, like drugs, where they can find trouble, and too many peer pressures. There are a lot of great people from the Midwest—not that there are not nice people here—but a lot of them are from the Midwest. I want to stay close to that grounded feeling I had growing up, because if I get too far from it, I end up going off in too many different directions.

There are many people who say, "Well, I want to be successful, I want to do that." If they want it too badly, however, they'll never achieve it. On the other hand, if they put time and effort into it because they love and have a passion for it, then good things will happen. They may not get high recognition, but they will be doing something they love and have satisfaction. It's a very lucky thing to be able to do something you like. To be successful, you need to demand a certain level from yourself—200 percent. I don't care if you are a dishwasher or a line cook, if you demand excellence from yourself, it will be a positive thing. People around you will also demand excellence of themselves. In whatever profession, if you give 200 percent and care about what you do, you will succeed. But you have to do that. You can't worry about little things, like working an extra hour. It's not going to be a 40-hour workweek. In this business, to be successful, it requires demanding excellence of yourself, and that means a commitment of time and energy. Too many people want it too fast, and they want it for the wrong reasons.

I've found the most successful people are also the most humble people. Their passion for life and the reasons that drive them are different from just the desire for money. Their goals are different. And those are usually the most successful people.

Conclusion

Being an entrepreneur usually means putting business first, as most of our leaders agree. Success can require a toll on a personal life, and Bradley Ogden is no exception. He seldom takes vacation and is on the road a lot of the time. What drives Bradley, as it does Wilkes Bashford and Howard Lester, is making people happy with a superb product and excellent service. Bradley describes his success as not what it brings to him, but the joy his food brings to others. And he achieves this goal by focusing on excellence in his food, and donating it to a variety of charitable organizations. Cooking is the way Bradley lives his values; just as quality merchandise and service is the way Wilkes and Howard live theirs.

Bradley was not immediately drawn to cooking. As he describes in his interview, he discovered his passion after he finished high school and started flipping eggs at a Holiday Inn. His father sent him to cooking school so he could have steady employment. Once there, he found he loved it, and thus began his marvelous career. The lesson here is that although you may not have a clear direction initially or at a midlife junction, it is important to try things and listen to your instincts. You'll find what's right if you just listen.

To succeed in the food business, Bradley reflects both passion and vision are essential. Vision to Bradley means imagination—what to do with the figs he finds unexpectedly at the market one morning—and the talent to think in terms of possibilities. He also believes hard work is an absolute necessity in the business. In the beginning of your career, expect to work harder than the boss. This is not a 40-hour job, and if you have friends in the restaurant business as I do, you already know this! As other leaders illustrate, Bradley shows knowing your strengths and weaknesses is essential. He brought in a partner who knew how to run a business so he could do what he loved, cooking and creating. Don't try to do it all. Finally, Bradley suggests if you own a restaurant, be realistic. It is difficult to find and keep good assistants. Therefore, make them your business partners so they have a stake and share responsibility.

In sum, perhaps the advice we can take away from Bradley's story is to explore and find work you are passionate about. And stay true to the expression of your values in that work. This is the way to business success and happiness.

VISIONARIES

ALLEN GROSSMAN

Former Director, Outward Bound
Professor, Harvard Business School

Allen Grossman is a senior lecturer of business administration at the Harvard Business School's Initiative on Social Enterprise and a visiting scholar at the Harvard Graduate School of Education. Grossman served as president and chief executive officer of Outward Bound for six years before stepping down in 1997 to work exclusively on the challenges of creating high-performance nonprofit organizations. Prior to his work at Outward Bound, Grossman served as regional chief executive officer of Albert Fisher PLC and chairman of the board of Grossman Paper Company.

In my search for interesting and accomplished people to interview, one of the people I consulted was my brother-in-law, Alex Sanger, then chairman of Planned Parenthood of New York, and Margaret Sanger's grandson. When I asked Alex about the people he had met during his career in the nonprofit world who impressed him, Allen Grossman was first on his list. I became immediately intrigued as Alex described Allen and spoke of his integrity, honesty, and intelligence. When I subsequently spoke with Allen and asked him to be in my book, the conversation was neither brief nor superficial. It was soon clear to me he would not agree to be included until he understood both my philosophy of life and my approach in the book.

Allen was still as passionate when I met him for the interview as he was on the telephone. There is a physical intensity about him. He engages in direct eye contact, and when he walked into the lobby of my apartment building in Manhattan, his lively gait reflected his energy and brightness. He warned me at the start of the interview that he is a talker, and I should be prepared to use a lot of tape. He was correct, but unlike many people, he speaks in completely lucid sentences with clearly expressed thoughts and ideas. I was impressed with his energy and excitement as he told his story, his hands moving about, and his eyes often crinkling with laughter.

Allen elevates the drive and initiative of successful businesspeople to a higher level of commitment to the world. I quote parts of his interview to my students because I find his words so inspiring. He's a do-gooder at heart and has lived his life according to his values.

Allen Grossman

. . . most people who are really successful are also passionate. It is the wonderful ingredient that brings happiness with success.

I never grew up, I just advanced in age. I was born in Newark, New Jersey, and we moved to a typical, affluent New Jersey suburb as my refugee father started to succeed in life. I went to a public high school and lived a very *Grease* life (as in the musical *Grease*). It was lucky. Being the middle child of five children was very special. If I had to choose again where I would be placed in a family, that's where I'd be. I had one brother who was perceived as the messiah in our family, and three sisters. I learned early on how to fend for myself, while still being within the security of my family.

My father didn't move to this country until he was 19, and his only education was religious. He was Jewish and from a shtetel (a Jewish ghetto), as were the characters in the musical, *Fiddler on the Roof.* When we were young, we sent my father and mother to see *Fiddler on the Roof* on Broadway as an anniversary present. The whole family pitched in to buy the tickets. That night, we stayed up, waiting for my father to come home and share his joy. When he walked into the house, however, he was very grumpy. It was such an illuminating experience. We asked him, "Did you love it?" He replied, "Love it? Those people were singing and dancing on the stage about our misery, our deprivation, our starvation, and brutalization. I was supposed to love it?" It was the first time I understood how people's frame of reference makes such a difference.

My father was a classic immigrant-entrepreneur. I worked in his paper warehouse when I was about 11 or 12 and did that virtually every summer, all through college. I never worked anywhere else. A very high value was placed on how hard you worked in my family. My father also had a keen sense of integrity and honesty. It was significant to him that he moved here from a different country and the only thing he really brought with him was his integrity and his name. He placed a great deal of emphasis on treating people fairly, and dealing with people in such a way you didn't end up with the full advantage. He had a long-term sense of what life was about. It was not only the effort that mattered. It was the amount of integrity that was attached to the effort.

As a child, I'm not sure I had an inner confidence or sense I was capable of success. I may have affected it more than I really had it. I was a second son in a family with traditional, European values. Women were basically expected to become homemakers and housewives. If they worked, they were supposed to teach because then they could be home in the afternoon when the children were out of school. For me, so much emphasis was placed on my older brother being smart and successful, that I was sort of an also-ran. Most people perceived me as cocky, but in reality, I harbored a lot of self-doubt about whether I really could make it on my own. This was exacerbated by the fact that, after college in 1965, I followed the family plan of entering business with my brother and my dad in the family's paper and packaging distribution company. It was quite small when my brother and I first went into it, and we were fortunate in our success. My father was a very, very wise man. Even though he created and loved his business, he knew if he didn't release some of the power to his sons, we would leave. So early on, he basically said, "Okay. Now it's your turn. See what you can do." Unfortunately, he died in 1972 when I was only 27. After that, my brother and I built the business into a national company, and it was quite successful.

I knew my father felt that of the two of us, my brother would be the leader. My brother, however, who was six years older, never thought he should be Number One, and I should be Number Two. He realized I would fight for equality and wouldn't accept a second position. In fact, he really enjoyed sharing, but at first I didn't realize that. What ultimately emerged was a terrific, complementary partnership. He is very smart, capable, tends to be more precise than I, and is perhaps more conservative. I like sales and am a little more of a risk taker. We balanced each other, and things usually came out (based on the empirical data) in the right place. It worked very well.

Having grown up in the Kennedy/Martin Luther King era, I always thought about doing public service. I wanted to make a difference and believed individuals could make a difference in society. I had friends who entered into some type of public work after college, but I, of course, took a different route. I went into the family business, married very young, and had a family early on. When I graduated from business school, most of my classmates went to work for large corporations. Now no one wants to work for them. Everyone wants to be an entrepreneur. It's now in. I became an entrepreneur when it wasn't in. I knew, however, that making a difference in the larger scheme was what I really wanted to do and always had the intention to eventually start another career even though that was not the norm like it is now. I was confident I could succeed in business, and then go on to pursue what I really wanted to do.

Confidence is an interesting concept. It's not a simple one. Perhaps one of the virtues of aging is understanding what confidence really means. For me, confidence has no absoluteness, it has always been a relative kind of concept. We're all, at some point, less confident than we might like to be. I think confidence is understanding yourself deeply enough and knowing you'll get through the times when you're feeling challenged or not quite as confident, as opposed to emanating the sense that you're always confident. When I was really young, I had bravado rather than true confidence. Then, the notion that I would ever lack confidence was unacceptable to me. Now, I can say, "I don't feel very confident, but I know I'll get through it." I think that's an important difference.

Early on I realized success in our business would require hard work, focus, determination, and weathering the inevitable setbacks

along the way. Of course, success always takes a little luck, and anyone who says it doesn't is a fool or a liar. You just have to keep plug-
ging. Another quality that made us a success in business was our
ability to motivate the people we worked with. There was a real
sense that our company was a good community, a good place to
work. Most of our employees were highly motivated because they
felt an attachment to the company. They didn't feel oppressed by us,
they were part of a team. That was a very important component,
because often, particularly in private businesses, people tend to
wrap their egos up so much in their companies they can't allow others to excel. My brother and I never had that problem. On the con-
trary, we used to feel that turning over more responsibility to others
was a great way to give us more free time or time to pursue more
strategic objectives. Also, having targets and high expectations for
ourselves as well as for the people around us was certainly important. And, of course, having integrity was essential. That's part of
building community. Finally, I haven't found a satisfactory substitute
for just working your butt off. Virtually everyone I know, whether
they get to be governor, president, the head of a public company, or
whether they're at Harvard, Yale, or wherever, the common denom-
inator is real commitment and focus. If you're not passionate, maybe
self-discipline or whatever set of emotions you have, including guilt,
might help you work hard. But most people who are really successful are also passionate. It is the wonderful ingredient that brings
happiness with success.

After about 15 years in the family business, I talked to my
brother about leaving. I lost my passion for the business, which was
one of the reasons I wanted to leave. He said, "Well, I don't really
want to stay on. It's been a wonderful partnership, and if you feel
strongly about it, let's sell together. We came in together, let's leave
together." So, we did. We sold the company, and it's turned out ter-
rifically for us both.

Right after we sold the company, however, it was actually very difficult for me. Looking at the landscape for where I could perhaps
make a difference, I decided it was in the nonprofit world. Although
I had served on boards and chaired a couple of nonprofit boards, I
now wanted to jump into a sector in which I had very little status. I
had to give up the ego gratification of having been successful in

another field, even though I didn't particularly love that field. For the next two years, I basically became a pro bono consultant to nonprofits and foundations. I was a hybrid. I got involved in international work on a project for the Rockefeller Foundation, helping the CEO of a nonprofit they were partnering with to get the project up and running. At the same time, I was able to go to the table with the funders. People thought, "Who is this guy? He's working for free? He must be crazy!" But it was a great opportunity because I didn't want to enter this world in a midlevel job. Since money wasn't the issue, I decided I would rather learn as much as I could at a higher level than just enter a more routine job. After two and a half years, I was offered several jobs in international development. I didn't accept because I was married and had two children, one still in high school, and my wife owned a bookstore in New York. Going overseas wouldn't really be conducive to maintaining a balanced life.

Then, serendipitously, the offer came along for CEO of Outward Bound. When I first heard about it, I thought it was not exactly in keeping with what I had been doing. Then I realized most of what I was doing concerned people and optimizing human potential, and that was what Outward Bound was about. I would be able to apply the management and leadership skills I had to an organization that fundamentally tried to change people's lives. So I did that.

Outward Bound was started by a man named Kurt Hahn, an educator whose philosophy is quite brilliant. The idea behind Outward Bound is you don't necessarily overcome fear—you're able to get through fear. I thought about that a lot the first time I was up on the well-known ropes course, rappelling down a 150-foot mountain with everyone looking at the new CEO of Outward Bound. The ropes course was actually easy, even though I'm scared to death when I go up there. It was more that my heart was in my mouth (I think virtually all my organs) but I didn't show it.

There were two challenging elements of the job. One was that I had come in as an unusual choice for a lot of the people within Outward Bound. They were used to either people who had outdoor experience or people who had an educator's background. I had neither. That was the initial challenge. I had to think it through, which was not terribly difficult except in the conceptualities. I needed to understand what values I added, how my skills were complementary to the skill sets of the organization, which were equally if not more important. That was the first challenge.

The second challenge was running an organization that's a federation. Outward Bound is a federation of independent 501(c)(3)s, the same as Planned Parenthood. Someone described the task of running a federation as herding cats. The people in the organization were wonderful, but they had a deeply held cultural orientation for independence on the local level. I was the national CEO. I had to build consensus and convince local groups to agree that organizational change was not only in Outward Bound's best interest, but in their own self-interest as well. It was a really overwhelming and, at times, daunting challenge. Faye Wattleton, and others who have gone into nonprofits that are national and have affiliates, also face that. That was by far my biggest challenge, and I think it remains the biggest challenge for Outward Bound.

When I entered Outward Bound, a man by the name of John Whitehead was a great role model and mentor. John was and still is on the Outward Bound board. A man who was able to move across sectors, John was successful as head of Goldman Sachs. He served as undersecretary of state under Reagan and then in the nonprofit world where he very deliberately dedicates about half his time, chairing boards and taking real leadership positions. John and I became friendly when I took the job at Outward Bound. In general, however, I'm not sure how important mentorship is in the lives of people who are very successful. I tend to think mentors are more adjusters. They help calibrate and adjust a direction you're going in rather than initiate things. That's often very important, because if you're a sailor and you're off course by five degrees, 1,000 miles later you're in deep trouble. I often look at people who don't succeed and try to figure out why. I don't know if mentor only has a positive sense. Mentoring probably helps you adjust your course as you go along, by looking at the mistakes others make as well as looking at them as role models. Most people who are successful would be successful anyway without mentors, given all the other components. From my perspective, mentors are good but not critical for success for people who have a certain set of characteristics and advantages from the beginning, such as education. But surely for some people, mentors are critical.

My major weakness in work situations over the years was being fooled by people. I'm a believer in human beings, so I'm really at a disadvantage and can be exploited. Sometimes I feel like a sucker. I have trouble with people who start out with a different set of ground rules. Either they're outright dishonest, which I've encountered, or exploitive and constantly angling for a better position. My sense, and it's not noble, is I won't change to gain advantage. It's simply a nicer way to live. I believe if you work with people, and you can truly create partnerships, it's fabulous. There are others who constantly use people to gain advantage, and a number of times over the years I was taken advantage of in significant ways. I look at myself and think, "You should have been smarter than that." But I haven't had any problems within organizations that were so hard I couldn't deal with them. Obviously, I've had many stressful times, but I believe people can accomplish a great deal together and get through virtually any kind of crisis. That's never been an issue that prevented me from moving on.

The route to success is always going to be different for different people. There are ruthless and not nice people who are perceived as successful by the public, but on the private side of that success, they're really miserable. They have miserable family lives or are unhappy with themselves, or are insecure. They have issues with self-confidence. Are they successful because they're insecure, or are they successful because they affect an arrogance? I don't know. There are a lot of lousy people in the world, but the majority of people aren't bad. The number of times, relatively speaking, I've been really taken advantage of is small. I'm old enough now to say, "Wow, over the years the percentage is in my favor." In retrospect, I wouldn't compromise my approach to avoid the few times I've been exploited.

Another thing I had to learn is to differentiate among the opportunities that came my way. If you don't differentiate well, you can, as I have, waste years focusing on activities or projects that, in retrospect, I should have been much more critical of. My screen should have been a lot less porous in terms of the projects I spent time on. That's one thing I haven't done particularly well.

My definition of success is multifaceted, but simple. I think professional success depends a great deal on the individual. For me, I like organizations, people, and communities. So success for me is to advance a community rapidly, in an optimal fashion. The other part of success is the part outside your profession. I don't know many happy people, and happiness is part of success, who are one-dimensional. It's the old conflict between love and work. Love, to me, is the people around you—family, friends, and self. To create a balance, you probably can't maximize your professional life. But to optimize your professional life while maintaining a balanced life is true success.

The advice I would give young people starting out today, whether in nonprofits or in business, is to find your passion. I don't think you always have to be passionate to be successful, but I don't think you'll ever be happy and successful unless you're passionate about what you're doing. Find something that feels right. Then test it and don't be afraid to change, but give it a chance. Career opportunities are not revolving doors. They are more like relationships. A good relationship doesn't grow by moving from person to person. You really have to work on relationships. You have to go through some tough times and some easy times, some joys and some sorrows. A lot of people do not give career opportunities the amount of time they should. There is a lot that emerges once you're engaged that you don't know about initially. So, find a passion, pursue it, give it ample opportunity, and test it.

Usually people don't just find their passion and immediately know it's right. They test out things and are willing to try different approaches. Most people don't know what their passion is. I certainly didn't. If you don't necessarily know what your passion is, you soon learn what it isn't. Some of the best management procedures are management by exception. In the same sense, there is passion by exception. When you don't feel a passion for your work, you'll begin to have a clue to what your passion might be. Sometimes people look at passion more as the specific job to seek as opposed to the function to perform. I think it gives a lot more latitude to look at the function you're passionate about doing. For example, if I like to work in communities or organizations, and my function is leadership, then what I apply it to is probably less important than making sure I'm exercising that function. If my function is to create beauty, the outlet may be very different. It may be in landscaping, or painting, or clothes design. Those are very disparate fields superficially, but they share a kind of functional satisfaction. I would start off a little higher, not at a ground level, but at 10,000 feet, try to figure out the activities that turn you on rather than a specific job. What activities make you feel good about yourself? Where do you think you can really add value? When you identify those functions, the application into a specific industry is a lot easier. Many young people say things like, "I want to go into banking." What does that mean? What part of banking? You can be in sales, you can crunch numbers, or you can be involved in organizational change. Even law, or any professional field, has a broad array of activities you might perform. That's the key for me— to identify that before identifying the specific job.

I won't massacre it in French, but there is this wonderful quote from Napoleon, in which he said, "Engage, and the possibilities will emerge." You'll certainly never find your passion standing on the sidelines. Many people say, "Oh, you're so lucky. You've had such interesting jobs." But if you wait for the jobs, they won't come. You've really got to go out there. The other piece of it is you have to be willing to swallow your ego. Ego locks people in and prevents them from taking risks. I see my peers now, some of whom are unhappy with what they're doing, but in order to shift their present situation in really meaningful ways, they have to take some risks that would, on some levels, challenge their identity, their ego, their sense of position in life. To the degree you can free yourself from that, you find a tremendously liberating dimension in life.

Conclusion

Allen Grossman grew up as the middle child of immigrants, and early on he learned to fend for himself and value hard work. His father conducted himself in business with integrity and honesty, and these traits influenced Allen throughout his career. Like other visionaries, he knew he wanted to make a difference in the world. He accomplished this by first growing his father's paper and packaging distribution business into a success and making it a place where employees felt attachment to the company. And then Allen focused on the nonprofit world.

Allen describes his skills and traits as selling, the courage to take risks, and an entrepreneurial spirit. It is interesting that several of the visionaries, like John Scully and Faye Wattleton, also describe themselves as entrepreneurs—the ability to turn their beliefs into a business! After 15 years with his father's business, Allen and his brother sold the company. Allen decided to jump into the nonprofit sector, where he had no status at all. He was strategic in his approach to establish himself as a potential leader in the field—he worked for free! He consulted CEOs in nonprofit organizations, and serendipitously became the CEO of Outward Bound. This position allowed him to directly help individuals optimize their human potential and help people learn how to overcome fear. Allen knew this kind of fear, self-doubt, as he grew up and is empathetic to the child in us all.

Allen's challenges in Outward Bound were first personal, namely that someone, like Allen, without an education background had to prove he could run the organization. Second, he hurdled the management challenge of building consensus for change in a federation like this in which each group valued its independence. Obviously, Allen's experience in an immigrant family who overcame cultural prejudice and his business skills helped him become very successful in his role at Outward Bound. Now he continues to generously give to nonprofit organizations by teaching how to become financially solvent.

Allen sees success as multifaceted, involving one's personal values and one's work. He calls the dilemma of success the old conflict between love and work, and comes to the conclusion that success is optimizing your professional life while maintaining a balanced personal and family life. Allen's advice for success is to find a passion, pursue it, and give it ample opportunity to blossom. He realizes many do not find it immediately and urges readers to not get discouraged in their search. As you explore, you will at least identify what you don't want, which gets you halfway there. Believe in the process, if not in yourself, Allen seems to suggest. Understand yourself, and have confidence that you'll get there. And you will!

JACK KORNFIELD
Buddhist Monk

Jack Kornfield is a clinical psychologist, therapist, meditation instructor, and author. During his career, he has written six books, among them *Seeking the Heart of Wisdom, Stories of the Spirit,* and *A Path With Heart.* One of the most delightful men I know, he has been a good friend of mine for quite a few years. I met Jack at Spirit Rock, the meditation center he founded in San Anselmo, California, where I went with a group of friends for a Buddhist meditation practice. The center is located on some of the most beautiful land in Marin County and is surrounded by rolling hills and grassy fields. With its many farms and horse ranches still untouched by the hand of real estate developers, there is a great sense of peace in the area. Horses graze beside the road and large boulders lie in the fields as you pass down the long and pleasantly curving drive to the center. Spirit Rock's buildings, which include a meditation hall with a small gift shop as well as office space and dormitories for those on a longer retreat, are low and unobtrusive to the countryside. On Monday nights, a large number of Buddhists gather to meditate and listen to Jack's talk.

I first went to Spirit Rock on a day when Jack held a daylong practice for some of his friends, who then invited some of their friends along. He started out by simply talking to us and guiding us through a simple meditation exercise. Then he spoke about his own life experiences with wonderful humor and compassion, even telling several jokes. I was soon completely sold. Through his humility and joy as a communicator, he captured the hearts of this diverse group. I really fell in love when he had us do a walking meditation, which is walking slowly around the large hall (like mental patients on thorazine in my view). Each time I ran into Jack, I had a hard time not grinning. He then made funny or stern faces to make me laugh. I felt like I was playing with a 10 year old, and that is always how I think of Jack. He seems like the kind of guy who would enjoy coming over to my house to sit on the roof and throw water balloons onto the cars below. We had a lot of laughs together over the years. Whenever I find myself whining about something, he always makes me remember it really isn't important after all, and he does so with his wonderful, light humor. Jack found a way to make my inability to concentrate during meditation and my refusal to obey the silence seem right for me and even helpful to others. He calls me Coyote Woman—the disrupter and jokester of the world of myth. It is a title I treasure.

Our interview took place in the gift shop of Spirit Rock, surrounded by books on meditation and objects collected by the staff during their travels to Buddhist countries around the world. Jack and I talked about his amazing life, and I was so enthralled with his story I forgot to turn over the tape at one point. Jack's story is fascinating because a sense of destiny runs throughout. His journey as a monk in Thailand for five years and later, his return to the States where he started the Insight Meditation Society is filled with encounters and lessons. He never doubts he is on the right path or that he will succeed in accomplishing what he needs to accomplish.

Jack has many of the same qualities as the entrepreneurs and CEOs interviewed in this book—a directness of purpose, dedication to his goal, and confidence he will achieve it. He also has a lovely, unassuming manner and a charisma that makes him a success within many different communities.

Jack Kornfield

... if you give yourself to your love and passion, eventually something good will come. And if it doesn't, you can change and do something else.

Today, I am one of the senior teachers and founders of Spirit Rock Center, for which I lead retreats and classes and participate in the teachers' council as a guide and director. Spirit Rock is a meditation center for a large community that offers a variety of inner trainings in awareness, mindfulness, and compassion so people can live a modern life from a spiritual perspective in their family life, business, creative arts, and politics. The teachings of Spirit Rock arise from the Buddhist tradition, but we are open for people from all backgrounds, religions, and parts of society. The idea is not that people come to Spirit Rock Center to become a Buddhist, or a meditator, or a spiritual person (God save their friends and family). But rather, they come to learn how to awaken their own Buddha natures, to live their lives from the values of their own hearts and their deepest places of wisdom. It is an American teaching center that uses Buddhist teachings in an American way, not the form one would find in a temple in Burma or a Zen temple in Japan. There is not the chanting or rituals one would encounter in a traditional Buddhist setting. Instead, it's very accessible and simple. Spirit Rock serves thousands of people, my guess is 10,000 people a year. Our mailing list is close to 40,000 people. Many who come here are involved in the world of service—nurses, teachers, therapists, doctors, and healers—and many are involved in the world of business. Our deepest hope is that we can provide a sacred space, a place where people can leave the complexity of their lives for a time to quiet their minds and open their hearts. And, from that stillness, hopefully live their lives in a wiser and happier way. The teachings we give are systematic trainings of how to work with the mind, body, and heart and how to develop a regular spiritual practice. We especially help people learn how to work with difficulties, everything from fear and worry to anger and restlessness.

I'm also involved in a number of other Buddhist centers in America. We have a large sister center I helped found in Massachusetts called the Insight Meditation Society. In addition to teaching and working individually with people, I mentor new teachers, work in community service, and write. For over 20 years, I've been writing a series of books, bringing the transformative teachings I encounter in Buddhist monasteries to the West. I've tried to translate them in a way that's really accessible for people in this culture. The recent books I've written have sold pretty widely. They include *Teachings of Buddha, Seeking the Heart of Wisdom, A Path With Heart,* and *Buddha's Little Instruction Book,* as well as a few others.

I'm also involved in other projects. I had the privilege of helping to organize and coordinate the first worldwide meetings of Buddhist teachers and leaders in the West and in Asia. We came together to discuss how we can serve modern society better, not through proselytizing, but through teaching compassion and awareness. We also want what's valuable in the teachings available for people in various disciplines, such as psychology, ecology, medicine, or science. We held a series of Buddhist teachers' meetings in India with the Dalai Lama and a number of them here. In June 2000, we held a meeting of about 200 Buddhist teachers from Europe, Asia, and North America, including the Dalai Lama, at Spirit Rock.

The Dalai Lama is a truly happy person. He says that even with the weight of troubles in Tibet, if you can't be happy, what use is all this spiritual practice? That belief is essential to our teachings. The Dalai Lama is quite wonderful in this way and so is another teacher, Maha Ghosananda, one of my mentors, the Gandhi of Cambodia. This religious leader just walks around, and smiles, and hugs people. You don't expect this little, tiny, old monk to come and hug you, but his spirit is just so buoyant, even in the face of grave difficulty. He says, "You must be happy. Just to be alive is a gift." He hugs you and asks, "Aren't you happy?" Even if you're a little depressed, he looks you in the eyes with such love that you start to smile because he's so happy.

My days are quite varied. When I teach retreats, I spend hours doing individual work with the people who come, as well as giving lectures and guiding meditations. On other days I might attend board meetings, mentor staff, write and work on my books, or meet with people of other spiritual traditions. We work with a lot of ministers, priests, and rabbis who want to learn the practices of contemplation and then teach them in their own communities. We offer a special training for this. We also have a family program and a series of trainings for youth from inner cities, with mentors from many traditions. I'm also on several boards and involved in international projects.

As a child, I didn't even vaguely imagine doing something like what I do now. I thought I would go into science or perhaps medical school. My father was a scientist. He was brilliant in some ways but very unhappy. He was actually quite disturbed. I saw at an early age that you can be brilliant and still suffer. My father taught in medical school and in academic settings, so I met people who were enormously successful in their field. Some of them were lovely people, but others were miserable or tyrants. I began to realize intelligence, or brilliance, or worldly success may or may not have something to do with happiness. The happiness of people really came from their hearts and the goodness of their beings and not so much from how brilliant or commercially or academically successful they were. I became really interested in this issue when I was a young teenager.

As a small child, I was often frightened because my father was violent, angry, and abusive. My three brothers and I would be okay and then suddenly it would be—Dad is home. Everyone stopped breathing for a second to see what mood he was in. He was so domineering and difficult. It was very painful. My mother was extroverted and a lot more sanguine and easygoing. My friends loved her. They would come and talk to her. When my father was around, however, they would disappear because he was so difficult.

We all tried different strategies to cope with him. I became the peacemaker who would try to keep things on an even keel. I still do that today—it's my job. You start early! One of my brothers would get angry and fight back as he got older. When I think about it now, that was probably the healthiest response. Another brother became depressed, it was just too painful for him. And another became very funny and cynical. He could sometimes diffuse things with his great wit. So we all had different strategies to deal with the violence and abuse in the family. In the end, I was very happy to leave for college.

When I was growing up, the only expectation about my career was that I should do something well. I should be successful, but there was no particular expectation as to a profession. I was interested in science because my father was a biophysicist who designed some of the first space capsules and some of the first artificial heart and lung machines. He also worked for the army's biological warfare section. He did all kinds of strange things. There was always science going on in our house. We'd go into the basement and we would find a new heart/lung machine my father was working on or some other kind of strange experiment. We were all interested in science in some way, but there was no expectation for us in particular other than school. We would be successful in school and then succeed in a profession. Nothing beyond that.

I left for college, Dartmouth, and enrolled in pre-med. I thought being a healer and doctor would be good for me. The first semester, I took organic chemistry and other science courses. Then I signed up for a class in Asian studies. It was partly out of my inner search. I had a sense there must be something else out there besides the mad scientist I lived with. The professor who taught that course, Dr. Wing Tsit Chan, had come to Dartmouth from Harvard, and he was already nearly retired. He was born in China before the turn of the century and before the Boxer Rebellion. He experienced the whole traditional, Confucian educational system and took the emperor's examinations. After the rebellion, he also obtained a modern education. Eventually, he moved to this country and taught at Harvard. Some days he sat cross-legged on top of his desk and lectured about Lao Tzu and the Buddha. My eyes widened and my spirit awoke. I came to his class from organic chemistry, and I thought this is what I'm really looking for. The organic chemistry was okay, but it really was just memorizing different kinds of molecular combinations. I was so much more taken by him. After a short time, I changed my major to Asian Studies. I started reading the *Tibetan Book of the Dead* and anything I could get my hands on about Zen. It was the 1960s, and there were a lot of other influences around for the expansion of consciousness, and I took some of them too. So I chose Asian Studies at Dartmouth, which I found really exciting and rewarding, not knowing what I would do with it. I mean, what do you do with it?

Actually, I didn't ever really worry that I wouldn't know what to do. As a kid, I worked a succession of jobs. Periodically, my father would either get fired or quit because he couldn't get along with other human beings. He did pretty well with animals when they were in his laboratory and he could control them, but that was as far as it went. So periodically, he would get fired or quit because of his unfortunate social skills. We'd go from having money to not having money, and I'd get a job. One thing that helped me over the years is that I've liked most everything I've done. I worked as a bricklayer's assistant and helped construct a big building in Washington, D.C. It was really a kick to learn how to lay bricks. I had a job working on an assembly line while I was in college studying Buddhism. I made it like a Zen exercise and would do this little mantra. It was amusing. Then I worked at Harvard Business School for a while running their very first major computer, which was an IBM 1401. It filled two huge rooms. What do you think Harvard Business School did with their first big computer? I thought perhaps they would analyze the market or something like that, but their first project was to computerize alumni giving. It is Harvard Business School after all. They knew who paid them. I thought that job was interesting as well. There is something in me that likes to learn, that enjoys the adventure of learning something new.

I'm a child of the 1960s and, like many people of that era, was never driven much by money. I also learned in my family, in the periods when there wasn't money, that you could get along fine without it. I was really driven by the excitement of life itself. I wanted to learn. I was also driven by a certain amount of pain because of how abusive my father could be. There was a lot of fear in our family. I looked for some healing from that fear and suffering. That was more important to me.

When I graduated from Dartmouth, I didn't want to go kill people—it was during the Vietnam War and there was still the draft—so I volunteered for the Peace Corps. I thought, I'll go and help people instead of shooting at them. I asked them to send me to a Buddhist country because I wanted to train in a monastery. After reading about Zen masters and lamas, I had an idea there must be people in the world who were wise, and I knew they weren't at the Ivy League colleges. I had to look elsewhere. I worked in Thailand for two years on medical teams in the Mekong River Valley, where there was still a great deal of fighting. It was a program focusing on tropical medicine in the villages, coordinated by both the Peace Corps and the World Health Organization. They gave us very good language training, and it was very exciting.

As soon as I arrived, I began to look for teachers and monasteries. I found that Buddhism is like Christianity. It's a big world religion with lots of temples where people go to pray or make an offering, then go home, feel like everything's fine, and don't change their lives. But in addition to those, tucked away in the mountains and the forests were these amazing ancient monasteries with great teachers, just like one imagines the Zen monastery in Kyoto. I started to visit these teachers, and it was wonderful. I was 22 when I met my teacher, Ajahn Chah, who was 47 at the time. Ajahn Chah was not very well known yet, but he did have quite a reputation for being both demanding and also very light-hearted. He had a wonderful sense of humor, a great twinkle in his eye, and yet a great depth to him as well. He would peer at people who visited like he was taking the cover off a watch to see what made it tick. Only one other westerner had gone to his monastery, and Chah tried to figure me out. I liked him a lot so I asked, "Can I train at your monastery?" He replied, "Well, maybe, if you can stand the discipline." He didn't immediately say, oh yeah, we want you. It was more like, can you stand it? Are you up to it? Then he laughed and said, "I don't know, you're pretty skinny, you might lose more weight. What will we do with you then?" I loved it. I realized he was someone who spoke straight. It was clear that he didn't want anything from me. He just looked at me and said, all right, are you up for this? That's the kind of mentor you want—someone who sees something good in you, but doesn't say, come along and we'll make you a star. Instead, he probed. Can you do something really deep? And really good? I loved that.

I was also inspired by a very wonderful and wise American who had gone before me, who is now the abbott of a whole series of monasteries. He's the first American recognized in Southeast Asia as an abbott, which is the equivalent of a Zen master, an elder in that community. He received an award from the king of Thailand in a royal ceremony because they recognized him as one of their Buddhist elders.

So I joined the monastery and trained. When I first entered, after my monk's ordination, Ajahn Chah looked at me and said, "Well, I hope that you're not afraid to suffer." He explained, "There are two kinds of suffering—the kind you run away from that follows you everywhere, and the kind that you turn around and face, so you're no longer afraid of anything. That's the kind we're interested in here. So if you're ready, come in the gates." As monks, we did some of the very traditional initiations, walking barefoot to get your food, carrying begging bowls 10 miles at dawn just as the sun rose. It wasn't difficult. It was a beautiful, moving experience. The villagers revere and love to feed the monks because the monks carry the teachings of the Buddha to the remote villages. The monasteries are the schools for wisdom and healing. Some of the monks are healers, using herbs and roots. We'd walk through the villages, and the people offered us food even if they were poor. I'd think, I'm an American, I have a lot of money compared to them, how can I take their food? But they'd look at us so respectfully, as if they were thinking, "You represent the Buddha, something so precious to our culture that we'll happily give of the little bit of food we have." You can't say, "Thank you for the mango." You're supposed to keep your mouth shut. What you can do is take their generosity inside, and it really inspires you in your monk's practice.

Sometimes we did long training periods in silence. We would perform funerals and sit in the forest at the charnel grounds where they would burn bodies all night, chanting and visualizing death. In this way, we consciously faced our own deaths. In the long periods of silence, we noticed every emotion that would come—our loneliness, fear, longing, ambition, hopes, expectations. We would see all the different parts of our mind. Then we'd go to our teacher and he'd say, "Tell me what you see in there. How do you work with it? Do you get lost in a particular mind state? Where do you get caught?" Gradually, we learned about the whole inner zoo, the lions and the tigers, the hopes and fears, and not fear them so much.

I lived in Thailand for five years. It was wonderful. My parents were supportive. They had four boys, so they probably figured somebody else would do something decent. Somebody else would go to medical school if I didn't. Then I came back and didn't know what to do. After five years, I realized I didn't want to remain a monk as some people did. I wanted a relationship and marriage. Celibacy was very hard in my twenties. At first, I came back as a monk and lived with my family in Washington, because I wanted to show them how I lived. My mother would drive me to the Thai embassy so they could put food in my begging bowl. She would feed me too, but for the Thais, feeding a monk was very sweet. Then I seriously contemplated what to do next. I decided to attend graduate school in psychology, partly to figure out what happened to me. I experienced a whole Buddhist psychology training and was somewhat changed, but still didn't really understand what to do with it. So I started graduate school, earned a master's degree, and then a Ph.D. in clinical psychology.

In the first years of graduate school, I started meeting other people interested in Buddhism and worked on my first book about the forest teachers that I had practiced with. This was the early 1970s. I met the Lama Chogyam Trungpa and Ram Das. Lama Chogyam Trungpa said he and Ram Das and others were starting the first big Buddhist University in America, the Naropa Institute. Since they didn't have anyone trained to carry on the Southeast Asian tradition, I was invited to join them and teach. The first summer, 2,000 people came to the big lectures of Ram Das and Trungpa. It was very exciting. Several of us, myself, Joseph Goldstein, and Sharon Salzburg, who became my colleagues and teaching partners for many, many years, found we were teaching a similar Buddhist meditation practice that we had each learned in Asia. After our classes, a group of people asked if we would lead retreats, or create a monastery to give meditation trainings. We rented Catholic monasteries and Boy Scout camps, and a lot of people started to come.

While teaching meditation at Naropa Institute, I finished my doctorate. When I first started my graduate work, I had to work to earn money, and I got two different jobs. First, I worked in a mental hospital. I thought I would teach meditation there, but I was really so naïve. The patients didn't need to close their eyes and meditate. They actually needed grounding, things like gardening and yoga, to bring them back into their bodies. I found a whole group of people in the hospital who desperately needed meditation, however—the psychiatric social workers, the doctors, and the nurses. They were often stressed, tense, or frightened. I realized there is a different place for meditation than I originally thought. I also drove a taxi in Boston during grad school. I liked it. You meet all kinds of weird and interesting people in a taxi.

After a year or so, many students who came to the retreats felt it would be good to have our own place instead of renting camps. A few students gave us money. It was very little, actually, but we hit the time when the Catholic Church had very few postulates anymore. They had some huge monasteries with no one in them. One nun who came to our first three-month retreat we offer in silence, a long deep training, suggested we talk to the monsignor in her diocese because they had some properties in Massachusetts that might be good for our retreats. The church had a huge, beautiful monastery—100 rooms, tennis court, bowling alley—and there were nine people living in it. They were old and needed to move. No one knew what to do with the building because it had all these little monks' rooms. We ended up buying, for only $150,000, a big monastery with a beautiful forest, 80 acres of land, and 100 rooms. When they discovered we were going to run it as a spiritual center, they left us all the furniture and things in the kitchen.

Our friends gave us $50,000 to put down, which seemed like a fortune in those days, and we just started. Many people came. Ram Das came, and at that time he was already a well-known figure. His book, *Be Here Now,* sold a million copies. The word got around that this place was a sanctuary where you could really go into yourself, and it became quite successful. For the first 10 years, I lived there half the year and taught by traveling around half the year. I worked individually with people as a psychologist, taught retreats, and continued to write. I published my first book and then a second and a third. My idea wasn't to somehow become hugely successful, but simply to teach what really touched me from my teacher. I wanted to communicate the level of compassion he had, the fearlessness he taught in the monastery, the practices that gave a sense of being free in yourself. I learned that even when there are painful or difficult circumstances, your heart can remain free. These teachings were important to me, and as I taught them to other people, they understood. It was very rewarding and nurturing, so I just continued to do it. I didn't plan for some special success. I remember talking to a good friend, who was the first manager of our center in Massachusetts and later became the president of one of the largest film and video companies in Hollywood. He believed success simply required finding something that is really good and just keep doing it. And that's what we did. We offered teachings and writings, and it seemed to serve people. Out of the devotion we had for our work, everything grew. It wasn't like we had some big game plan to become more successful, build more centers, sell more product, and things like that. It just happened.

There was always basically some trust. In the first year after we opened our center, we had very little money. People were paid a pittance to come and help. One of our friends' parents gave him a new car and when our cash grew short, he sold his car and donated the money. We used that money to pay everybody for six months. Then, the center grew. We had some of the folly and pleasure of youth as well. There's a kind of immortality you have, a sense that you can and should do what you love, and if you give yourself to your love and passion, eventually something good will come. And if it doesn't, you can change and do something else.

One quality that enabled my success is a certain kind of trust and flexibility. The trust is not that things will work out, but that if things don't work out you can do something else! That's the real trust. If this doesn't work out, I'll simply go back and study some other thing. I felt there would always be something interesting to do—that was all it took. It's one of the good lessons I received from my family. My wife complains about it, but among my brothers and myself, we feel we can do anything we want. My wife always teases me, "You Kornfields think you can do everything." One of my brothers is the chief building inspector for the city of San Francisco. He does earthquake preparedness and 100 other things for the whole city. He's extremely competent in a huge range of things from architecture to engineering to boat design to gardening aesthetics. He was a master ski instructor and a professor of landscape design. He's done all kinds of things. Actually, it is a little hard for his wife because she'll wonder what to do about something and he'll always reply, "Oh, I can do that." The problem is, of course, that (being a man) he will sometimes say that even when he can't do it. There was just some trans-mission that happened to make us believe, "You can do it, or you'll figure out how." Although he was very difficult, that was one of a number of gifts from my father. Another gift he gave us was an inter-est in and curiosity about the world. That was a great gift.

Work and teaching alone wasn't a very complete life for me. Although the work was really rewarding and rich, it was only half of me. It wasn't until I married and had a child that I felt my life was whole. This might not be so for everyone, but I needed that. I feel like the training I received in the monastery, the training to be a psy-chologist in graduate school, and my work as a teacher was really a warm-up for being a husband and a father. I learned more in my marriage and in parenting that helped me be even more useful to people as a teacher and a guide.

If I look back, would I have done anything differently? I don't think so, really. I feel there's a certain way I've been guided, and things unfolded as they should. There's some way my own trust was met by the world. I really wanted to go to Harvard, but my grades were low so I only got on the waiting list. I did well on every kind of test, but I was really undisciplined. It turned out to be a good thing because at Dartmouth I met the man who became my mentor, Dr. Wing Tsit Chan, and the others who followed. Dartmouth was a rather small pond where I could do exactly what I wanted. There were no Asian Studies majors. I was the only one at the time. I could study whatever I wanted, and it was perfect. So I look back and think, I wouldn't change it. Even the pain in my family led me to search some other kind of wisdom. This trust is another gift I learned from my teacher, Ajahn Chah. He started out relatively unknown and yet, when he died, nearly a million people came to his funeral. He was beloved because he was wise, compassionate, and very funny. His tapes and books were spread all around the country. He would just tell the truth. He saw things as they were and wouldn't censor what he said, but did it with a good spirit in order to help people awaken. He was a fine mentor, because when he worked with people, he would see the possibility—some spark in them—and he would place them in difficult situations to make that come out. He made my American friend an abbott very early, after only five or six years as a monk, which was unheard of. But he saw the possibility, and my friend became a brilliant abbott. I learned from watching Ajahn Chah the pleasure of seeing gifts in others and then fostering them, mentoring them. That's been one of the great joys as a teacher—I get to do that with a lot of people. I don't know if I would change anything.

Conclusion

A quote I like most in Jack Kornfield's interview is from one of his mentors, Maha Ghossananda, which is, "You must be happy. Just to be alive is a gift." It seems to sum up Jack's personality and the message he shares in his meditation centers and books. Jack is very dedicated to Buddhism's central message and encourages others to live based on the values of their own hearts and inner wisdom.

Jack's initial career plan was to enter science or medical school, but a chance class in Asian studies changed the path of his life. After college, he joined the Peace Corps, lived at a Buddhist monastery, and eventually returned to the States and established meditation and retreat centers around the country.

In his reflections on how to achieve success, like so many other interviewees, Jack says you just have to find something you love and keep doing it. He adds what helped him build on that principle was his trust in life's experiences and his flexibility. Jack learned this trust from his childhood. As the family moved from place to place, Jack found he could always find interesting work to do. And he survived a volatile home by creating harmony where he could. Now he is grateful toward his father for the gifts he gave him—a sense of curiosity and a self-confidence that he'd always be able to figure things out. Jack enjoys passing on what he has learned from others and from his own inner journey.

ROBERT MONDAVI

Founder, Mondavi Vineyards

Robert **Mondavi, who comes from a family of winemakers and** entrepreneurs, is actively involved in the California wine industry today as its foremost spokesperson. Robert's parents, Cesare and Rosa Mondavi, immigrated from Italy in 1910 and moved to California, where they began a business shipping grapes from the Napa Valley to the East. Robert grew up helping his father in the business. He graduated from Stanford University, and then worked at the Sunnyhill Winery in St. Helena, which his father purchased. The family winery produced bulk wine, but Robert soon became interested in producing fine wine. In 1943, Robert convinced his father to buy the Charles Krug Winery. He studied many aspects of winemaking, and determined to increase the quality of wine produced, he upgraded the technology of winemaking in the family business, becoming the first of the winemakers in the Napa Valley to use cold fermentation extensively. He was also a skillful marketer. He changed the branding of a white pinot wine into a chenin blanc and its sales quadrupled. He employed other new marketing techniques such as blind tastings for the public and for those in the trade, believing that this public exposure would be the most successful sales tactic.

In 1966, Mondavi built the Robert Mondavi Winery in Oakville, California and is currently chairman of the board. Mondavi is the largest exporter of premium California wines, now in 90 countries. The company went public in 1993, and its stock is traded on the NASDAQ exchange.

Robert and his wife, Margaret Biever, actively participate in several organizations promoting food and wine, among them the Great Chefs Program, the Robert Mondavi Missions Program, designed to educate Americans about wine and food, and the American Center for Wine, Food, and the Arts in Napa, which he founded. He is founding chairman, with Julia Child, of the American Institute of Wine and Food, a member of the American Wine Society, the Brotherhood Knights of the Vine, and the Chaine des Rotisseurs.

I interviewed Robert in his office in Oakville, California where his winery is located. The buildings, located adjacent to the winery, are a handsome collection of Spanish style stucco. An appealing air of informality and quietness pervades the place. It was easy for me to find the correct office with the friendly help of several people passing by, and I found his office interior to be quite lovely. Robert is a very charming, attractive man with a warm smile. He has a head any sculptor would love to shape. His cheekbones and nose are wonderful and strong. His handshake was firm and very friendly, and he immediately insisted I call him Robert. During our interview, he showed a very sharp memory for details and told his story with humor and liveliness. He seemed to love telling his quite remarkable story. He also just completed a recently published autobiography, so the memories of his life are fresh.

Near the end of the interview, his wife, Margaret, entered the office from a door on the terrace and kissed him. There is an obvious tenderness and passion between the two. I was reminded of the part of the interview when Robert spoke about the importance of keeping a relationship alive when one is very involved in a business. He has clearly thought a great deal about marriage and commitment and understands the importance of balance in life. As he admits, he learned this from his mistakes. He is humble about his accomplishments and his personal weaknesses. I found him to be a truly fascinating man and was particularly impressed with how he taught himself to be flexible and change his mind when he needed to. His intellect, curiosity, and openness to new ideas provided him a full and passionate life.

Robert Mondavi

Now I realize you cannot change people, and now I'm living in a state of nirvana.

I'm a competitive person. Ever since I was a child, I wanted to excel in everything, whether it was swimming, football, rugby, or simply nailing boxes for my father. I wanted to be the best in all my classes. I always tried to be in a position, physically and mentally, to excel. I'm not a brilliant person, just above-average intelligence, but I have a lot of common sense. I always look at my competition to see whether I have an opportunity to succeed.

As I observed the world in my youth, I saw that many people were basically lazy, afraid to gamble, and unwilling to work hard. Common sense told me if I worked hard and applied myself to something that had a future and stayed with it, I could eventually succeed. Those were the basic principles I followed, and I had enough self-confidence to succeed if the conditions were right.

It was never my concern *what* I would tackle. I always wanted to see first what the playing field was, and measure my chances. For example, I played football in high school. I was 140 pounds and a full-back. I must have been pretty good because we won the northern California championship. When I went to college at Stanford, however, I saw the other football players were about 180 to 200 pounds. I realized my chances of really doing anything great on this team would be very difficult. So instead, I played rugby, where because I was pretty quick, I did quite well. In fact, in my senior year, I received the gold football for being the most valuable rugby player. So, this was my attitude. Nothing else, except perhaps my gene structure, gave me the ability to excel.

My parents came from Italy in 1906. My father moved here first and lived here for two years. He then returned to Italy, married his girlfriend (my mother), and brought her back here. The family was raised here. I have two sisters and a brother, who are completely different from me. I wanted to excel much more than any of my siblings. In fact, my brother was very conservative—just the opposite of me. I looked at my brother and sisters and thought that if I use common sense and have patience, they'll eventually think as I do because we were brought up in the same environment. That didn't work, however, and it took me 75 years to learn that.

I realized the gene structure in each individual human being plays a very important part. I thought I could change my brother and sisters to think the way I did. I found out that they didn't change, and I didn't change that much either.

We can influence people, but we can't change them. When I realized that, it made life much easier for me. I always tried to change people to think my way. Now I realize you cannot change people, and now I'm living in a state of nirvana. As you get older, you get a little wisdom. I accept people's differences now. There are always many differences of opinion, and I accept those and live with them. So I'm at peace with myself and a very happy person in that regard.

In business, I would always discuss things openly with people and explain my philosophy. I would try to find out what they thought. We'd come to a common understanding on how I run my business. If someone didn't agree with me, I felt that they'd be better off going elsewhere, because there's more than one way to run a business. What you need are people who understand and believe in your philosophy—bring them in and you'll succeed. I learned that but didn't practice it until the last few years of my life.

My father came to talk with me when I was at Stanford in 1935, after the repeal of Prohibition in 1933. He wanted to know my plans for my career and had enough foresight to come to me in my junior year. I told him I was either going to be a businessman or a lawyer. He used to call me Bobbie. He said, "Bobbie, I think there's a future in the wine business, and Napa Valley is the outstanding wine-growing region in all of California."

We lived in Minnesota in 1919, when Prohibition took effect, and people were allowed to make 200 gallons of wine per family. My dad would go to California and buy grapes. He was very knowledgeable about all the grapes grown in California. Before we moved to California in 1923, he purchased grapes from Napa, Sonoma, and as far south as Fresno, so he knew Napa Valley was one of the outstanding wine-growing regions in the world. I agreed with his idea when he said, "Why not enter a young industry and grow with it?"

I drank wine since I was a child. My mother and father fed me both wine and water from the time I was three or four years old. I looked at wine as liquid food. When I went to Stanford, and we went on those so-called beer busts, I was dumbfounded. They would drink beer, scotch, bourbon, and gin—no wine—and over a third of the people got plastered. And I wondered, are these people civilized? They didn't know how to drink alcoholic beverages, or how, in moderation, wine could be good for you.

I never went to enology school. I basically learned the hard way. I was tutored by a professor who taught enology and viticulture at the University of California at Berkeley. He was very, very good. I spent two hours a day several days a week for two months during an entire summer learning the wine business. I studied the book, *The Principles and Practices of Wine Making*. If you follow that book meticulously you can make good wine. I also visited all the principal wineries in the state of California. When we came to Napa Valley, there were only 20 wineries. Now, there are over 250 wineries, so there's been a big, big change.

When I first came into the business after Stanford in 1937, we only made bulk wine, which we shipped in tank cars to the East Coast. I realized we had to go into the fine wine business in Napa Valley if we were to succeed over the long run. I talked to my father about buying the Charles Krug Winery, which was one of the oldest wineries in Napa Valley. It was built in 1861. In 1943, I convinced my dad to buy that winery so we could go into the fine wine business in addition to shipping bulk wine. The bulk wine business actually financed us in the fine wine business.

To go into the fine wine business, you had to either be a rich man or make money to feed it. When we first bought the Charles Krug Winery, we bottled our bulk wine, shipping it in gallons and half-gallons. After we made some money, we started in the fine wine business. I became more knowledgeable about the wine business by visiting other wineries and comparing our wines. We grew our business that way and were quite successful. At wine judging contests at state fairs, we did much better than most other wineries, and we built a reputation. So, little by little, we grew.

It was very difficult during those years. Up until 1966, we had many lean years. We had two good years during the war, 1943 and

1945, but after that, it was difficult because wine was not generally accepted by the American public. It was a long, hard road.

The big change came about 1966. That year, I sold my interest in the Charles Krug Winery to my brother, and built the Robert Mondavi Winery. That was the beginning of a revolution in the wine business in California.

As I mentioned, I compared our wines constantly. First, when we had bulk wine, I compared our wines to what I thought were then the truly fine California wines (Inglenook, Berringer, Beaulieu, Wente, and others). After we began to produce wine equal to theirs, I began to compare our wines with the great Bordeaux and Burgundy wines of France, which were considered the outstanding wines of the world.

I realized they were doing something in their wine making that we weren't doing. I took my first trip to France in 1962 to discover what they did and found that they made their cabernet differently from their pinot noir and their chardonnay completely differently from their Riesling. We made all our red wines exactly the same and all our white wines more or less the same. They, however, aged each of these varieties differently.

So I experimented with changing the technique of making each kind of wine—cabernet, pinot noir, zinfandel, petite sirah, chardonnay, Riesling, and the other varieties of grapes we had. Suddenly, our wines had a lot of character that they did not before. We improved our wine making by being very clean, topping our barrels, and understanding what kind of barrels produced the best results.

We also realized we had to grow our grapes naturally in the vineyards. We learned, after many years, to stress our vineyards so we could get the maximum quality, not the biggest tonnage but the best quality grapes. This took a lifetime of work, but as we did each of these things, it added character, depth, and drinkability to our wines.

We now grow our grapes naturally and make our wines naturally. We are not even filtering it. Our wines became ranked with the greatest wines of the world. Today, we produce wine in Napa Valley equal to the great wines of the world.

The main reason we outpaced the other wine makers was the others were not applying themselves to the small differences. They weren't willing to gamble or take a risk by doing things a little differently. I was willing to do that, and that's one reason why my family eventually split. I constantly wanted to experiment, to spend money to try this and that, whereas my brother was not of the same frame of mind. We finally split, and I formed our winery here. He's doing his thing, I'm doing my thing, and everything goes very well now.

Communication is a problem you have all the time in business. It's another one of the things I've learned. I realized my brother and I were talking, but we weren't understanding each other. He didn't understand what I was saying, and I didn't understand what he was saying.

What I later taught my children was to ensure what you say is understood by the other party, whether it's your family or anyone else. If there's something important you want to communicate, be sure they repeat it or in some way show you they understand. I have done this with my own family, Mike, Tim, and Marcia, and we are still together. If I hadn't done that, I don't think we would be together. As with all families, all people, sometimes we think we hear each other, but in fact we misunderstand each other. We close our minds. We all do. We don't mean to, but we do. After a number of years, I realized even I do things like that. I thought I had an open mind, but even I sometimes close my mind.

People often ask me the secrets of my success. What are the biggest lessons I can share with people who are starting out or who are remaking their lives? There are some basic tenets I believe lead to success in business and almost every other life endeavor.

To succeed in business or in life, you don't need fancy schooling or high technical experience. That helps, but what you need most is common sense, a commitment to hard work, and the courage to go your own way. That is the necessary foundation. On top of this foundation are 15 other qualities that served me well. I think of them as basic components of my philosophy for success. I learned these lessons from my own experience, and I put them down to teach my grandchildren. So, here's my philosophy:

First, and foremost, you must have confidence and faith in yourself.

Second, whatever you choose to do, make a commitment to excel. Then pour yourself into it with your whole heart and soul, with complete dedication.

Third, interest is not enough. You must be passionate about what you do if you want to succeed and live a happy life. Find a job you love, and you'll never have to work a day in your life.

Fourth, establish a goal just beyond what you think you can do. When you achieve that, establish another and another. This will teach you to embrace risk. I always strove for something just beyond what we were doing. When I first went into the bulk wine business I wanted to have the best bulk wine. Then, when I achieved that, I wanted to enter the fine wine business. Then, I wanted to make the best fine wine in California. As I began to do that, I looked at the great bordeaux and burgundy wines and wanted to do that too.

Fifth, be completely honest and open. I never had secrets. My family used to get mad at me because I told everybody our secrets, but I felt they would learn them sooner or later. I was always willing to share my knowledge and experience with people if they would share theirs with me. I had confidence there was enough room for all of us.

Sixth, generosity pays. What you give will enrich your life and come back to you many times over, if you have the desire and will to stay with it. So, learn to initiate giving.

Seventh, only make promises and commitments you know you can keep. A broken promise can damage your credibility and reputation beyond repair.

Eighth, understand you cannot change people. You might improve them, but you can't change anyone but yourself. Accept people the way they are. Accept their differences and work with them as they are. I learned this after about 70 years of life, and it is amazing what peace of mind I found when I finally understood it.

Ninth, live and work in harmony with others, don't be judgmental. Instead, cultivate tolerance, empathy, and compassion. Never berate people. With my family and other people, I used to say, okay, let's be open and honest so we can excel. I would ask, Why did you do this? I would belittle my own children. I didn't mean to, but I thought it would encourage people to do better. I found it doesn't work. You must bring people in and talk with them alone. People are too sensitive. Never berate people in front of their cohorts. This can be dispiriting and damaging to them, and it's counterproductive for you. If you want to teach someone to fly, you don't start by clipping his wings. I learned that late in life also.

Tenth, human beings experience the same thing in different ways. Two people can live the exact same experience and come away with very different understandings of what happened. So there's always a large space for misunderstanding. Always stay alert for misunderstandings and tread lightly, especially when it comes to politics, religion, or moral standards.

Eleventh, it is very important to understand one another. We need to learn how to bridge those spaces of misunderstanding. To do this, we must listen carefully when we talk, and be sure people understand us. On important issues, have people repeat back to you what you've said to make sure there are no areas of confusion or conflict.

Twelfth, rarely will you find complete harmony between two human beings. If you find harmony, maintaining it requires individuals or soul mates to have complete confidence in one another. You must make time to share experiences and appreciate precious moments and the beauty of life together. Open yourself to that person emotionally, physically, spiritually, and intellectually. Always allow time for playfulness and laughter. There's no better tonic for keeping love alive and vibrant than laughter and good cheer.

Thirteenth, in both life and work, stay flexible. The same holds true for a country, company, or family. Dictatorship and rigidity rarely work. Freedom and elasticity do.

Fourteenth, always stay positive. America was built on the can-do spirit and will continue to thrive on it.

Fifteenth, the greatest leaders don't rule, they inspire. Out of all the rigidity and mistakes of my past, I learned this one final lesson, and would like to see it understood by every business leader, teacher, and parent in America. I was raised Catholic and learned the fear of God, not the love of God. If I did this, I'd go to hell. If I didn't do this, I'd go to heaven. Then I went to Stanford where the professors told us to use our own heads. Don't just believe what people write in books, those are their own ideas. They may be right, but use your own head and decide.

I began to think about religion again. I realized there were other teachers in the world, in addition to Jesus Christ, who taught love. And love was an entirely different story. It's so much easier to rule by fear. Although I always realized the need for a supreme being who creates things, I didn't agree with the church teaching the fear of

God. I realized it was much more difficult to teach through love, but when a child grows up with love rather than fear, you have a different child. This applies in business, too.

So, to be successful, you have to enter a business in which you feel comfortable and in which you can excel. Then you must learn to excel. There are many intelligent people, but few with common sense. There are many visionaries, but few can execute their vision. When you look at the world and see that, you begin to realize there are many different ways of doing the same thing. Yours is not the only way, but by dedication to hard work and motivating others who believe in your philosophy to work with you, you can eventually achieve success.

The other part of success is learning how to live with people in a happier, more loving way. There are very few people who can do that. I love my wife more now than when I married her 18 years ago. People look at us and wonder how that can be. I used to try to change my dear wife. I learned to accept her the way she was. That's a small thing, but once you step back and realize how silly some things are, you get along beautifully. I've had a long life, and I've learned some lessons. Hopefully, they can help you, too.

Conclusion

Robert's initial career goal was to become either a lawyer or a businessperson. His father convinced him there was a future in the wine business of northern California. He learned the business the hard way. He studied with a professor from the University of California at Berkeley, visited wineries and made comparisons with his wine, and traveled to Europe where he learned their unique techniques for winemaking.

Robert was different from other winery owners because he was curious, willing to learn, and open to experimenting with his vineyard's techniques. Basically, what differentiated him from the mainstream was his ability to take risks, a key trait of all the entrepreneurs in this book. The result, of course, is that Mondavi wines are world famous.

Through his career, Robert learned the softer side of business acumen, namely the importance of communication skills. He reflects that the simple intention of speaking to be understood, and listening to understand makes all the difference in his business success and family happiness. He adds that after a good many years, he also learned that as much as he might try to have his staff accept his management style, he could never expect them to share all his opinions. Ultimately, he said, there will be differences of opinion, and learning to accept them is important.

Robert summarized the key ingredients to success as common sense, a commitment to hard work, and the courage to go your own way. In addition, he generously offers his more in-depth philosophy regarding success in the 15 points he shares at the end of the interview. These are beautifully expressed and a true gift to readers and to his grandchildren for whom I sensed he wrote them.

FAITH POPCORN

Futurist

Faith **Popcorn is a well-known expert in predicting trends and** chairperson of Faith Popcorn Brain Reserve Inc., a marketing consultancy that she founded in 1974. She has written two best-selling books on future trends entitled, *The Popcorn Report* and *Clicking: 16 Trends to Future Fit Your Life, Your Work, and Your Business.* She has served as a consultant to many corporations, predicting future consumer needs and behaviors. She identified such widely used societal concepts as cocooning, cashing out, female think, and pleasure revenge and predicted the advent of stay-at-home shopping, fresh foods, fresh delivery, and interactive TV shopping. Her predictions are documented as having a 95 percent success rate. Faith is a graduate of New York University and New York's High School of Performing Arts.

I first met Faith Popcorn at the home of my sister, Olive, in Manhattan. My daughter and I were there for dinner. Faith arrived, dressed in black and looking very avant-garde and chic. I thought she was quite interesting as did my daughter, Annabel. Annabel, who is always ahead of her time in fashion, was wearing a deep blue shade of Hard Candy's nail polish. This was before alternative nail color hit the streets, and Faith was fascinated with Annabel's choice. The two shared an instant bonding experience and spent quite a bit of time talking fashion and comparing notes on their preferences. Faith, who is very interested in almost everyone and everything, is great with people of any age. She communicates easily, which is certainly one reason she succeeds like she does. She is thin, wiry, intense, and moves quickly with a lot of energy. She looks hip, but in a subtle way.

I interviewed Faith at Brain Reserve headquarters in New York. The company is in a townhouse on Manhattan's Upper East Side. It occupies the first two floors, and Faith and her family live on the upper floors. From the outside, the townhouse seems dignified and traditional like its neighbors but, once one enters, the atmosphere is very untraditional. Everyone who works at Brain Reserve wears black, and most of the people I saw in the office were under 30. Faith expects her employees to dedicate their life to the company and therefore attracts young people who want to be on the cutting edge of trend prediction. The atmosphere in the office is energized and bustling. There is a keen sense of egalitarianism, and there didn't appear to be any special back offices for upper-level management. Everyone operates as a team and dresses in the team uniform. Even Faith's adorable daughter dressed in black velvet.

While waiting for Faith's meeting to end and our interview to begin, I was completely entranced playing with her delightful daughter. Faith is a concerned and attentive mother, and very happy to have a little girl. The room we met in was a living room in the townhouse, which was creatively furnished with round ottomans and a combination of old and new furniture. Faith is very professional and easy to interview because what she sells in the world is herself. She created and promoted herself, Faith Popcorn, as a symbol of the future. Like a seasoned performer, she presents her life in a certain light, promotes her ideas clearly and concisely, and is alert and conscious of her listener's reactions. Faith is an inspiring woman, entrepreneur, and visionary because she is a complete original.

Faith Popcorn

The way women run companies is to give the people in their companies a vote. Everybody has a vote here, because you can't make anybody do their best for something they don't believe in.

My company, which I started in 1974, is called Faith Popcorn Brain Reserve. We consult with Fortune 500 companies. They retain us, usually at the chairman or president level, to help them see the decade ahead and invent products or strategies to fit the future. Chairmen of companies are focused on today and yesterday and really don't have the time to look forward. So we help them and have very unique ways of doing this, a 38-step methodology that enables us to see the future consumer and market space. I would describe what we do in more detail, but it would take 20 hours. We've been 95 percent accurate in all our Trend predictions. They are all recorded in the books. It's not just me saying we are correct. So our methodology works. We tell companies, "Don't be in this, be in that," or, "Reposition your cookies to deliver this message," or, "Have this formulation."

My next book, which I think is the best book we've ever written (my coauthor Lys Marigold agrees), is called *EVEolution—The Eight Truths of Marketing to Women.* It discusses how men and women are different and how one needs to market to them differently. Women buy 80 percent of consumer goods. They're powerful. *EVEolution* will be a hard book for many people to swallow. It presents a new marketing model containing eight case histories of companies and products we've EVEolved—from GE Capital to Jiffy Lube.

The Trend we're best known for is called cocooning. The stay-at-home trend. What's interesting about it and what a lot of people don't know is that we named it and framed it in 1981, when everybody was still having sex, drugs, and rock 'n' roll. We said consumers were going to stay home, and if they do, companies (depending on who we were working with) should think about take-out food, gardening, or home offices, and computers for the home. That was a very early take. We saw it before it really happened—just before. If we were working with a restaurant, let's say a fast-food company, we'd say, "Here's why home delivery is going to be so important. How do you reformat your service or product so you can take advantage of it?" First, companies must see what the future is and what consumers will be like, then they can reformat their products and services to fit, even if it means changing something so that it will fit.

I backed into the idea of Faith Popcorn's Brain Reserve, a future-focused consulting company. I was a copywriter and creative director in an advertising agency and was fired for being "out there." I even started a very small advertising boutique. I soon realized whatever I predicted, happened. For example, I'd say, "You know, it's going to be hot to be older in the future. Gray will be okay." Then, a gray movement came on the scene. Or, I would say, "Indian food is going to be hot. So is Mexican food" and it was. I could tell you what car would succeed. I realized I was informally using a methodology. I'd talk to friends. I have thousands of friends just to talk to and brainstorm with. That ultimately became our Talent Bank. It's currently 7,500 experts, globally. We also talk to a lot of consumers—4,000 per year in 16 categories, for the last 20 years. I read everything, about 50 magazines and newsletters a month. Now we read them in many languages, including Chinese and Japanese. That's our Knowledge Bank. I'm just one of those people who can sense something about to happen. Somebody else can go into a store and just see stuff, but I'll notice something else. I'll see the future of the shelf. So I knew women would leave Fortune 500 companies in droves and want to have kids and start their own businesses. Now, female run and owned companies employ more people than the Fortune 500 combined. We predicted this 10 years ago. I'll even know when a company's employees are going on strike. I just talk to people. I told a guy who ran an airline, "You know, your flight attendants are going to go on strike." He said, "What? We aren't talking about a strike." They striked two weeks later.

I was always like that. My parents were both attorneys. My mother was a negligence lawyer. My father was a criminal lawyer with the CID, the Criminal Investigation Division of the U.S. Army, in Shanghai. I have a younger sister, seven years my junior. I was raised in Shanghai and was intrigued by the mystery of discovery in China, which may be why I ultimately adopted a Chinese child. I wanted to be a private detective. I used to follow people on the street that I found interesting. I just followed them. I think it's fascinating what people say they're going to do and then what they really do. I could be a private eye, and actually I am a cultural private eye. That's what this business is about—what people say and think and what they will think in the future. I'm putting together clues and predicting how they're going to think. I would also read about 30 books in a week. I was just voracious. I read magazines on clothes, electronics, food, sports. Maybe the brailling of the culture, the private eye thing (which I always had) is the key to my profession.

Also, it helps to be a woman. Women read faces. That's what makes women very good salespeople. They're incredible. Because they've been silenced for so long they developed an incredible ability to see what's on people's minds. Women just braille naturally. We feel with all our senses.

I actually find it very annoying to do this all the time. It's unnerving. I can't go anywhere or do anything without thinking, "What does this mean? What are they thinking?" It's like those couples who say they're happy, but you can see they're not. When I was a child, that's what I did, observe and watch. I was always too old for my childhood body.

I wasn't allowed to work as a child. My parents thought it was terrible for a child to do. I wanted to be an actor for a while, so I went to the School of Performing Arts in New York and to NYU for acting. After college, I was supposed to go to law school but didn't. My father died in an automobile crash when I was 19. It was a very defining moment in my life. If my father lived, I would have been a criminal lawyer because I worshipped my father. But when he died, that was it. My boyfriend was in advertising, so I took a course in advertising and was really good at it. I'm a very good writer—a short, brief writer. So I was offered an opportunity in an advertising agency, and I took it. It sounded good, but I actually never really wanted to work in the advertising business. I didn't want to be told what to do and what to tell a client to stroke his ego. Also, as a businesswoman in the 1970s, I don't think I was regarded very seriously.

In 1968, before I started my own company, I changed my name to Popcorn, which was my nickname. My name was Plotkin. My boss used to call me Popcorn. He didn't like to say Plotkin, so he'd say, "Popcorn." So, I said, "Okay, I'll call myself Popcorn." And it was the best thing I ever did. It's so memorable. It's on my passport. So many people ask me if it is my real name. Well, it will be much easier for my daughter, g.g., because when people ask her if it's her real name, she'll be able to answer honestly with a simple yes.

When I started the company, I had no money. I didn't make any money for 10 years. There was me, my partner, Stuart Pittman, and a secretary. Stuart and I were both fired from the advertising agency and were good friends. We started this thing, but he really wanted to be in advertising, and I really wanted a consulting company. So we eventually parted ways. It took me a long time to grow this company. It made some money, but not a lot. I just decided it was going to work. I didn't care if it took me 50 years. I put my head down and said, "This is going to work." They may not have caught up to me out there, but I knew companies should look at the future. It was and is obvious to me.

One of my earliest clients was Campbell's Soups. They really understood my work. The chairman was a lovely guy named Gordon McGovern. The president was Herb Baum (who has since hired me at Hasbro). Even though Gordon was almost retired, he completely understood and really let me go to work for the company. My Trends didn't have names then, and they told me I had to call my Trends something. So I defined the Trends, named them, and really worked them through. A Trend is simply a future consumer direction. An example is 99 Lives, the Hurry-Up Trend. For that, we had to think about how to deliver products faster. So, for Campbell, we figured out (and this sounds so obvious now) that cans were over. They were frustrating. They were annoying. We recommended soft cans for soup, and then 10 years later somebody else did it. We recommended Food-for-One. We predicted women would be living as singles, on their own. They weren't then, but we showed the demographics and how we believed women would be living alone.

So many women have started their own companies (at twice the rate of men). That will be the big purchasing power in the decade ahead. We are a predominantly female company. The way women run companies is to give the people in their companies a vote. Everybody has a vote here, because you can't make anybody do their best for something they don't believe in. We have a lot of fun here. I don't hire people who say no or it can't happen. They don't have what I call the track, the willingness to keep going around the track. When I hire, I ask people what is on their night table—what they read. I also like it when a client walks in and sees a unified look. It came from the concept of dress codes. I love dress codes. IBM almost invented them, I think, with the guys having to wear ties and blue suits. Schools that require uniforms are great, because you don't focus on what people are wearing.

I am a very impulsive person. An example is this house. I was with a real estate broker looking for a two-bedroom apartment, and I walked by this house. I said, "My God, if I could get a house like that, I would buy it." This was four and a half years ago. So she said, "Well, this house is in foreclosure." It had no sign on it or anything. It was impulsive. Predictive. An instinct. I figured if I moved my company into this house, I could do it financially. I bought at just the right time.

I would have been absolutely one of the worst lawyers. I'm the kind of person who feels bad if I insult someone or say the wrong thing. I would have made a better Save the Poor crusader than a lawyer. I probably would have gone into criminal law, but wouldn't be one of those wealthy lawyers. There's so much injustice. People buy their way out, and the bad guys do finish first a lot. I don't admire rich people. People like Eleanor Roosevelt are my heroes. I admire her enormously. And, my daughter is my hero in the making.

Success, for me, is creating this business and making it successful. It's not only a business; it's an industry, and it's my life. There's no Trend industry except us, really. I would love to say I left a new industry behind, and it's starting to happen. Harvard asked me to teach a course and that was very rewarding—seeing a high level of interest on the students' faces. I want to leave the legacy of future sight. I want it to be a serious profession. That would be success for me.

Another part of success is just to see what kind of mother I'm going to be. I hope a very good one. Beyond that, I can't imagine what would really, really make me any happier. I want to do a newsletter now. I have to do this. I need to do it. I'm also creating products based on Trends, like Faith Popcorn's Home Office Cocoon with Hooker Furniture—a home office created for women. Another product is Faith Popcorn's Cocooning Chair with a La-Z-Boy—a recliner created for women, and a chair created for their kids.

A lot of my friends study Zen Buddhism, and that's a good thing.

It's a Trend we call Anchoring. I need more of that in my life. If I died right now, would it be okay? I don't know, maybe. But that peaceful place inside us they talk about—well, it's not in me yet.

I would advise young people starting out today wanting to be an entrepreneur to get a partner who does something you don't do terribly well. I wish I had a financial partner early in my career. Another thing I would suggest is to have a really clear idea of your goals. Write a business plan, I didn't. Use some of the really good disciplines out there and available, and stick with them. One thing I did was to meet a lot of smart people who helped me. Dale Carnegie did that, too. I love Dale Carnegie and his book, *How To Win Friends and Influence People*. It's the best book I've ever read. Early in his career, Dale Carnegie wrote to about 100 people he admired, people like Thomas Edison, and asked to meet them. They all met with him. I'd tell young people to meet the people you admire. They will take the time. When kids write or e-mail me, I meet them. They come here. They want to see what we do, and I invite them in. I think that's important when you're a young entrepreneur. Meet people who are good in your field or a related field and ask them a lot of questions. When I was young, I had no money. But, my lawyers worked for me for free. I always had a lawyer on my team. A family bias, I guess. I didn't have any money, and they didn't charge me. So I suggest to people, meet people who are good, and they'll help you. I don't really like being called a mentor. It makes me feel old, and I always think it's going to take too much time. But if someone says, "Can I talk to you about what I want to do, about my business plan?" I'll say, "Well, okay, let me see it." So I always tell people to meet the people they admire and ask them, "How did you get here? What's your advice to me?" That can be very useful. It can create an industry for you.

Conclusion

Faith Popcorn did not begin her career intending to own a company predicting future trends. She began in advertising, and discovered over time that she had a talent for knowing what the public would want—and labeling it.

Faith grew up wanting to be a private detective and had planned to be a lawyer until her father's untimely death when she was in college. Faith defines success as making her business work. She is passionate and totally committed to her company, and when she hires staff she wants them to share the same total dedication. Faith advises young people who want to be entrepreneurs to write a business plan, find a business partner with complementary skills, and meet good people who will help you. Also, she adds in her interview, have excellent communication skills and ask a lot of questions.

Faith's interview was exactly as she presents herself to the public: bright, snappy, and very self-confident. I think readers will learn as much from her presentation as from her words. I know I did!

JOHN SCULLEY

Former CEO, Apple Computer

John Sculley became CEO of Apple Computer in 1983, when Apple's revenues were $600 million. Under Sculley's leadership, the company's revenues grew to $8 billion and Apple's advertising campaigns won several advertising awards for television and print. Sculley is well known for bringing brand marketing to the personal computer industry. Several major marketing brands were created during his tenure at Apple, including Macintosh, Apple Desktop Publishing, and the Apple PowerBook. *Advertising Age* and *Adweek Magazine* both voted him Advertising Man of the Year, and he was chosen CEO of the Decade for Marketing by the Financial News Network.

Sculley came to Apple from PepsiCo, where he was president and CEO for five years and held marketing and management positions for 16 years. While Sculley was CEO, the company passed Coca-Cola as Number One in the packaged foods market share in the United States, as measured by A.C. Nielsen. Currently, Sculley is involved with his own venture capital company, a partnership with his two brothers, Arthur and David. The purpose of the company is to build new companies for the new economy. They search for promising companies in the initial stages of development that can benefit from their expertise in the fields of marketing, business strategy, and development. They are particularly interested in virtual company business models, such as People Link and Sirius Thinking.

I first met John at a dinner in San Francisco in the early 1980s. At the time, he received a great deal of publicity in connection with Apple, and

I felt sure he would be self-absorbed and conceited. I was seated next to him and saw immediately that I was very wrong. I found him modest, unassuming, intelligent, thoughtful, and quite interested in what I had to say. John is an attractive man, tall, slight, very fit, with reddish hair and chiseled features. He always seems to dress in clothes that don't quite fit right, as though he couldn't care less about what he wears or how he looks. As a result, he looks very charming. He approaches every new person he encounters with the same sense of curiosity and delight. I have introduced him to a number of people over the years, and everyone is impressed with him. One of the people I introduced him to was my father, Thomas Watson Jr., who really liked John, despite the fact they were competitors. One of John's real business strengths is that so many people like him. In his current work, he interacts with many young people and has many young friends.

Last fall, he spoke at the Technology Conference at the Haas School at Berkeley and was very well received. During the hour-long speech, he never once consulted his watch or his notes. At the end of the speech, I asked to see his notes, and he showed me an index card with a list of topics and the amount of time for each topic. I've never seen anyone come so close to his notes without ever consulting them. He's a remarkable man in many, many ways.

John Sculley

. . . anyone who is successful in business today must be able to deal in a risk environment, and I can't imagine they don't experience some fear in the process. Learning how to cope with your fear doesn't mean the fear goes away. It just means you learn how to succeed anyway, with it.

I've been working enough years I can look back and see what I liked, what I didn't enjoy, what I did do well, and what I didn't do well. I learned that I'm essentially an idea-driven, creative person. I like to build. My best moments in business were building through marketing ideas. That's what I do now, and I really enjoy it. I spend all my time building new companies for the new economy. We look for companies in the first stages of development and help build them by assisting with the marketing, recruiting management, and bringing in investors. In the past, when I ran a large company, I could only spend a small part of my time on these things.

I'm a lot happier now than when I ran a large corporation because I don't have the stress of dealing with a wide range of administrative and operating tasks. I can spend 100 percent of my time on things I really like to do, whereas when you are a CEO, by definition, you are a generalist. You probably were promoted because you excelled in a particular area, but when you are a CEO, you must work in all areas. It is actually less fun being a CEO than it is working to become a CEO. What I do now takes advantage of my several decades of experience working all over the world. It allows me to apply those experiences and my interest in building to a whole series of ventures. I'm working on about a half dozen different companies.

For me, entrepreneurship is more fun. In business, there's no such thing as no accountability, but it's a lot more fun to pick the people to whom you're accountable. You don't get that choice in a large corporation. You're hired by somebody else. As an entrepreneur, I'm accountable to myself because I invest my own money, but I'm also accountable to the other people who invest and trust I will work hard to make a particular venture successful for all of us.

I think timing in life is everything. If I could do anything differently in my career, I wish I would have left Pepsi and become an entrepreneur earlier than I did. I also wish I left Apple earlier than I did. For several years, I thought about leaving and starting what I do now. I wish I followed my instincts and did it sooner. What prevented me, both at Pepsi and at Apple, was the people I worked for didn't want me to leave. I grew up with a set of values in which loyalty was extremely important, so I let loyalty be the guide instead of my own instinct.

I don't think anyone is ever successful in business without running scared all the time. That's always true, it's still true in what I do now. If you take risks for high rewards, you're always concerned about who might come after you as a competitor or how conditions might unexpectedly change in the marketplace or what could go wrong in your own organization. Throughout my life, I always experienced a bit of fear. I think you deal with that fear the same way an athlete deals with the tension before an event or game. It actually is positive because it helps build your adrenaline and in some ways sharpens your senses.

There are different kinds of fear and different ways to focus. Some people play it safe and avoid situations that put them at risk. You usually don't find those people very far up in an organization, particularly, I think, in this era where the whole ground rules of our economy are shifting toward chances for incredible wealth creation in business. At the same time, the risk has risen as dramatically as the rewards. Consequently, anyone who is successful in business today must be able to deal in a risk environment, and I can't imagine they don't experience some fear in the process. Learning how to cope with your fear doesn't mean the fear goes away. It just means you learn how to succeed anyway, with it. That's probably positive in the sense that you remain alert, because in today's environment things change so quickly—they can change day to day. What you thought were the ground rules for your industry one day can dramatically change the next because a competitor introduces a new product or the pricing structure shifts in the industry or scarce commodities suddenly become more scarce. Those things happen instantaneously, so I think learning to live with fear and managing it is actually an important attribute to success. It's not something to be embarrassed about.

I also have tougher skin today. The kinds of things I would have feared 20 years ago don't really bother me as much today. You learn to essentially handicap the situation and think, "Well, if that goes wrong, can I tolerate it?" You've been through enough situations in the past and have enough experience to know what kind of events you can tolerate and what to stay far away from. The biggest advantage I have today in business versus 20 years ago is experience. There are lots and lots of very bright, creative people in business today. The ones who perhaps have the most energy are the younger ones, but they don't have the experience yet. I've seen situation after situation, just in the past year, where I've been working with bright, young people who because they lack experience are fearful of things those of us who are older do not because we've been through it a number of times.

The advice I have for young people is—it's more rewarding and a lot more fun in business to take chances and make mistakes. The consequences of mistakes are nowhere near as bad as you fear they are. Even in the toughest situations, the downside turns out to be more manageable than a lot of young people expect. I found that I learned far more from my mistakes than from my successes. In fact, you don't really remember your successes, you remember your mistakes. So, I would advise people not to be afraid to make mistakes.

The worst kind of mistake I made was misjudging people, trusting people I shouldn't have trusted. And then, after trusting them and being loyal to them, having them turn around and stab me in the back. If I look back and ask, what sort of blind spots do I have that were really the most serious, it's misjudging people.

As a child, my interests were inventing. I wanted to be an inventor, or an artist, or a designer. I was really interested in anything creative, and I never dreamed I would become a businessman. My father was a New York lawyer, and my mother was an artist and a horticulturist. I think I inherited my creative streak from my mother and her family. Almost all the relatives on my mother's side were very visual and able to draw, as I can. There were a great number of artists, engineers, and architects. Those on my father's side were all very left brained. None of my father's relatives can draw at all. My father was a very good student, but not in any way creative. He wanted my brothers and I to succeed by his definition, which is really about business. I had two brothers, and he wanted at least one of us to become a lawyer because he was a lawyer. I think I would have been a terrible lawyer and never had any interest in it. None of my brothers became lawyers either. They all became very successful businessmen.

I'm the oldest and, of the three of us, I'm the only one who is artistic. When I was a little kid, I spent a lot of time on creative things. I was always building, or drawing, or sculpting, and I was also interested in electronics. I used to go to Courtland Street in New York City where all the secondhand radio, television, and surplus electronic equipment from the military was sold. I bought parts and built televisions and transmitters. From the time I was 12, I was a ham radio operator and talked to friends I met over the airwaves. We used to try to pick up signals from as far away as possible. We recorded who they were and then sent a card to them saying we received their signal from 500 miles away, or 1,000 miles away, whatever the case was.

I grew up a bit of a loner, or like an only child, because I was so much older than my two brothers. I spent a great deal of time alone reading, building, and sort of living my life in my head, with fantasies created in my mind. Yet, there was also another side to me. While one side was totally content alone dreaming and creating, the other side enjoyed meeting people. When I was 11, I was sent to boys' school and spent six years there. I was president of my class all six years. I was on the soccer team and was a member of several different associations at the school. I had a mix of interests at that time. Even when I was head monitor at school, however, I never thought I would be in business. I still thought about being an inventor and had several inventions by that time, but no idea how inventors made any money. I never really cared about making a lot of money. I was more concerned about doing things that were interesting, and thought that would make a difference.

My grandfather on my mother's side was very much a mentor for me. He was an inventor. Around the turn of the century, he worked on the team that built the first submarine. In my early teens I would visit him, and he and I used to get up early in the mornings, about 4:30 A.M., and talk about all kinds of fanciful ideas like building desalination plants to transform saltwater into freshwater, or reclaiming land. Or we would discuss the theory of relativity and space-time travel and things like that. Those were wonderfully exciting years.

I didn't want to go to college. I wanted to go to art and design school. My father was outraged I would even think about that. Eventually, we compromised and I enrolled in a joint program with Brown University and the Rhode Island School of Design. My ideas changed when I studied architecture in graduate school. I realized I really didn't want to be an architect if I had to work for someone else in a large organization, either in city planning or an architectural firm. The more I learned about the field, the less I liked it, and eventually I decided architecture wasn't a very good field for me. First, I wanted creative work, and I didn't think the field offered that opportunity. Second, there were very few jobs, and nobody made any money. Finally, from what I saw at architectural firms, it was not the kind of life I wanted. I decided that what I really wanted to do was work on my own. And about the only way I could do that was to learn business. So, I went to business school and earned my M.B.A. At that time, marketing was not yet a well-understood field. It was just an adjunct to sales. In those days, consumer product marketing was really not done inside companies, but in advertising agencies. So, after I graduated, I worked for an advertising agency. I had worked in the summers for an industrial design firm and enjoyed it. When I was at the advertising agency, I was primarily interested in the creative side, but for some reason, I ended up also doing market research. I was always good at math in school. Mathematics is actually pretty creative. The further you delve into mathematics, the more conceptual it is. So, I did market research on Coca-Cola. Eventually, I switched from advertising to the company side, the product side of the business, and worked for Pepsi.

When I worked in advertising as an industrial designer, I was on the team that changed all the mechanicals on Procter & Gamble's packaging. I was on the drawing board when the company decided to put the American Dental Association claim on their toothpaste packages. Inside the design firm, however, they said they weren't going to do that. So I realized decisions weren't made in the industrial design firm, they were made back on the company side, by the businesspeople. At that time, I was married and the stepfather of my then wife was the head of Pepsi-Cola. He told me I should really move over from the creative side and learn marketing because that's where the future was, particularly if I wanted to be independent and on my own one day. He was also the person who, some years later after I was divorced, convinced me to leave advertising and work for Pepsi.

Working for Pepsi was totally different because it was working for a product company. I was the first M.B.A. Pepsi ever hired, and they really didn't know what to do with me. They put me out on a route truck to learn the business, and I loved it. I always had an insatiable curiosity, so I learned everything I could. I was running routes and changing merchandise sections in stores. The more I did, the more interested I became in redesigning the merchandising equipment. Ironically, some years later, when I became head of marketing for Pepsi, one of the first things I did was use the experience I gained in the training program to redesign all the merchandising equipment for Pepsi. My designs eventually became the designs used by the soft drink industry around the world.

There was always one consistent pattern in every job I had—I always redefined the job so I could do what I liked. Sometimes that turned out to be wildly successful. When the business I was in required new creative marketing ideas to change the ground rules of the business or the industry, that's when I had the most fun. That was true at Pepsi and at Apple. When the jobs required sticking to the rules and doing the same thing over and over, but better and better, it wouldn't work out. That's why I think at this point in my life, I value the flexibility of picking and choosing the opportunities where a lot of change is going on, where creative ideas can make a difference, and where my experience over the many decades can hopefully give high-risk situations a better chance to succeed.

When we were kids growing up, we had heroes, but in this day and age, I don't think people give much thought to heroes. My heroes as a kid were people who were essentially inventors or artists. I was fascinated by Leonardo da Vinci because he was so inventive and able to see beyond the possibilities, and also invent solutions to problems long before there was enough information for anyone less than a total genius to imagine. Today, however, things change so quickly, it's very difficult to find heroes anymore. Someone once said you really don't understand something unless you understand it more than one way. Things change so rapidly now, and if you only see events through television or reading newspapers, you often have distorted perspectives. What seems very obvious now about what happened three or four years ago, didn't seem at all obvious three or four years ago. So I think this is a particularly difficult time to figure out who the heroes are, given the context of events and what they really mean. Decisions must be made so rapidly. There's a paradox that it's better to have more and more information to make better decisions, but in hindsight, it's almost always the wrong kind of information. Therefore, people depend more on their instincts than on role models or on an ability to use the predictability of past events as an indication for the future. It's an unsettling time.

Earlier, when I talked about the biggest mistake I made, I said it was misjudging people. When I think back on things, however, in many of the cases when I trusted the wrong people, if I had followed my instincts better, I would have done things differently. I would have moved on to other things when I wanted to. The problem, and I guess other people have this problem too, is that we often have conflicting first principles. One first principle is to follow your instincts, and another is loyalty. Those two can conflict. When I've misjudged people, it was usually because I was too loyal or gave my loyalty too quickly. More than once, I did not follow my instincts, but instead remained true to my sense of loyalty. Maybe we're destined to repeat our mistakes if we don't really learn from them. That's why I said earlier the experience from mistakes is far more valuable than the experience from successes.

Conclusion

John Sculley found his niche building new companies for the new economy. He loves helping start-ups with their marketing, finding management talent, and bringing in investors. John also loves being accountable only to himself and the investors who trust his business judgment. Like Nick Nickolas, he wishes he used his entrepreneurial talents sooner! One other subtheme that resonates with other interviewees is the motivating role fear played in their careers. In John's venture capitalism business, taking risks is essential, and with the unknown often comes fear. Success to John means living with fear and managing it.

One pattern in John's career was how he defined the job around what he liked to do, both at Apple and at Pepsi. His mentor was his grandfather with whom he would walk in the early morning and talk about all kinds of fanciful ideas.

John values his experiences throughout his career and sees that in today's competitive workplace, youthful energy and intelligence are not always the defining factors in business. Decades in the marketplace and experiencing a fair share of success and failure, he reflects how each experience helped him develop a tougher skin, and not be afraid to make mistakes. Just as John was able to articulate his creative strengths and talent for visioning, he readily discusses his mistakes in misjudging people.

This ability for self-reflection and honest self-appraisal is another recurrent strength of many leaders, entrepreneurs, and visionaries in this book. John sees the source of his mistakes in judgment as conflicting first principles. For him, the conflicting principles were trusting instincts and loyalty. John doesn't present a formula for resolving this kind of conflict. Instead, he ends the interview on an almost wistful note that seems to convey the message—be aware of what's happening, do the best you can, and be patient with yourself.

ALICE WATERS

Founder/Owner, Chez Panisse Restaurant

Chef and restaurateur, Alice Waters, is the owner of the world-renowned California restaurant, Chez Panisse. Next year, Waters will open a restaurant for the French government in the Eiffel Tower.

I first met Alice one summer evening at the home of my friend, Susie Tompkins, in a small, coastal town in Marin County, California. When I arrived, Susie was making dinner while listening to a commentary by Alice. I remember thinking at the time how brave Susie was to risk cooking dinner for Alice Waters! Alice is a very petite woman with an elfin face, short, straight brown hair, and an enchanting smile. She looks like someone you would like to get into a little trouble with or one of the teenage orphans in the musical *Oliver*. She often wears a little cap on her head like a flapper from the '20s, and peeks out at you from beneath it. Looking at her, it's sometimes hard to remember she is an incredibly capable woman. The dialogue about the dinner went back and forth between the two with Susie constantly telling Alice what she was doing and asking if it was okay. (Our dinner turned out to be delicious.) Alice seemed perfectly happy to wander about the spacious kitchen drinking vin rosé, chatting with Mark, Susie's husband, and me. I soon fell under Alice's spell. She talks about life and her daughter, Fanny, in such an enchanting way and seems surprised and delighted by almost everything she encounters.

Alice and I met the second time for her interview at Chez Panisse during lunchtime. Chez Panisse has stood in the same location in Berkeley since it opened in the 1970s. It retains the character of the town with its brown-shingled exterior and angled rooms with nooks and crannies. One almost drives past it without noticing the small sign unless one knows the location. The restaurant opens daily for lunch and at night serves a casual dinner as well as a fixed-price menu. Guests make reservations many days in advance for the dining room and visitors to Berkeley still flock here to eat the delicious and world-famous food.

When I entered the restaurant, the manager greeted me and assured I was taken care of during my brief wait for Alice. When Alice sat down, I was dismayed to realize she was intending to hold the interview there, in the dining room. I knew immediately the recorder would not function very well in the middle of restaurant noise. Alice noticed the dismayed look on my face and immediately asked if I would prefer to interview her downstairs, which was quieter. This awareness of others is what makes Alice special. She reads people just as she reads their appetites and prepares an extremely enjoyable meal. We moved to the empty downstairs dining room where one of her assistants set our table. Alice asked what I would like for lunch. She quickly answered her own question, "Just a little of this pizza, I think, don't you? It's very good, unusual, and then maybe a little soup, just a drop to get the flavor. I haven't tried it yet today and I simply must." She rambled on about the food, and I thought I must be in heaven. I just wondered how I would eat all these incredible treats and still keep my head for the interview.

As she began to talk about her career, it was evident this was no inexperienced woman. She had a very clear story to tell and thought a lot about how to tell it. As we progressed through this delightful meal, we were interrupted often by her assistant and the restaurant staff, needing her to solve various problems. Alice treated them all with the same courtesy and patience. She considers her staff part of her family and her interactions with them reflect this. The restaurant is staffed with both young and old people, and all share a devotion to Alice and her vision. When she opened the restaurant, the idea of fresh food was new in California, and she pursued it with a vengeance. I have the feeling Alice pursues everything she undertakes with a vengeance. Just before this interview, she was offered the opportunity to open a restaurant in the Eiffel Tower in Paris—the pinnacle of success for an American chef!

At the end of our lunch, Alice asked if I was interested in a little dessert. That is like asking a thirsty woman on a desert if she wants some water. We had three desserts! It was heaven. Alice took a small taste of each and made careful comments about flavoring, color, and taste. I just took my time and ate them all.

Alice Waters

I think you really have to love it, whatever it is you do, all the little parts of it.

I grew up in the late 1940s and 1950s in Chatham, New Jersey, 17 miles northeast of Newark in a little, small town. It was small enough you felt like you knew a lot of the people and your neighbors. It was a pretty normal kind of childhood. I have three sisters. I'm number two, and there are four years between my older sister and my next younger sister. And then my youngest sister came two years after that. We did lots of things together as a family.

My father worked for the Prudential Insurance Company. They had a big old victory garden during the war, and my mother canned fruits and vegetables from our garden. That was a very early memory of mine. My family was lower-middle class. Incrementally, we moved to a bigger house, but it was very, very simple at the beginning.

When I was a teenager, my first job was (believe it or not) at a drive-in, called The Country Cousin in Michigan City, Indiana. I was a carhop. The place had everything you can imagine but the roller skates. We wore straw hats and took fried chicken, honey, and biscuits out to the cars. The second job I had was at this hot dog stand called Whiskey & Whiskey Enterprises. Those were both very short-lived.

I didn't have many expectations for my life. I thought at the time I would do exactly what my older sister did, which was get married right out of college and then have a family. I don't think I saw the future very clearly. I guess I thought I would be taken care of somehow. I knew I would go to college. I never had any doubts about that.

I just thought somehow it would all unfold. But I don't think I worried about it very much.

My life really changed, however, when I went to France when I was 19. I had worked a little in restaurants during college, but when I went to France, it was a revelation. I was a very picky eater all my life. I liked certain things, like green beans, tomatoes, corn on the cob, but I wouldn't eat everything, only what I really liked. For my birthday, for example, I wanted to go to the automat in New York so I could choose exactly what I wanted to eat. My parents got off very cheaply, but I loved the automat. Back then, they actually cut pieces from real pies and put them in those little baskets. It was great. But France opened my eyes. I felt like I was almost asleep before that. All my senses were stimulated. Everything was so beautiful and tasted so good. I was initiated into the whole experience of food. I fell in love with it and wanted to know everything about it, just like when you fall in love. I wanted to know all the details—what everybody ate, what every restaurant was like. I wanted to go to all the marketplaces. So instead of going to school, which I was supposed to be doing, I explored the foods in France.

I visited France for a year to attend school, but I didn't learn very much French. I was very intimidated about speaking French. I absorbed it as if by osmosis. I was with a friend, and we traveled together all over Brittany and Normandy. There was something else about being there. I didn't know what it was. I thought it was just the food, but there was something else I wanted as part of my life. I think it was the sense of being together around the table and knowing the guy who sold you the bread, having friends connected in that way in my life.

I taught school right after I graduated and cooked on the side for friends. Happily, or fortuitously, I chose the right cookbooks to learn from, the books of Elizabeth Davis. I discovered them at a little cooking store in Berkeley run by a friend. I went in there and asked if she had anything French. And she replied, "Well, I've got this great cookbook by an English writer who wrote about her experiences in France." So I bought those little cookbooks, one on French food and one on French provincial cooking. I cooked everything from beginning to end. I cooked for my friends. Then I realized,

"Ah, I like cooking better than I like teaching!" So I thought, "Well, why don't I open a little café?"

One important step before this was the experience of writing a column for an underground newspaper called *The San Francisco Express Times*. Somebody there thought I knew how to cook and should write a column with my friend David Golds, a calligrapher. He illustrated and I wrote the recipes. I didn't really know anything. I called up friends and consulted *La Rue Gastronomique* and all the books I needed to find out how to do whatever it was. That educated me and prepared me a little bit for the restaurant.

I started the restaurant on borrowed money, $1,000. I was 26 and just obsessed. I wanted to cook meals like those I ate in France and wanted everybody to like them. I thought, foolishly, I would have my friends come in, and they would all eat and pay so I could make a living. Well, I never saw my friends again for probably 15 years because I was so absorbed with the proposition. I didn't feel like I could cook in the beginning, so we hired somebody. He was my first partner.

The cook dropped out probably eight months after he started because he really wanted to make films. So we hired someone else. It was all done absolutely by the seat of our pants. We were open from 7:00 in the morning until 2:00 at night. Very quickly, we were $40,000 down. So I called my only friend who was in business, the woman who owned the cookware store in Berkeley. She came to the office and started picking up little pieces of paper off the floor, receipts and so forth. She liked the restaurant so much she put her own money into it to pay the bills. She ended up owning a big share of it, and ultimately a group of people here bought her out and became partners of mine.

It took about eight years for the restaurant to get into the black. It was very rocky. We were in a kind of gray zone after five years. I never thought we'd make it five years, but as soon as we got to five, then I thought we'd be there forever. I don't remember too much about that period because I was just driven, from one aspect to the other. I didn't go about it in any logical way. I just tried to make people who came in happy.

I never could imagine giving up. It never crossed my mind. I never, ever wanted to give up, no! It was an obsession. I knew I wanted this thing, and I was just determined to make it work. And if

I hadn't found that woman, I don't know what would have happened. I think I was very lucky to find her right away.

The restaurant, in a funny way, was successful right from the beginning, and I've attributed that to very good timing. I do think I have a good sense or an intuition for timing. Some people are too soon, and some are too late. I feel like it was the right time, and in fact it was, because people supported the idea. I never compromised about the food. I would cry if somebody didn't like it. I'd look at every plate, and if somebody didn't eat their food, I wanted to know why. I went right out there and boldly asked them. And they'd say, "Oh, I just didn't like this, or I thought it was overcooked." I'd cook it again and give them a free dinner, and they came back.

My father was a management psychologist, which ultimately turned out to be his greatest skill. He had his own business, and maybe I got some of that in my genes. He was certainly obsessed with his work. I never thought I would make money at the restaurant. That was never part of the package. I figured that would just happen if it was good. But I wanted the restaurant to be perfect. I'd rather fail the business than ever compromise the food. I was very lucky.

I never wanted another Chez Panisse because I think a very important part of a restaurant is that there is somebody home. I go to restaurants where I know the owner. I want to know who is responsible. Somehow you lose that when you have all these other places. It's very hard to seriously stay connected to places when there are too many of them. There are very few restaurateurs whom I think can carry that off. Also, there was always this atmosphere of family among those who worked here. I hired all my friends.

I was lucky because James Beard came here very early—probably about 1975 or earlier. He wrote about the restaurant and how these young chefs were trying something new. Then I went to New York, to one of those events where you cook for hundreds of people. That was a really big moment for me because I never did anything like that before. I was selected, along with another guy from America, and three French chefs. I had a very good menu. It was the first day of spring in Central Park, and I cooked outside. Everything clicked. All these people came. It was a very good experience.

At some point, American Airlines asked me to participate in a consulting group of chefs. It's called the Chef Conclave, and there are about 12 of us. I attend a meeting once a year. Some of the chefs consult on a regular basis two or three times a month. I don't do that and don't make any of the recipes. I couldn't be involved in that way. But what I do is go to the meetings and say, "I think you need the support of partners who take care of the land around the country. Host an apple campaign and pick up apples from all those farms. Have a big poster, American Airlines Supports American Farms." I'm almost a broken record. They listen very patiently, and say, "Thank you so much for all your comments." Then I leave, and they give me some wonderful tickets.

The first American Food & Beverage person I worked with about eight years ago ultimately ended up with Swissair. This last year, he put all organic food on Swissair. It was in the newspaper, and it said, "Swissair Promotes Organic Foods." So I brought it back to the Chef Conclave and told them that's exactly what I was talking about.

I realized I can't do what I'm doing, and won't be able to do it well in the future, unless I pay attention to the bigger world. I couldn't be an island here. And that is why I got involved with the King School and the Edible Schoolyard project. I think the only way we're going to change things is by teaching children certain essential values needed to live in the world. We must teach them how to care for the land, how to feed themselves, make the right choices, and have pleasure at the table. They need to connect with nature. That connection, that stewardship, is what will allow us to live on this earth beyond our generation. The Edible Schoolyard curriculum has children working in the garden, growing food, understanding where the food comes from, taking care of the land, bringing that food into the kitchen, and learning how to cook for themselves. Eighty-five percent of the kids in this country don't eat one meal with their family. This is the first generation that has not been asked to come to the table. Ultimately, we want this as part of the school lunch program, so kids can actually sit around a table and communicate and know the pleasure of eating what they cooked. That's the idea.

We've received private support and also some government support. I hope we get a lot more. Ultimately, this is the kind of program I would like to see in every school. In the same way they're putting computers in every classroom, they could put gardens in every school. It really has to happen because these kids are not prepared to live in the world from the current school experience. A lot of things that happen in the world, the very brutal kinds of behavior, are a reflection that these children haven't received any sort of human connection or understanding of where they are in time and place. Kids don't play outside anymore. They sit inside, watch television, eat fast-food, however it comes, whenever it comes. They feel left out. I feel that it's neglect. People think kids only like hamburgers, hot dogs, pizza, and pasta, because that's all they're given. In fact, we found through this program that children are hungry for all kinds of other foods.

I think getting involved in the world is seeing how we're all connected, how life is a big web. The Web of Life. It's seeing and knowing that you are a part of that, you have to pay attention to that bigger picture. I find it very unsatisfying to just be involved in my own creation. I love to collaborate with a whole group of people and make something greater than the sum of the parts. It's so exhilarating to make that happen.

Starting a restaurant, I never worried whether it was going to be successful. I didn't feel the risk. I just felt if I did the right thing, we'd succeed. People will come. I didn't think of it in a business way. I don't know how to describe my relationship with money, but I don't think about it very much. If I have a small amount of money, I live on that. I never spend more than I think I'm going to have. I never thought about making money. I let other people operate that part of the business. I think if there is a good idea, the money will come forth. If the money doesn't come, it makes me wonder whether the idea is good, and I change my course.

I feel I was lucky to go to France at that very formative time in my life. I just absorbed things like a sponge. It completely gave me a sense of purpose. It put things in context. I was a Montessori teacher, and I use a lot of that philosophy in my work. One thing she very strongly believed was that every kid can connect with this feeling of finding what you really love. It takes a while. When I work with kids—even little tiny kids from three to five—I always find something they like. I had to really put my mind to it, but when we found what they liked, it just clicked for them. The children could just go on and do that all day long.

The potential is there in college also. I think programs must be opened up in different ways so students can find other avenues to learn. That's why this sensory experience of gardening, cooking, and eating opens up those pathways in their minds. That's how the information gets in. It helps to not just intellectually understand, but to involve your whole body to really feel and learn in a whole different kind of way. The more education can be three-dimensional, or six-dimensional with all the senses, the more possibility there is to really connect with kids. When you take a kid on a boat trip around the world, that's an extraordinary thing for some kids. I think teachers should be paid the most money. The folks who have the passion should do the teaching, because those are the ones that make a huge impression. That's why I feel so lucky with the Edible Schoolyard project. We have extraordinary people, and I hope we continue to gather people.

Starting out in business today, or starting your own business is such a hard thing. One certainly must have passion. I don't think it can be just to make money. Maybe you're not successful—some people are that way—but really satisfied. I think you really have to love it, whatever it is you do, all the little parts of it. I thought, "I'll give up this restaurant when I'm not connected with it in that way." And I've actually said that. I've said, "We're going to close the doors." It's always been a challenge. It never ever felt like a completed thing. It's hard to tell somebody what those elements really are that make a business work.

For me, it is "Go with your passion." And also be completely aware of the circumstances around you, not just the people and the environment you work in. I felt like I knew people would come here because I knew the people in this neighborhood. I think it must be terribly risky for those big companies that make decisions about businesses in other countries where they're not familiar with the people who live there, but it's based on a marketing evaluation of what they think people might like. I'd feel so insecure in those circumstances. That's where the risk is. It's not a risk when you know there are people who want to eat the food you cook, or who really like the way you sew a dress. You've done your own sort of marketing survey. You're very comfortable with that.

The way men and women grow up in this world leads to different ways they run businesses. I think men have been programmed in one direction and women have another purpose. For women, it's much more nurturing. I like to have both in this restaurant. I like both men and women in the kitchen, especially when they collaborate, because it makes something better. I've always run it myself, so men had to respect my work. I had very good relations on the whole with the men who worked for me. Because women aren't used to executive roles, I think they're trying to find their way, and it's more humanistic. They feel their way along. It's hard for them to remove themselves and make cold-hearted decisions and that kind of thing. They are, I think, naturally better communicators and nurturers just because it's in the genes, especially when it comes to the restaurant business. It's an extension of feeding people at home, and it's all, I think, an expression of love.

Another important element is to never feel satisfied that you've arrived. It's just a constant refinement. When people figure they have reached the goal, they just go on automatic. It changes, certainly in terms of a restaurant, the vitality of the business. People do not put themselves in it in the right way. They just go through the motions. Everything you do, you need to focus on it, try to figure out how to make it real and interesting for yourself.

I think people have a natural curiosity, and they can find great pleasure in the simplest things. We had that taken away from our educational process—finding pleasure in the very simplest things—and I think we should put it back. It's coming to every task as if it's new. Having great pleasure in polishing the silverware, putting on the table, thinking about their relationship to the whole presentation, and putting it all in context, seeing its worth, its value. I think people often do things they don't understand the value of. So it doesn't give them a sense of accomplishment. It doesn't feed them. When you are fed in a conscious way, and you feel like what you do is important, your self-confidence builds. You take pleasure from that and want to do more. You want to do more and different things.

Making things meaningful for yourself, knowing how to make them meaningful is something I think you really have to be taught. Some people get it through their family or their friends, but it is something that can be taught. It's certainly part of what we try to do at the Edible Schoolyard. You can enjoy washing dishes if you just focus on what the thing is. For me, it's very important that all the spaces in this restaurant are beautiful places to work, aesthetically. I don't ever want to have a back of the house and a front of the house—up here it looks good, and back there it doesn't—because employees are the ones who need inspiration. The cooks need those circumstances and that environment. It helps them. They have to know they're taken care of. It's important for my business that every person really likes to work here and really wants to work here. It's about finding the right place for everybody, so they can get legitimate recognition for what they do.

Conclusion

Alice Waters describes a sense of being asleep before a trip to France awakened her, and she fell in love with the art of creating fine food. It was then that her obsession began, and she started to create wonderful meals and atmospheres for people. Alice opened her first café on borrowed money, and never worried about success. She felt if she had a good idea, the money would come. Eventually it did, but not for several years. At a critical junction, she brought in a businessperson to help balance her passion for food. She has been successful ever since.

Like other visionaries, Alice had purpose once she discovered her calling, though growing up she did not see her future clearly at all. Alice attributes her discovery to a kind of sense or an intuition for timing. She notes that finding your career path can take a while. Unfortunately, there is no magic formula. Like other leaders in the book, she suggests a willingness to try things out and a little bit of luck!

Alice suggests a secret to success is curiosity and the ability to enjoy pleasure in simple things, waking up the senses to life. She further suggests following your passion while staying very aware of the context within which this passion exists, the bigger world beyond one's immediate environment and people. She models this awareness in her many contributions to community, especially her Edible Schoolyard project. It is here that Alice teaches children values for living. She also helps awaken their senses by engaging them in gardening, meal preparation, and enjoyment of whole foods.

Self-confidence, to Alice, comes from approaching every task as if it were for the first time and taking the time to understand it in depth. Alice, a humanitarian and master chef, exemplifies this philosophy in her approach to cooking, teaching children, and life.

FAYE WATTLETON

Former President, Planned Parenthood
Founder/Executive Director, Center for Gender
Equality

Faye Wattleton was president of Planned Parenthood Federation of America from 1978 until 1992. During her tenure, she played a major role, influencing the status of reproductive rights and family-planning policies worldwide. For seven years prior to her work at Planned Parenthood, she was executive director of the Planned Parenthood affiliate in Dayton, Ohio. In the fall of 1996, she published her autobiography with Ballantine Books, entitled *Life on the Line*.

Faye has been widely recognized for her exemplary achievements. In 1993, she was inducted into the National Women's Hall of Fame. She is a recipient of the 1992 Jefferson Award for the greatest public service performed by a private citizen, the 1992 Margaret Sanger Award, the American Public Health Award for Excellence, the 1989 Congressional Black Caucus Foundation Humanitarian Award, the 1987 John Gardner Award, and in 1986, Women's Honors in public service from the American Nurses Association. *Business Week* magazine named Ms. Wattleton one of the best managers of a nonprofit organization in America. *Money Magazine* selected her as one of the five outstanding Americans who help shape our lives. She has appeared on numerous public affairs and news programs and in national publications. Faye has a bachelor of science in nursing from Ohio State University and a master of science in maternal and infant care with certification as a nurse midwife from Columbia University.

Currently, Faye Wattleton is president of the Center for Gender Equality, a not-for-profit research and development institute dedicated to illuminating the status of women in the United States and creating strategies for dismantling the obstacles that impede women's full equality. She also serves on the boards of directors of the Estee Lauder Companies, Empire Blue Cross and Blue Shield, Quidel Corporation, Leslie Fay Inc., the Henry J. Kaiser Foundation, the Institute for International Education, Women's Environment and Development Organization, and Thirteen/WNET.

I met Faye for our interview at the Center for Gender Equality, which occupies a suite of offices on a high floor of an office building in Manhattan. I was immediately struck by her beauty, poise, and grace. My first impression was of a woman with spirit who carries herself with pride. At six feet tall and quite lovely, she could easily have worked as a model instead of devoting her life to improving the status of women. Though she commands respect and is not an informal woman, I felt comfortable with her immediately. An excellent communicator, she is articulate, concise in her speech, and displays clear thought patterns. Nothing she says is irrelevant or superfluous. It struck me during the interview that she would make a good politician because she is open and honest, yet what she reveals is carefully chosen and moderated.

She discussed the successes and failures in her life with equal detachment. Faye is someone with a secure sense of herself. Whether this is due to the values she learned from her parents or other factors is hard to say. She has a stateliness about her that commands immediate respect, and she projects success. When she discussed her failure to make a television show work and the reinvention of herself during that difficult time, there was not a shred of self-pity in her story or demeanor. Like other interviewees in this book, she knows the ropes of failure and never allows herself to dwell on bad luck. Failure was never an impossible impediment, only an opportunity to be creative in moving forward.

Faye Wattleton

The top person has it all. It really is a seat apart from every-thing else. Unless you sit in that seat and walk in those shoes, it's impossible to fully appreciate the toll it takes . . .

I was born in St. Louis and spent my early years there. When I was about six or seven, my mother decided she wanted to devote her life to the ministry full time. At that point, we started traveling, and she ministered to various churches all over the country. I'm sure I get along well with different people from different cultures today because we were all over the place when I was a child. We lived for two years in an all-white town in Nebraska when I was 10 through 12. In the summers, we went to church meetings in the South, Mid-west, and the East.

I don't ever recall not wanting to be a nurse, or not saying I wanted to be a nurse. This was, in part, certainly my mother's influ-ence. She wanted me to be a missionary nurse. It wasn't sufficient just to be a nurse, I had to commit to a religious cause as well. Mis-sionary nurses work in church hospitals, in Africa and all over the world. I suspect this was suggested to me before I even understood the power of suggestion, and I always grew up saying I was going to be a nurse. I earned two degrees in nursing, but never practiced as a nurse. In the broadest sense of the word, you could say I have nursed all the time, but not in the technical sense. After undergrad-uate school, I taught nursing for two years. Then I went to graduate school at Columbia University and earned my master's degree. Fol-lowing that, I moved to Dayton, Ohio to work in a public health department. There, I was asked to join the board of the local Planned Parenthood. Two years later, I became executive director of the local chapter. Then, seven years later, I became the national president of the organization.

My family are immigrants from the Deep South. My mother is from Mississippi, and my father is from Alabama. They were strivers in the classic sense of the word, part of the second wave of immi-grants who moved north in the late 1930s and early 1940s. Though they had few skills, my father was a laborer and my mother was a seamstress, there was a sense of independence and an expectation to carry your own weight and do whatever was necessary to make ends meet. You were obliged to provide for yourself. That clearly defined my framework for approaching life, as well as work. Everyone in my extended family worked very hard and sent the kids in my generation to college, so there was a sense of upward mobility in our family.

I'm sure the suggestion to become a nurse was colored by the limitation on women's options in those years. Women were nurses, social workers, or teachers. I don't ever remember being explicitly told, "Oh, you can't be that because you're a girl." It just was. Before we started traveling around, we lived in a large, multifamily house in St. Louis. My mother and my aunts were quite independent. Their husbands went to work, and they labored in the home in the dress-making business. It was never conveyed to me there were any limitations on what I could do and what my work could be, although I'm sure the idea that I be a nurse, as opposed to a doctor or something else, was due to the limitations on the role of women at that time. Living in a house with so many relatives during those years was really the foundation that held me together during the ensuing years of traveling all over the country and being displaced and dislocated.

My early imagery was women. Not only the women of my family, but the women who came into the dressmaking room for their fittings. In those years, there was a great deal of emphasis on fine dressing and appropriate attire for various events. Even though we lived in a working class community, there wasn't as much integration, so blacks of all economic levels lived in the black community. My father was a laborer, and my mother was a seamstress, but I went to nursery school with our doctor's son. The doctor's family lived a few blocks from us. This was before the Civil Rights movement, and before blacks moved into white or integrated neighborhoods. That experience also played a very important role in my sense of who I am ethnically, as well as what the possibilities were for me. We lived next door to professionals, as well as the housepainter who had the most beautiful house on the block because he painted and decorated it beautifully.

So there was a combination of imagery for me. Because the church was the center of our family's social life, the influence of the religious community in our family was also very strong. Ultimately, with my mother deciding to commit her life to and become involved on a full-time basis in the ministry, it became an overarching, dominating influence in our family.

The differences between religion and spirituality are increasingly being made more distinct as people search for those things they don't find in so-called mainstream religious institutions. We all need a more spiritual, ethereal kind of experience to somehow satisfy us or give us a certain psychological comfort. The Center [Center for Gender Equality] is about to release a poll on religious organizations, specifically on conservative religious organizations and women's attitudes about women's rights. As one of our national committee advisers remarked, "Women have always been the keepers of the faith." From this poll, it seems that women are much more religious or spiritual, and see religion or spirituality as much more important in their lives than they ever have.

When I faced opposition from religious fundamentalists at Planned Parenthood, I understood it because it was what I grew up with. My mother was not an Episcopalian priest, she was a fundamentalist Protestant minister, so it was the material of my upbringing that these people promoted. I intuitively understood not only from whence they were coming, but also the dangers of their zealotry. I lived with a very zealous mother who gave up everything, including me and my father, to pursue her religious teachings. When you hear the call of God, nothing stands in your way. I understood that, perhaps better than most people at Planned Parenthood. I knew it was a very dangerous combination, which is why I promoted the idea of the organization becoming more heavily involved in blocking the ascension of fundamentalists in the political process. Unfortunately, I wasn't able to prevail.

I got my master's degree in 1967, and then became the associate director of the Public Health Department in Dayton, Ohio for three years. My public health professor from college recruited me out of graduate school to come to Ohio to work as her associate. Then I became the deputy director of the Visiting Nurses Association in Dayton and Montgomery counties. While I was in that position, I was asked to serve on the board of the local Planned Parenthood affiliate. The people on the board got acquainted with me during the time I served and, in 1970, I was named executive director of the local chapter. I was an administrator. In those years, if you had a master's in nursing, you either ended up teaching or being an administrator. That is not so much the case now, with so much emphasis on clinical nursing specialties today. Then, nurses were pretty much guaranteed those two tracks, because there were so few nurses who had higher degrees.

I took the position as head of the national office of Planned Parenthood in March 1978, and I left in March 1992. I was there 14 years. It was a long time, and it was always very interesting. There was never a dull day, never a day that was the same. I think now I needed to leave earlier, because I had been there so long and it became so difficult—not the external work, but the internal conflict. Even though I really did want to move on, it took something major to get me to leave. Actually, from about the tenth year on, I was really tired of it and wanted to go, but there always seemed to be another battle around the corner. And, frankly, there weren't many options out there for me. That's one of the things women in higher positions find, certainly women in the nonprofit field. You get into a strata that is very narrow. If I were a man who had run the seventh largest charity in America, a $400 million company, and as successfully as I had, I believe many offers would have fallen at my feet. I would have had to stay up nights trying to figure out which one was the best. But that was not true when I left Planned Parenthood. The thing that interested me the most at the time was the possibility of having a nationally syndicated television show that dealt with women's issues. I felt it would give me an even broader platform to promote the debate and dialogue about women.

Business Week voted me one of the best managers of nonprofits, which I think they did because I ran a very well-managed organization. I believe I have the ability to articulate and convey a spirit of mission, a vision. People really respond when there is a leader who has a vision and says, "This is where we're going." My style is not of a dominating leader, although some might tell you I am very controlling, which I always find mystifying. I would have had to stay up 48 hours a day to control everything that went on in an organization like Planned Parenthood. There were some things, of course, I was controlling about because I felt those were the critical issues. My basic style, however, is to organize a support management team, give them clear expectations, let them perform, and judge them on their performance. I support them even when they make mistakes, as long as I feel they are really trying to carry out the objectives of the organization and the mission. I am also a leader who listens to other people's points of view. In fact, I solicit them. I try to find the best people I can in various specialties so I can learn from them. I want people who are better than me in their specialties, maybe not better than me in running the whole shebang, but better than me in the communications field or legal field. Stitching everything together to make it work as a machinery is, for me, the challenge and the excitement. To some degree, I suppose I want people around who support me, but I also don't want people who say yes to everything. I will get into trouble if that happens, because then I don't have any check on myself. Even if I listen but don't follow their advice, I want to know they're checking me, even if they can't checkmate me. Because people can trust I am who I say I am, they don't feel they will be undermined or sabotaged. If I was unhappy, they knew it. If I was happy, they knew it. It created an atmosphere of security and trust that resulted in a pretty good team. The various acknowledgments I received were really a reflection of the management team's performance and the distinction the national organization held among other nonprofits. In the end at Planned Parenthood, I had tremendously loyal staff, some of whom were with me the whole time.

I try very hard to listen. If there is conflict, I want to hear what the other side says. I'm, of course, speaking about professional experiences. When it's personal and on an emotional level, it can be more difficult. I have a lot more capacity to detach my emotions in a professional setting than I do when I'm emotionally engaged. As long as I feel there is mutual respect, it does not hurt me to listen to someone with whom I am really in conflict, to hear what they are saying even if I disagree. If it's a conflict I really want to resolve, I try to find ways we can come to mutual points of agreement. One thing I always believed is if you talk long enough you can almost always reach a resolution. Just the process of talking has a defanging influence. I have great faith in human beings finding ways to relate if they have enough contact with each other. That's not always true because there are some really despicable or completely rigid people. I don't suffer fools gladly and don't like being patronized or not treated with the respect I am due as another human being and as somebody who has accomplished something in life. So there are times when I have to decide I just can't resolve the conflict. But in most cases, if you talk long enough, you can find a way to somehow adjust and accommodate each other on some level.

To some degree, that was really a major theme of my work. I certainly found myself in the midst of one of the most severe national conflicts of the latter part of the twentieth century. When I was hired at Planned Parenthood, they wanted me to straighten out the place from a management perspective because I had already established a record in Ohio as a strong manager. They wanted somebody from within the organization and thought it was time for a woman to be president. There was nothing on the horizon about the moral majority. There were some conflicts going on at local levels, but not to the level and intensity that would emerge after Reagan was elected. When I took the job, I didn't expect to be in the midst of one of the most intense social conflicts of our time, and would end up spending a lot of time speaking in public. Rather than hollering back, I tried to talk in a reasonable way even when the unreasonable ones didn't want to listen. While they didn't agree with me, I think even the unreasonable people would often concede I was a reasonable person. That is less important to me, however, than to be perceived as a principled person. I don't really care whether somebody considers me reasonable in those kinds of situations. It really means a lot to me, however, to be perceived as principled in a conflict.

I suffer self-doubt all the time. I don't suffer self-doubt on the principles, on the basics, but I certainly do suffer self-doubt in terms of whether I've done the right thing in a particular instance, or whether I could do better. I worry about what lies ahead, and whether I'll be ready for it. Creating this new organization stirred up a lot of those emotions, but that's one of the things I've lived with, to just keep going. Even if you fear and worry that you may not pull it off, tomorrow's another day, and if you can just keep going long enough, before you know it you pick up more steam.

When I left Planned Parenthood, I was really sick of the internal strife, and sniping, and attempts to undermine the success of the national organization's work. The organization was never more prominent since Margaret Sanger founded it. It had never been more successful. It became increasingly difficult, however, for me to tolerate the internal viciousness, which I describe in my book. So much is invested on a personal level when you're involved in a cause like this. The end for me came at the last annual meeting we had. The affiliates voted to reduce their support to the national organization. I felt this was such a flagrant slap in the face I didn't see any reason to continue.

I left Planned Parenthood to do a national syndicated television show, which did not work out. I was under contract with Tribune Entertainment. The show we talked about creating before I left Planned Parenthood was not the show they were ultimately willing to do. They wanted me to do Jerry Springer–type stuff, which I am temperamentally incapable of doing. In the test shows, I would get bored to tears with somebody talking for an hour about not having sex for six months—that kind of stuff. Even before we did the first test show, I knew it was doomed. They convened a meeting of their station managers, who apparently did not support the show and questioned whether I was too classy or intelligent for their morning audience. They felt I was better suited for an afternoon audience and wanted me to do shows that would get them high ratings. One of them asked, "Are you willing to do women with big breasts during sweeps week?" I said no. I came home that night and told my daughters the show was not going to happen. And it didn't. Then Tribune tried to cheat me out of part of my option. I was also under contract to write my book, which I then really had to concentrate on. And more than that, I had to really focus on restructuring my life, because I thought the show was going to be my life. I need to earn a living in addition to pursuing a cause. While you can never depend on television going very far, when I left Planned Parenthood I never thought it would not get on the air. I felt my strength had always been communicating with audiences, and if I could get on the air, the show would be successful. You only need a few years in television to be very comfortable financially. I figured after the show ended, I would write the book, and then do the type of international work that I like. I assumed I would be financially secure, which would give me latitude and flexibility to do the projects I wanted to tackle.

That didn't happen, and since my daughter was about to begin college, it really meant doing what women do all the time—reinventing ourselves. My options were pretty limited. I did have the book, and that was one of the main objects of my attention. And I had several opportunities for management consultancies. I began to network with friends and old colleagues, indicating an interest in corporate board work, which was sort of a challenge to me. I always chafed at the notion that successful nonprofit organizations were different from successful for-profit businesses. Nonprofits are businesses, and if they don't make a profit, they don't last very long. So it was a challenge. Would anyone see my talents and value for a for-profit? I was restructuring my financial base and my life. Also, interestingly, I was achieving one of the objectives I set when I left Planned Parenthood, which was for my life not to be defined by one thing, one focus of work. I didn't want my intellectual life to be defined by only one area of work. I wanted the challenge of multiple experiences, and was able to create that. I had not really reckoned how hard it was to work individually and have four or five different clients. It's a much different kind of work, much harder in a way than what I was doing at Planned Parenthood.

Starting the Center [Center for Gender Equality] has really been a challenge. We're creating something very unique. It's not easy for people to understand why it's important, how it can make a difference, and how it can influence the public dimension about women. We understand how right-wing think tanks work, how they influence things and impose their agendas, but we can't understand how something of a similar structure, pursuing a similar strategy for a different agenda, can work for the issues we care about. So it has been a very interesting experience in entrepreneurship. Running a big organization is very different than starting a new one. Running one with a well-established name and history is different than a newly established name that may, in fact, change in time. Trying to convince people to invest in ideas and research for creating change is difficult. I had no doubt the Center was the right thing to do—the only doubt is whether I can pull it off. As with anything in life, none of us succeeds alone. It takes help and support, and the support has not been as forthcoming as I hoped or expected, given the early generosity of the start-up funding. But we'll still get there.

In the last three years, I certainly have felt alone here, but the Planned Parenthood situation was also a very lonely spot. Even though I had an excellent vice president who was very supportive and we became like each other's second skin, ultimately he was not the one who had the buck stop on his desk. He was not the one who had to deal with the stress of the picketing, and violence, and death threats. The top person has it all. It really is a seat apart from everything else. Unless you sit in that seat and walk in those shoes, it's impossible to fully appreciate the toll it takes, the emotional toll, particularly if you're not someone who is always going around erupting.

All the signs are very disturbing and point to the fact that women are regressing. You name any indicator, and it looks bad. The wage gap is widening again. Women are still in the minority percentages in professions for which they had really been making progress. Our access to healthcare is still very unequal. We are comparable in terms of getting college degrees, but our wage earnings are not. In academia, the disparity among the tenured and the untenured is widening. Women account for only 5 percent of top-level management. You can still count Fortune 500 women CEOs on one hand. When we're 50 to 52 percent of the population, they still have to publish a list of women who are at the top. Finally, reproductive rights, as we knew them in the 1970s, are really pretty eviscerated. Late-term abortion is under fire. We might be facing the passage of a law that will make it a crime to take kids across state lines for an abortion, unless they have their parents' or the court's permission.

My view is there is an attitude of complacency. Young women are living in a fantasy world about what the possibilities are for them. Women have made progress and that leaves an impression, without more valid information, that things are fine. I just spoke to a group of informed women working on women's issues. I asked, "Do you know what is happening to women in this country?" And they just sort of sat there and said, "Oh, I didn't know that." I went to Arizona and spoke to Hearst magazine editors and publishers. I rattled off all the concrete evidence of where women are losing ground. These were women who write for women's magazines who knew nothing about what was really happening. There will be some big surprises for young women today who are taking a lot for granted in terms of what's possible for them. It just isn't reality.

I also fear there's a lack of understanding of where power really still resides in this country. It doesn't reside at the middle-management level where women achieved progress. It still resides in the boardrooms. It still resides at the top levels of national government. That's where the ultimate decisions are made. As long as women represent a tiny presence in those echelons, we simply will continue to confront the very hard ceilings that are so frustrating in different stages of our lives. It will become more acute as the population ages and older women come face-to-face with real limitations on what's available to them in our society.

I hope this institution will have a much greater influence in the long run than one person can have, that we will be able to speak across many issues and influence many political forums. In the end, however, women just have to get up and do the work. We have to take responsibility for our state. Unfortunately, the middle class doesn't feel the pinch—the battles are more individual. It's not like we do combat in the foxhole to break down restrictions on reproductive rights. When there is just flagrant and structural discrimination, it doesn't necessarily work like a war. It doesn't have quite the same dimensions, so it is a much more difficult fight we're engaged in.

Conclusion

Clearly the childhood of many of the interviewees impacted their careers, whether it was learning farm skills like Don Kendall, or creating harmony in a volatile home like Jack Kornfield, or developing a sense of striving, responsibility, and resiliency like Faye Wattleton.

Faye trained as a nurse, yet she never applied her degrees directly to the field. Instead she nurtured others in her work in the nonprofit segment. Faye says that when she accepted the key leadership position at Planned Parenthood she never imagined she would be involved in one of the most intense social conflicts of our time. What Faye brought to Planned Parenthood was a reasonable voice in all situations, and a principled approach to her leadership. At times, she admits to having self-doubts regarding management decisions, but never about her management style and principles. She managed her team by giving clear expectations and then letting go. Evaluations were based on the impact of their own decisions, giving them the freedom to implement as they chose. Faye strongly believes communication skills contribute to a sense of security and trust in one's staff, and attributes her belief in honest communications to her good staff relations.

Regarding success, Faye states that vision, trust, teamwork, honesty, and listening skills are key. She also urges readers not to avoid conflict, but to get parties to talk it out. Similar to Robert Mondavi, Faye firmly believes if people express their thoughts and feelings, and truly listen to each other, most conflicts can be resolved.

Faye's life story illustrates the challenge many individuals face when reinventing themselves in midlife. It is inspiring to hear how she handles her disappointment with a television program that was to guarantee her financial security and allow her to continue living her values by promoting the advancement of women. When the program was not aired, Faye networked and found ways to work with various kinds of projects, a lifelong dream of hers. She decides to join several corporate boards, write an autobiographical account, and start the Center for Gender Equality. Now Faye is still in the lonely position at the top of her organization, but as she shows so clearly, she is energized by this entrepreneurial experience to continue the work of helping women gain equality.

EPILOGUE

Thomas J. Watson Jr.
Former Chairman, IBM Corporation

Growing up as the daughter of Thomas J. Watson Jr. was a magical experience. Children never really see their parents as the world does, so I was rather sheltered from the fact that I was the daughter of "The World's Most Successful Capitalist," as the cover of *Fortune* magazine once billed him. We were not as spoiled as some might imagine. In fact, mother bought us new clothing only once a year and a single new pair of shoes in the fall. We didn't always get what we wanted for Christmas, and our allowances were rather meager.

Nonetheless, the world we lived in was full of wonderful surprises. One never knew who would visit for a meal. My father loved to befriend people, whether they were heads of government or Swiss ski instructors. He was an intensely curious man. One year he gave me a beautiful harpsichord to entice me to learn the piano. I hated the piano, but I hated his bribe even more. My father decided it didn't matter he had five daughters and one son. He treated us all like boys. As girls of 11 and 12, my sister Olive and I shared our very own motorcycle. We drove it all over the backwoods of Greenwich, Connecticut, making a mess of our neighbors' lawns. My father enjoyed his wild girls.

It was good to have freedom as children. My parents were not around much to supervise us, so we supervised ourselves. I was the middle child, and in my opinion, the best position in a large family. You can get away with murder. I was also my father's favorite. From an early age, he took me with him on business trips all over the world. I think he liked me because I argued with him. People in positions of power can really be bullies. As I tell my students today, there's nothing a bully likes more than to be stopped and stood up to. Often, that is the key to success in business—learning how not to be intimidated by the powers that be.

I remember the time I introduced John Sculley to my father. We were at our family place in Maine, and I invited John and his wife to lunch, which was served on the deck overlooking the ocean. My father was late. Suddenly a small red plane appeared in the blue sky above us, trailing a line of smoke. My father maneuvered the plane through a series of stunts—loop-the-loops, barrel rolls, and what have you. John turned to me and in a most bewildered tone asked, "What is going on? Who is that?" "Oh," I replied, "That's just my father trying to show you he still has a few tricks up his sleeve!"

I found it odd that my father cared so much about proving himself to John, who was in fact the more powerful executive at the time. Of course, it all was a joke (of sorts), but I think my father's real point was to show John although Apple was big then, IBM could match any stunt they could devise. My father may have suffered from an inferiority complex throughout his life. He always believed other people were smarter and more talented. I think the only place he felt confident was in the cockpit of an airplane. At the age of 55, he was the oldest pilot in jet school; at 65, he learned to fly a helicopter! Stunt planes came later still. To him, flying represented freedom. He found the confines of corporate life very restricting and was only able to escape by flying to some exotic spot or sailing his boat halfway around the world following the old course of Captain Cook.

My father wanted to be an airline pilot, but my grandfather, who founded IBM, would never allow that. My father entered IBM and initially hated every minute of his working life. As he became more successful, I know he enjoyed the challenge of running a large company, but in his heart of hearts he dreamed of being airborne. In his last year, the doctors told him he could no longer fly, and his desire to live left him. He loved challenges and physical tests, and if he was denied them, he saw no real point in living. He was a driven man, haunted by many demons. He was volatile and loving, humorous, and vindictive. I don't think he ever found a place within himself where he could relax, look back on his life, and simply be content.

My dad would have categorized himself as a CEO, but I would argue with that. Though his life's work was running IBM, his dreams were greater than corporate life, and his interests reflect this part of his personality. He was a man who couldn't sit still, a trait most of my interviewees had in common, nor could he contain his dreams within the four walls of a corporation. His interest in world peace and nuclear disarmament were reflected in his involvement with the Salt Talks and his ambassadorship to Russia. He started an institute at Brown University, the Watson Institute for International Studies, whose sole purpose is to study ways to reduce conflict in the world. Despite these many and varied endeavors, however, he never felt at peace with himself. This is what makes him different from many of the CEOs, entrepreneurs, and visionaries I interviewed. He was never a political animal and had a hard time not speaking his mind on issues. His passion for his work was transitory and depended on whether there was sufficient challenge present. Perhaps that's why he often felt more passionate about his hobbies, flying and sailing.

Long before I considered the prospect of writing *How They Achieved*, I interviewed my father. He was in his last years and was clearly grappling with his own mortality. The interview was short, but I think dad had a number of important things to say.

A Brief Interview with Thomas J. Watson Jr.

For many years, I ran the IBM corporation and was responsible for its entire operations in the 50 states as well as overseas. It was my life, the company, and it took all my time. I was with IBM from the time I got out of the air force until my retirement after a heart attack in my fifties. Now I mainly fool around, as I call it, with several boards that I'm on and with my sailboats and planes. I get a big kick from my sailing adventures and spend a good deal of time planning them and going around the world.

As a kid, I didn't think about much—except that I was in trouble a lot. I really didn't think I would amount to much. I wasn't a good student and was always in trouble for not doing my homework or not paying attention in class. I didn't have a lot of confidence. My dad was always mad at me. I stole a car from up the street and drove it into our garage, and he was pretty mad about that. When I got to college [Brown], it took me six years to finish. The only thing I really loved was flying; it was all I wanted to do. I joined the air force when the war was over and decided to become an airline pilot, but my dad wouldn't allow it. He insisted I join IBM, and so I did.

In the early years, I was pretty unhappy. I had to travel all over the country meeting people. I really didn't understand how things worked. My dad and I fought all the time, and I really didn't like the job. That's why I kept flying and sailing, I guess, to have some time off from what I viewed as pressure. In retrospect, I think my dad knew what was right for me. He was right to push me into IBM, but I never saw it that way at the time. I wanted to pretty much do what I wanted and what I loved, but there wouldn't have been much satisfaction in that.

I suppose I had a choice, but then again, maybe I didn't. In retrospect, I liked what my life became, but in my heart I always wondered if it would have been better if I had just been able to do what I wanted. I wasn't good at much except flying, and that's why I was so interested in it. I think you are interested in what you are good at. At IBM, I liked talking business, but I didn't much care for the day-to-day aspects of the job.

My heroes were adventurers and explorers, like Captain Cook, and guys like the Wright brothers. I always loved Lindbergh and people who lived their dreams. History always interested me. I guess I loved the idea of exploring places where no one had ever been. Going to the Arctic Circle was a big dream of mine that I actually fulfilled, and it was great.

I made a lot of mistakes. I made them out of stupidity, or anger, or whatever, but I certainly made a lot of them. If I hadn't, I never would have tried anything. I think fear is a great motivator. You keep trying, and you just get used to it. You have to fail, and that makes you tough. If you never get tough, you never believe you can do anything. I didn't have a lot of confidence as a kid. I thought I was dumb and probably lazy, too. But somehow I kept at it and wasn't afraid of failing too much. Perhaps that's because I failed a lot. I made people mad. I would say to be a success you have to be willing to fall down and get up again, or you will never move beyond a certain place.

I had a great mentor when I started out at IBM. He really made me feel I could do it, and so I tried. Mentors are really important, and I try to be a mentor to young people. I spend a lot of time with my grandson. I would tell young people starting out today to dare to do what they really want to do. To not be afraid. To try new things— even if they're ultimately not successful. To be ready to see an opportunity and take a risk. I think I probably took too many risks. I talked my father blue in the face about taking IBM public. He never wanted to borrow that money from Morgan, but I finally persuaded him to try it. My father thought I was totally wrong, but he gave me the chance. Obviously, it was a good thing. But it wasn't easy to build a company, and I still think maybe I could have done it better. I never really believed in myself over the years, and I think that's what caused so much trouble with my temper. Life goes by while you're living it, and sometimes you do things wrong and have to back up and start again. I started again a lot.

My definition of success? Wow—that's a tough one. Success is doing the right thing, I guess. Making an impact. Building a company like some of these young guys out there today are doing. Or maybe success is raising some good kids. It's always been hard for me to answer that question.

I remember building the house we all went to in Vermont and running out of money halfway through and thinking, "What a dope I am to have thought I could do it." I went on to finish it. You remember all the good times we had there? I loved flying you all up there, getting away from IBM and really having fun just being with you kids. It was success to have a place to be together as a family and enjoy the sport of skiing. That is what I really liked.

INDEX